Praise for *Dead White Men and Other Important People*

'I read this book with great pleasure, enjoying how it ... reader on a voyage of sociological discovery. The co... ...arrative with the systematic presentation of sociological ... ...er and is a neat way of encouraging the newcomer to apply su... ...r own circumstances. The book is a really novel, pedagogically effica... ...ntellectual means of stimulating thought within and about sociology.'

David Inglis, Professor of Sociology, University of Aberdeen, UK

'I found the book engaging and wholly appropriate for the sorts of things I cover with fresh students, and that's where I think the beauty of this book lies: its accessibility to those alarmed by the task ahead because they feel not quite prepared for the rigors of a sociology degree.'

Joel Nathan Rosen, Associate Professor of Sociology, Moravian College, USA

'I really do think this will be popular because [it has] some great hook lines and clinchers as well as a really neat way of applying the big ideas to everyday life. Every lecturer in every land will be borrowing material ... this book is a real winner.'

Adrian Franklin, Professor of Sociology, UTAS, Australia

'The authors have a knack for presenting ideas in dramatic dialogue. The text conveys the interest and the central thoughts of sociology and sociologists in very graspable ways and with entertaining characters.'

Gregor McLennan, Professor of Sociology, University of Bristol, UK

'A thoughtful, engaging and lively contribution to the teaching of sociology. *Dead White Men and Other Important People* certainly is a novel approach to writing sociology for students and one that I found provided very clear with succinct explanations of the material covered. The style, tone, level of sophistication and the type of ideas being discussed are perfect for junior sociology students.'

Catriona Elder, Senior Lecturer in Sociology, USYD, Australia

'This book has a completely different approach to anything else I've read on the subject. It's really refreshing and makes theory a lot easier to understand because it's written in language that means I can concentrate and take it in for longer than with other textbooks.'

Holly, a sociology student

'*Dead White Men and Other Important People* really helps me to understand complex aspects of social science and the theory behind it. I found that other textbooks over-complicate theory, but this book gives me a broader understanding of each topic as a whole and helps me to understand parts that I haven't been able to grasp before. And I really like the modern-day comparisons. It's really easy to dip into certain chapters, or to read the book as a whole.'

Katy, a sociology student

'I think this book is absolutely fantastic. The idea of structuring social theory around conversations works really well and the style makes it both easy and exciting to read.'

Tony, a sociology student

2ND EDITION

DEAD WHITE MEN AND OTHER IMPORTANT PEOPLE

SOCIOLOGY'S BIG IDEAS

ANGUS BANCROFT & RALPH FEVRE

macmillan education   palgrave

First published 2016 by
PALGRAVE

Palgrave in the UK is an imprint of Macmillan Publishers Limited,
registered in England, company number 785998, of 4 Crinan Street,
London, N1 9XW.

Palgrave Macmillan in the US is a division of St Martin's Press LLC,
175 Fifth Avenue, New York, NY 10010.

Palgrave is a global imprint of the above companies and is represented
throughout the world.

Palgrave® and Macmillan® are registered trademarks in the United States,
the United Kingdom, Europe and other countries.

ISBN 978–1–137–46785–0 paperback

This book is printed on paper suitable for recycling and made from fully
managed and sustained forest sources. Logging, pulping and manufacturing
processes are expected to conform to the environmental regulations of the
country of origin.

A catalogue record for this book is available from the British Library.

A catalog record for this book is available from the Library of Congress.

Printed in China

Ralph dedicates this book to Claudia Fevre (because she has big ideas too).
Angus dedicates this to the loving memory
of Betsy Addison.

Contents

sex and gender – hermaphrodite sociology – Judith Butler and
performing femininity – being a drag – career opportunities –
masculinity and singing the blues

mind and society – group formation and getting closer – being on
the same wavelength – Charles Sanders Peirce, signs and living
together – semiotics and the science of signs – Charles Horton
Cooley and knowing how to fall in love – masquerade, secrets and
imagining people

George Herbert Mead, Herbert Blumer, the self and symbolic
interactionism – the individual against the crowd – making
choices and making society – seeing ourselves and others in the
mirror – being different with different people – interaction and
accomplishing meaning – the Generalised Other and the secret self

working at making things normal – Alfred Schutz, making sense
and looking away – Harold Garfinkel and ethnomethodology –
the illusion of order – definitions of reality – talking politics and
giving directions to nowhere – Alvin Cicourel, stimulating the
senses and breaking into laughter

Erving Goffman and pretending to be yourself – making a drama
and an impression – frontstage and backstage – playing different
roles – the odd one out – stigma and spoiled identity – passing –
asylums and the total institution – resisting institutionalisation

the persona and the real me – Erving Goffman and identity –
Michel Foucault and the panopticon – surveillance and
discipline – sex, power, the body and appearance – liberation,
repression and resistance

science, medicine, proof and evidence – the Forer effect – is
sociology scientific? – quote-ology – common sense and

data – Noam Chomsky and universal grammar – epistemology
and acquiring knowledge – Harry Collins and science as a social
construct – bad science

doing what you are best at – Talcott Parsons and functionalism –
structure, values and action – sociology as a priestly caste – the
sick role, medicine as morality – functional differentiation and the
professional ethic – society as an organism

can sociology make you a better person? – respect and the code
of honour – Pierre Bourdieu, disposition and habitus – structure,
agency, social capital and field – the rules of the game – second
nature – language as an instrument of power

race, ethnicity and post-colonialism – Edward Said and
Orientalism – Frantz Fanon and critiques of the Enlightenment –
Gurminder Bhambra and critiques of modernity – racial science –
Globalisation and the global supply chain – development and
undevelopment

Karl Marx and Friedrich Engels – surplus value, labour and
exploitation – materialism and the social relations of production –
serfs and lords, bourgeoisie and proletarians – the contradictions
of capitalism – ideology and class struggle

Max Weber, rationality and the origins of capitalism – the
Protestant ethic – bureaucracy and disenchantment – the prison
of rationalisation – markets, monopolies and social stratification –
class, status and party – the state and geopolitics

Eleanor Marx and Marianne Weber – listening to hidden
voices – observer bias – inadequate categories – limits of the
Enlightenment – universal truths – speaking for others – feminist
standpoint epistemology

Georg Simmel – the stranger – intimacy, fashion and obedience –
following the crowd – the universal rule of money and the search
for stimulation – gossip, confession and possessing secrets –
making new things

Preface

We wrote this book because we knew sociology had some big ideas, some of the biggest ideas you were ever likely to come across. But we also knew that these ideas sometimes passed people by, even when they were studying sociology. We thought a good part of the fault for this lay with people like us, the professionals who were meant to do a better job of explaining those ideas in the first place. We therefore set out to find the best way to explain both the ideas themselves, and how we hoped that people who came across those ideas would receive them, not just remembering the ideas but arguing with them, wrestling with them, and applying them to their world and their problems. For us, this is what learning is actually about.

If you are starting out on a sociology course at school or university, or are already on a course but do not always feel that the books you are asked to read are helping, then this book is for you. It is also for anyone who might just be interested in good ideas, anyone who thinks that there is more to explaining the way the world is, and the ways people behave, than saying, 'that's just the way things are'. Whatever your background and your interests, the aim of this book is not to tell you how to think, or what ideas are best, but to show you how to think with ideas.

Acknowledgements

We would like to again thank everyone who contributed to the first edition, especially Emily Drewe whose vision and drive made it happen. Lots of people commented on the first edition and the proposal for this edition, in various ways. Thanks are due to the many students and teachers who used it and provided thoughtful, constructive criticisms, and the anonymous reviewers contracted by Palgrave. Lloyd Langman steered the new edition home and we thank him and Palgrave for the vote of confidence.

Many of our friends and family gave inspiration, ideas, and succour during the production of the book. Thanks to Elise and Steve Kemp for some smart ideas, and to Kim, Colin, Martine, Elwyn and Lanya for their loving care. We are very grateful for the editorial support provided by Natasha Fevre.

In writing the first edition we learnt a lot from Jostein Gaarder's *Sophie's World: A Novel About the History of Philosophy*. He and we write in a long tradition of illustrating ideas and provoking thought through dialogue, which stretches back to Socrates. In times when debate is ruled out of bounds and statements of fact are rendered suspect we celebrate the sociological and philosophical tradition of provoking, unsettling, and discomfiting.

0
Making a Start

Sociology aims to explain the actions of human beings in society, to describe social problems, and look for ways of solving them. As C Wright Mills put it, more than any one topic or approach, Sociology is about how we imagine the world. The sociological imagination means taking what we do every day without thinking – those routines of brushing our teeth, traipsing to work or college, arguing with boyfriends, girlfriends, husbands and wives, or going out for a night – and understanding how all these mundane activities are shaped by history, economics, culture, social structure, institutions, and other factors that only become apparent when we ask 'why'. Why is it done that way? Who said that is the way it has to be Has it always been like that? Can it be different? The question also works the other way round. People can feel themselves trapped by the weight of traditions, institutions, laws, and expectations. When these questions are asked it becomes apparent that 'the way things are' is not 'the way things need to be'.

Sociology does not stand apart from the world it studies but is immersed in it. You will come across a thousand clichés and stereotypes about what life is like for people – 'what everyone knows' about it. Sociologists seek to find out whether what everyone knows is the truth. For example, Everyone knew that drug dealers and traffickers have huge amounts of cash and use violence to enforce their will. Sociologists who wanted to know what drug dealing is really like went and spent months and years with dealers. Sudhir Venkatesh was so trusted by the urban, crack-dealing gang he studied that they asked him to be their 'leader' for a day, and the people in the community relied on him to resolve disputes. He found that many were making less than the minimum wage. Another sociologist, Jennifer Fleetwood, found that drug traffickers were organised more like a social network than a mafia-style gang and avoided violence when they could.

In this way, sociology is an investigatory discipline. It dives into social life to ask why the world is as it is. It shows that what might feel like the effects of impersonal social and economic developments, and what might seem to be the inevitable and unchanging facts of life, are the results of decisions taken and choices made by human beings. We can feel ourselves to be buffeted by forces beyond our control but if we can investigate them as the outcome of human process, human institutions, and human choices, we can understand them and perhaps control them too. For example, financial markets have shaped and reshaped the world in recent decades. It has appeared as if individuals, businesses and governments are entirely at their mercy. If a nation wants to borrow money it has to show it is credit worthy according to what is presented as an objective set of value judgements. What sociologists have shown is that what happens in these markets is not only the result of objective judgements about monetary value. Like any human activity, they depend on cultural value judgements, anticipation about what other people might do next, and understandings of what is possible and what is not. One sociologist, Donald MacKenzie, found that the computer models they used to describe the financial markets were also changing what the market was, because market traders were acting in anticipation of what the model would show. That has implications for everyone because significant financial risks can be taken because everyone involved thinks that the models and equations they are using keep them safe. The global financial crisis of 2007-8 happened because of this exact reason. Human beings forgot that technology and institutions were human creations that could run away from them.

How to use the book

We have written the book as a novel. It follows our character, Mila, and her friends and family through university life. You will read several different voices throughout the book. There are the authoritative voices of Mila's teachers and textbooks. We have put names to them - there is a textbook Mila reads called 'Fussein and Stein', and a tutor she likes and listens to, Dalina. They are the kind of voices you will come across when you read textbooks and listen to academics. We also show you other voices that you do not often read in textbooks but we hope you do come across in your life - students, people who question, who talk back, and who challenge these voices of authority. As sociologists, we all started out as one of these other people. Your voice might be one of them too. You might read the book thinking you are like Mila, or like Jasmine, or like Mila's brother, or one of her aunties, or all of them at different times.

We know you will want to dip in and out of the book as needed so here is where to find what you need. The book covers the themes sociologists think are important and also the disagreements between them. Since the world changes rapidly, and since every way of looking at the world changes what it is, there are vast disagreements between everyone about some very basic questions.

If you are using this book with a conventional textbook that describes different theories and research topics then there are some ways you can combine them. This book introduces each problem and how the ideas can be used. Textbooks are good for setting out the evidence by which people arrive at different perspectives and back them up. So for example, you could read about the debates about what social classes are in Chapters 14 and 15 and then look at your textbook for the ways researchers have investigated social class, the effect social class has had on inequality and politics, and how social change has altered what social class means. Textbooks can be used to link the ideas you find in the book to your own context – the society, the nation, the state, and the community that you are part of.

What's in the book

We introduce you to social theories. A social theory is a framework for interpreting the context of human behaviour. We start small and build out. The different theories outlined in this book take different approaches to this, and work on different levels. Some examine human interactions. Others look at institutions, economics and society itself. We wrote this book to show how you can use your own life to explore sociology, and vice versa. The book follows the journey of our character, Mila, as a learner. She begins to make connections between ideas and fit them into her evolving picture of the world.

Sociology came into being to answer the problem of how society could work while the past mechanisms that it had relied on – tradition, family, religion, deference – were either falling away or being radically changed in the modern workplace. That constant state of change, what we call 'modernity', is the first big idea, discussed in Chapter 1. Sociologists argue over whether there is one kind of modernity, or if there are many, and if it even applies to the world as it is today.

If you ask people who they are, they will often say something about where they are from – the place, the community, the nation they grew up in. Sociology studies *what* they are from – the society that creates, shapes, and supports individuals. It is easier to give this object of study a name than to agree on what it is – and what it does. Chapter 2 takes the work of Émile Durkheim, who said that modern society had a very special quality of creating social relationships which could work without the people involved ever meeting. He called this 'organic solidarity'. That sounds very pleasant, but Durkheim also wanted to know how these obligations could harm individuals. Suicide is thought of as the result of people feeling so detached from the world they have nothing to live for. He showed that was an example of a common social condition called 'anomie' meaning – living without expectations.

Following on from that example you can see that sociology looks at the big and the small. Chapter 3 examines that most personal of experiences: emotions. It presents the division between emotion and reason, which often stands for other contrasts: the division between female and male, nature and culture, barbarism and civilisation. These are social distinctions, not naturally occurring divisions. It shows how emotion and reason are in fact intimately connected. One becomes impossible without the other. Emotions are culturally shaped and created. They are often ignored in academic study, other than as possibly troublesome responses to psychometric tests. The chapter shows that the founders of sociology and psychology took emotion seriously as part of the texture and fabric of social life. Sociology looks at how these everyday aspects of personal life are shaped by often hidden divisions and inequalities. Feminist approaches tackled in Chapter 4 highlight gender as a division that cuts right through the middle of every other institution in society – it runs through social class, workplaces, the education system, and the family. Gender is treated as a natural, genetic, fact of life. We show gendered roles and expectations are constructed. The more that individuals act towards gender as if it is real, the more real it becomes.

The qualities and experiences that we consider most individual and specific to us might be products of the way we interact with others. Chapter 5 begins with the relationship between mind and society as studied by Charles Sanders Peirce and Charles Horton Cooley. It shows how ideas do not spring fully formed from the mind but come from symbolic reflection. That relies on the existence of signs, shared symbols which give meaning and shape to the otherwise formless plasticine of life. The chapter shows how in order to relate to someone in reality you must relate to them in your imagination. That is why fictional or mythic entities have such power and influence. The imaginary is more powerful than the real. To make these signs meaningful we have to interact with them. Chapter 6 discusses George Herbert Mead's claim that to become thinking adults, individuals have to relate to the world as an object, as if they were looking down on it from outside. The chapter then introduces Blumer's symbolic interactionism. Every activity is an interaction. All the big structures that sociology studies – gender, social class, religious beliefs – consist of interactions. None of them exist outside of what individuals do with them. Symbolic interactionism takes that as the starting point for its study of how people relate symbolically to one another and to their experiences in the world.

What we learn from these writers is that everyday life is made up of the work individuals do to make it seem effortlessly normal. In Chapter 7, Alfred Shutz calls these the typifications individuals bring to bear on situations – which explains why people can tolerate the most outrageously intolerable situations. The chapter explores what is called ethnomethodology, which argues that social life is created out of our reluctance to question what is normal, and society is an illusion built on that. Chapter 8 moves outwards again from the mind to discuss more of the work people do in the roles they perform. It uses Erving Goffman's studies of behaviour in public places and the presentation of self to show the ways in which social life is a performance. People present a front, which they hope convinces others. It presents an example of when this does not happen and people cannot control their 'front' and 'backstage' – in total institutions like mental hospitals.

The example of people who are inmates of institutions shows how power is key to understanding the gap between people's desire to live out their lives as they want and their ability to do so. Michel Foucault, discussed in Chapter 9, argued that those very 'wants' are created and shaped through power. An instance he used is how different identities and ways of being are created through medical and scientific discourse. We use his studies of sexuality and madness to show how the way a topic is talked about and written about changes what it is. The same goes for individuals – how we are talked about, written up, processed, identified, and categorised changes who we are. Power – the ability to get people to act in ways that are to others' advantage – works more commonly through persuading people to think and act in the right away, rather than forcing them to do so.

When sociologists like Foucault comment on medical and other kinds of science they are arguing that what we know about the world is key in controlling what it is. As sociology is a discipline which investigates problems directly, it examines the kinds of knowledge and evidence people use and value. Chapter 10 takes up the study of science. This is the most authoritative form of knowledge in most modern societies. Science deals with facts, not feelings or subjective judgements. The chapter introduces sociological studies of science, medicine and technology. It discusses the claim that scientific knowledge is just another kind of social knowledge – one that has a special privilege in society because of the convincing story it tells about itself. It uses the example of the placebo, which shows that knowledge and reality are not entirely separate.

You will have picked up from these examples that nobody is quite sure whether they act and make decisions out of their own volition, or because there are deeper forces that in some way 'make' them act in a particular way. That is called the debate between 'structure' and 'action'. Chapter 11 uses the example of medicine and sickness to introduce this and the work of Talcott Parsons, who tried to bridge this gap with his structural-functionalist approach. The chapter asks to what extent this was successful. It presents criticisms of the ability of sociology to understand conflict and division. Chapter 12 moves onto another writer who examined how structure works through action, and vice versa: Pierre Bourdieu. It uses his study of the use of honour in Algeria to present his ideas of habitus, field, and social capital. These can explain how behaviour is both actively chosen and structured.

Examining structure means we have to discuss what the big structures that matter are. Sociologists often study national societies as 'the places that matter'. Chapter 13 puts sociology in a global perspective. It looks at how social thinkers have been embroiled in colonialism and post-colonialism. It presents the work of Gurminder Bhambra and others who have sought to show how the structure of ideas in European thought reflects something particular rather than universal. Globalism is relevant because many aspects of our lives are affected by global changes and we often interact with each other using global systems. For example, you may use a social network to keep track of your friends that is owned and operated by a company in a different country. That means your data – your private knowledge – can be kept thousands of miles from where you are and may be read by employees of that company. Data about your personal life – your friends, your family – can be mined for valuable advertising or sold on.

That aspect of life, the way in which more and more people become defined by their monetary worth, was studied by Karl Marx, who we discuss in Chapter 14, and Max Weber in Chapter 15. Marx's innovative idea was that the economic system was not a machine following everlasting rules, but a set of social arrangements relying on the power of ownership. From that, many other facts of life came such as the need to sell one's own labour power and the experience of alienation in work and personal life. In his time, ownership meant owning factories, machinery, and land. In our time, it can mean owning data and software. Max Weber presented a novel idea about the relationship between economic development and religious thought. He said that what mattered in the development of the capitalist economy was not what people did with the money they made but what they thought it symbolised. Those who thought that possessing money showed them to be holy would use it to create more.

The final two chapters bring us back to the story and the question of who is who, who speaks, and who is a stranger. It shows how the contribution of women, people from ethnic minorities, and non-Westerners to social thought has often been hidden. It introduces feminist epistemology as a perspective. We finish with Simmel, a writer who saw how personal life and its strangeness were fundamental qualities of life in modern society.

Doodles make the abstract concrete

At the end of each chapter you will find one of Mila's Doodles summarising it. If you are taking a degree you will find yourself doing a lot of writing. You take notes when you go to a lecture or read a book or research article. Some of this writing is more useful than others. We have found that the best kind of writing to help you learn is when you put your books and lecture notes aside and write down what you have learned, in your own words and in terms that make sense for you. Everyone learns and recalls information differently. You will know yourself. Some people seem to pick up a tune immediately or recall song lyrics. Others can tell you exactly what someone was wearing or how they wore their makeup. Academia tends to emphasis abstract, textual forms of learning. However, we have more tools at our disposal to learn, using sound and visuals. Our spatial awareness is one of the best honed and least used parts of the human mind. So use those millions of years of evolution to draw out what the ideas are. We would like you to use the Doodles and try to do the same. When you are grappling with an idea, think of a doodle or a sketch for it. It does not have to be artistic or profound – it only has to have meaning for you.

The characters

Our friends:

Mila is a sociology student finding out who she is and how to make sense of her life.

Jasmine is studying astrophysics. She is as constant as gravity and just as forgiving.

Tuni is a student of fashion and design. She knows that while what counts may be on the inside, what matters is on the outside.

Circe and Ana, who know the meaning of true friendship.

Arun, Mila's intellectual foil.

Mila's family:

Her father, who may be going from selling stocks to being in the stocks.

Her mother, who keeps it all together.

Doni, her brother.

A collection of aunties: Aunt Enid, Aunt Bee-Bee, and Aunt Ima.

Mr Lee, a family friend.

In support of Mila are her teachers, Dalina, Randolph, and Amram. Well, mainly Dalina.

● ● ● ● ●

1
In at the Deep End

Mila had at last found the lecture theatre after hunting along dusty corridors and wandering past blank-faced portraits. Her bag was weighed down by her shiny new textbook, proudly purchased at the university bookshop. *Sociology and Its Problems* by Fussen and Stein was comfortingly bricklike and imposing. A thin tablet was loaded with classy novels that were in danger of remaining unread for the next three years.

She opened the door to see ranks of seats filled with students messaging, flirting, gossiping, and in some cases dozing. It looked more like a stadium than the intimate classrooms of her school. Where to sit? There were lots of free seats at the front but it looked quite lonely down there.

The lecturer appeared on the stage and tapped the microphone. The theatre quickly hushed and Mila slipped into the nearest front row, feeling slightly exposed as she caught the lecturer's glance.

'Hello, I am Randolph and welcome to the first day of your sociology class. Now, one of my colleagues, Amram, has suggested we use this Twitter thing to have a conversation. It seems you can tweet with the hashtag #dwm and it will appear on the screen behind me.' He glared at his colleague in the front row. Clearly not his idea, thought Mila. Someone else was feeling exposed today as well.

Randolph began with a glance at the screen behind him.	#dwm
'Let's start with the holy trinity of sociologists, Karl Marx, Émile Durkheim, and Max Weber.	Is this the psychology class? Who are these old guys? #beards
	What is sociology? #confused
The study of sociology is the study of human beings in society.	Is this an easy course? #needthecredit
	That's why I took it #don'twanttogetupearly
It's the hardest of the social sciences because it asks, what are the problems of the age? What shapes our minds, our lives, our souls, unknown to us?'	Is there a textbook for the course? #readitforme
	Fussen and Stein #readthehandbook
	Where can I get a decent coffee?

Amram came up to the podium as the lecture ended.

Randolph started, 'Yuck, I feel like I just googled myself. The students only seemed interested in how to get through the course, not what they could learn from it.'

Amram said, 'They do have other thoughts on their minds! You have to work the backchannel in, prompt them with problems and questions. Otherwise they have nothing to go on.'

Mila overheard them while she was gathering her stuff together in the front. She couldn't help but feel sorry for Randolph, stuck in front of several hundred people with varying degrees of interest in what he was saying, from the blank to the fading.

She took a deep breath. 'You're talking one level, but just now students are on another level. You can't assume that we all have the same interest you do, or speak the same language. People come here from all over the world. The problems that Weber and Durkheim might have worried about are not the same, but the questions they asked could be.'

Both of them stared at her. Oh, now they expect me to have a magical solution, she thought. Bigmouth strikes again.

She thought of one of the books she had uploaded to her tablet by a Danish philosopher. He had expounded his ideas through a novel, to show how they worked in the world. Ideas were a part of the world they lived in.

'So what if you showed them how someone like me grapples with the fundamental questions that bothered the sociological thinkers? It doesn't have to be a textbook with lots of information. You could tell it as a story.'

'It is more like how students actually learn. Talking at them is not teaching. Listening is not learning. It is when students talk back that they learn. And we learn from them, more and more,' Amram reflected.

'Just don't write me into it,' Randolph said.

'Oh, I definitely wouldn't do that,' Mila smiled warmly.

***

Another student interrupted Randolph to ask him what a theory was. He replied. 'It's like an explanation for something that we don't know is really true yet.'

Another fresh-faced student dived in, speaking very quickly.

'It's like your best friend stops speaking to you and you don't know why and you say to another friend "why is she being like this?". And the other friend says they don't really know but maybe it's because she's angry at you because of something you did before, or maybe she's ashamed of something *she* did. So those are two different theories, aren't they? Maybe one of them explains what's going on but you won't know which, or either, until you find out ...'

Mila was thinking, when your best friend doesn't speak to you, and some other kid says it's because they don't like you anymore, that was how children ended up being horrible to each other. Then you make it worse by being bad to your friend, and it turns out that wasn't what was going on at all. Randolph was now telling the young-looking student that he agreed with a part of what she had said: 'A hypothesis is a proposed explanation that you can test; a theory is a hypothesis with force – an idea that structures other ideas, that has withstood at least some engagement with reality. You are right when you say we are waiting to find out if the theory will turn out to be true but instead of explaining what your best friend does, there are theories to explain what atoms do, or the stars or our genes, or ...'

The first student saw a chance to jump in now and show how intelligent *she* was: maybe, she seemed to be thinking, more intelligent than this lecturer. 'So theories are never about what *people* do? How can sociology have theories, then?'

'Yes, sociology does have theories but in sociology you need different kinds of evidence to work out whether a theory is right or not. When you deal with explanations about people it can be trickier deciding what the right evidence is and that's one of the reasons sociology can never be a science like physics.'

Maybe student number one *was* smarter than Randolph. 'But scientists, psychologists even, say that we do stuff because we are programmed to follow stimuli. They think we are all like big bald mice or rats who fight each other and are only interested in passing on our genes.'

Mila thought she had better say something and, without thinking too hard about it, she remembered something she had read in a magazine: 'Some psychologists say that's why men can't help being promiscuous – because they are programmed to have lots of babies with different women – so then it's OK for men to behave in this way. It's just an excuse for bad behaviour. Men can choose to live like people; they don't have to behave like rats.'

This was pretty daring for Mila, but she liked the joke about rats. Randolph brought her into the conversation. 'Sure, well some theories are better than that. They help you to judge a situation as well as explaining it – help you to make life better and not just keep life as it is. Theories should not be about justifying the way people's lives are lived, but about making them better.'

Mila thought this was familiar. It sounded like what her old sociology teacher used to say about sociology being able to make the world better and fairer, but, all the same, she was confused. Wasn't it what sociology found out, what it told us was true, that helped us to make the world a better place? To her surprise, Mila now found she had a genuine question. 'You are saying theories can change the world, then. I thought it was what we found out about the world that changed the world.'

Randolph focused more closely on Mila. 'Theories *have* changed the world. They do it by changing how people see the world. When they see it in a different way, it's like they want to change the way they act or the way other people act, maybe even corporations and governments. You need these theories to make all this change possible.'

The first student thought she had been out of the conversation for much too long. 'How do you know which is the right theory – what about all the theories, the ideologies, that are making trouble? They won't make the world better, will they? How do people know they are not going to change the world in the wrong way, and make it worse?' This question pleased Randolph too. He smiled again as he answered.

'This is why you need to test the theories to see which ones are right, which ones help and which ones cause trouble. If you think people are just like big rats, you can test your theories in a laboratory, but with most theories about people it is a bit more like finding out why your best friend won't talk to you. You have to ask around and see what other people think, and you go on how they normally are. You never know for sure with people, the theory is never 100 per cent right. And sometimes you can only test the theory by trying it out.'

Mila felt that what he was saying mattered to her in a way she was not yet sure of. 'And that's when all the bad situations happen – like bad governments and dictators that kill all sorts of people? They're doing a kind of experiment with people?'

'Yeah, it's true: that can happen. There have been attractive theories that turned out to be very bad when people tried to live by them.'

'And you still think if people want to make life better they need to come up with more theories?'

'Well, that's a bit of it. You've got to have new ideas about how to live.' To Mila this sounded lame and Randolph seemed to notice because he hurried on. 'But you have to know which questions to ask. You can't make theories out of nothing. You make them out of questions like the ones you are asking. You have to have questions to start with. You can't have theories without questions. We need more questions to make us think of more theories.'

Student number two decided that asking questions might, after all, make her seem smarter than answering them.

'Where do the questions come from first of all?'

'Some of the best times for new theories are when lots of big, exciting changes are going on because the changes make people ask questions they haven't thought about before. In sociology you've got to go back 150, maybe 200 years, to understand this. Go back to the time before electricity, and antibiotics, and when hardly anyone thought women should vote.'

The first student wasn't having any of this. 'But how can something written a century ago help us now? If I wanted something fixed, or I had something wrong with me, I would want the latest ideas, not what people knew centuries ago.'

'OK, I know what you mean, but, as I said just now, sociology isn't like those other kinds of knowledge – medicine, chemistry, pharmacology. Science really does build on previous scientific work but this kind of process only produces small changes in sociological theories. Sociological theory changes in a radical way only when its subject matter – society – changes. That's when the new questions come up. For scientists, every problem has a built-in solution. For sociologists, every solution comes with built-in problems.'

Mila had heard little of this. She had not been able to sustain her interest in this conversation and was feeling deeply frustrated. Still they carried on showing off to each other. Student number two thought the time was up for questions, and it was now time to show Randolph that she understood all of this and more. 'I get it. You are saying that what happened in history gave people new situations to think about but we are still supposed to be basically the same.'

'That's it. Our times are not yet different enough to produce hugely different theories. Or just maybe there are big changes going on but we haven't yet come up with the right questions about them. Sociological theories from a 100 or 150 years ago have plenty to say about the economy and also the family, but economies and families are so different now that it's probably time to start coming up with some new theories again. But you still have to understand what the old theories say to understand what we are changing from. You can't see what is changing if you don't know how life used to be. And there are plenty of facts of life that are still basically the same – but look at the time! I'm late for my next lecture already. Nice talking to you all.'

***

Mila was exhausted by the time she got back to her new accommodation. As she got nearer, she saw the light was on. She was learning that students left lights on everywhere they went – but she realised there was someone sitting at the kitchen table. Someone was sitting on her own, snacking and reading the big book on the table in front of her.

'Hi. I'm Jasmine, are you hungry, too?'

'No, I just want a glass of water – I'm on my way to bed; I'm so tired after today – oh, I'm Mila.'

Mila was turning on her heel, but trying not to be rude by turning her back on the woman before she looked back down at her book. 'Where are you from, Mila?'

Jasmine wasn't really interested in the answer Mila gave (and when Mila politely asked where *she* was from it was no place Mila had ever heard of). But when Jasmine asked what Mila was here to study it was clear this was an answer that she was interested in hearing. Mila guessed that what she said now might keep her in the kitchen for at least another few minutes and she hoped utter indifference was the shortest route to end the conversation. In the throwaway (and sleepy) manner of someone with no interest in what she was going to be doing for the next three years, Mila said: 'Sociology. It's all I could think of doing.'

Jasmine made a sound that might have been a snort and looked at Mila more intently. 'I'm studying astrophysics; it's what I've wanted to do since I was ten. It's why I stay up late to read about it. Why did you bother coming if you don't really want to study your subject?'

Mila might have said, 'I don't know, see you in the morning,' but she was not sure of herself in her new surroundings – maybe there were lots more women like this one (with an unhealthy interest in books) at university – and Mila did not want to risk seeming dumb. She did not want to risk doing anything which might make her stand out and draw attention to herself.

'Well, I do want to study it. I studied it for two years before I decided I wanted to do it at university. It's about people, and most of it is interesting. It was not about how individuals behaved because of *who* they were – that was psychology – but because of *what* they were. You could say sociology was about how people's behaviour was shaped by the time and place they lived in. If the people who were asking you what sociology was about also wanted to know what it was good for, you could tell them sociology could make the world a better place.'

'OK, so that's what it's about, but what sort of facts do you learn from it? Astrophysics is *about* understanding the universe and how matter in the universe behaves – like how stars are born and die – and where it comes from and where it is going. But that does not tell you what you get out of studying it – that's another list of problems altogether. That's knotty questions like, what evidence there is for and against the Big Bang, and black holes, and dark matter. Those are big ideas that are really exciting because they could explain so much – maybe everything – but we don't quite know how to put them all together yet. So what are sociology's big ideas?'

Mila noted the challenge in Jasmine's voice and she thought she had the beginnings of an answer. Sociology's big ideas were theories. Jasmine had given her an injection of curiosity that would spread through her head and get under her skin and give her an itch she had to scratch.

Mila went back to her room and before turning in for the night she looked at the newsfeed on her tablet. The trial of the last of the four defendants had begun. Her father's picture seemed to be on the front page of every website again. It was the same old photo from the first day of his trial (his was the first case to come to court). In it he was frozen in mid-stride up the courtroom steps, apparently striding confidently to vindication, but the smile for the camera did not look easy. Her mother was on the step behind him, looking defiantly at the camera. They both looked too young to have children of her age, yet there was Mila in the photo behind her mother: a young woman with round shoulders and a square jaw and, just like her mother, staring stupidly, straight at the camera.

Mila had no idea now why she had offered herself up for identification by anyone who bought a newspaper. Of course she should have thought of the press and their cameras before she got out of the taxicab, or her mother should have. If only she had put on sunglasses, a hat, or a scarf, it might have made all the difference. But even as unprepared as she was, she could have turned aside instead of looking straight at the camera. Doni, a yard behind her, had saved himself – he had his hand up to his face to brush the hair out of his eyes and you couldn't identify him at all.

Six weeks ago, as she stared at her face in the bathroom mirror, Mila had anticipated her first day at university and realised that she could not endure it without making some attempt to undo the damage done on the steps of the court. She had her hair cut and coloured and she stopped wearing contact lenses. Now she was never seen without the glasses she had last worn when she was 13 years old. Then she changed her name. So Mila was born, a young woman wearing a child's glasses who was starting university and praying that nobody recognised her as the person in the infamous photograph.

This morning she had lost faith in her disguise. She found herself copying (six months too late) Doni's gesture from the court steps – her hand constantly fussing around her face. She was holding her stomach muscles in tight, preparing for the lurch inside that she would feel when someone showed they recognised her. She kept telling herself it wasn't instant recognition she had to fear but the teachers and fellow students she would be sitting with in classes with, week after week ('we were talking the other day, you know, you look like the daughter of that man who stole all those poor people's money'). Nevertheless, she was close to running away throughout that first morning. Up to that point, most of the commentators in the media had implied that his guilt or innocence was a matter of fine judgement. Looked at in one way, they said, it was a felony, but looked at in another way (and this was just as easy) there was no crime at all.

They said he could easily be what Mila still knew he was – a falsely accused man who should feel terribly aggrieved for all the pain and anguish that he and his family had endured. But when the announcement of her father's guilt opened the floodgates, the family were submerged in torrents, which soon became deep, slow-moving floods, of other people's judgement. Now there was no thin line between innocent man and criminal. Mila could see it all being replayed on the screen in front of her: 'disgraced business man', 'notorious fraudster'. Since the trial, the media had called him the embodiment of self-serving duplicity; they called his crime heinous; they said that all right-thinking people would think of this as the trial of one of the most notorious white-collar crooks. They revisited their judgement on the arguments of the defence too – there it was on a screen again now: 'defence claimed he did not know his actions were illegal'; 'common practice'. Before the trial, it had seemed they agreed with this but now they said his defence had been as shameless as his crime: he had had the audacity to claim he did not know it was wrong. What a bare-faced liar – to rob from the poor and then, unashamed, say he did not know he had done wrong at all! This showed, they said, that he had no understanding of the meaning of morality, or, worse still, thought he was not bound by it.

Mila still believed her father had done no wrong. He had explained to her when the charges were first made public that he had always told everyone the truth, including those people to whom he sold the stocks. It was because they were poor that they had to provide for their sickness and old age and he was helping them to do this by making an investment they could rely on in the lean times. He told them they might lose their money, and that they made their choice freely, and that is how the world went in business.

For her father (and in fact the family) the risks were not so great. They stood to gain whether the stocks made money or not, but that was the advantage of having professional expertise which no ordinary investor could acquire. In what her father insisted was an entirely separate arrangement, he and his friends were to be remunerated by a third party if the price of the stocks they were encouraging people to buy should rise.

According to her father, the stocks themselves were a sound investment and it was on that basis that her father had been happy to sell them, and he would, he insisted, have done exactly the same even if it were not the case that he and his friends might benefit if the buying power of the people boosted the price of the stock in question. And yes, it was also true that he and his friends, who were also now to be put on trial, had all bought the stock cheaply and taken their profits before the slide began. But this was what everyone did: it was common practice; there was nothing wrong and certainly nothing illegal in it.

In the news feed and in any search engine, the killer quote about this now, the one that the prosecutor had given them on the courtroom steps after the trial, was that her father was guilty of 'an obscene confidence trick'. This was the accusation that the Twittersphere had been using ever since to turn her father into a hate figure.

***

A few weeks went by and Mila had to return to her home for the night because she had a family duty to perform: her mother needed to show her off to her three sisters. None of the women in her family had been to university, and Mila was quite a novelty. The three aunts had made the trip from different corners of the country to Mila's house for a special celebration meal to mark Mila's achievement. It was more than likely, Mila knew, that this meal would give her the first opportunity to find out whether the first big idea she thought she had learned in those first two months was big enough and important enough to justify her being at university at all.

Modernity, she was pretty sure, was a very short way of describing a big sociological theory. It was like the Big Bang in astrophysics, a short label you could remember for something that was actually huge and could predict lots of observations we did not know – it could be complex enough to make your head spin. Mila had wanted to be sure that big ideas were always theories and she had actually asked Jasmine about this in the kitchen again, this time over breakfast.

Mila asked her what those big ideas in astrophysics were, such as the Big Bang, and Jasmine said the Big Bang was an idea about how the universe started. She explained that nobody just 'knew' that the Big Bang was the point at which the universe was created, but there was evidence of the Big Bang all around us: in the way the universe was expanding and in the measurement of background radiation (the 'echo' of the Big Bang). Some scientists still weren't convinced and there were gaps and observations that didn't fit, but maybe the Big Bang was a major part of the explanation for the origin of the universe and what you needed were other theories to fill in the gaps. Even if you needed to ask what came *before* the Big Bang, you would still need a theory which explained the origin of the universe we now live in.

So now Mila knew what she was looking for – an idea that was a label which led you into a theory about something big. Modernity was certainly the biggest idea she came across in those first few weeks. She knew that some ways of behaving were called 'modern', which usually just meant 'new' or 'unconstrained by convention or tradition'. Modernity was a term that described how many societies around the world came to value novelty – making new things – and abandoning tradition – making things new. It described a historical change whereby more than 200 years in the past, European societies underwent a significant and quite rapid change in all aspects of their social, cultural, political, and economic lives. This involved getting rid of old traditions and relationships – such as relationships of obligation and deference between a feudal lord and his serfs. It also meant creating new conventions and obligations, and new ways of thinking.

Modernity was also exported to other parts of the world, either because it was so successful – as in the case of the United States of America in the eighteenth century or Japan or Singapore in the twentieth century – or by force. Some countries, such as China during the nineteenth century and the first half of the twentieth, were simply made to accept the new way of doing it all. Modernity meant new ways of organising thought and belief, so it was secular – private, religious beliefs were not to be allowed to influence politics, law, or intellectual inquiry. It meant new ways of organising time. Once, the day, the month, and the year were organised around religious festivals and agricultural seasons. Now, they were organised around the precise rhythms of the clock, so work and leisure started and finished when they were scheduled to. At all points, modernity involved tearing up the old and established, not accepting that something should be done a certain way because that was the way it had always been done.

That was all modernity was, in a way: the idea that all the major changes that men and women had been through in the last few hundred years were part of an even bigger change, a massive revolution, in which the world was turned into a new kind of place. It wasn't such a difficult sentence to say in your head, but Mila thought that to persuade people why it could give you a completely fresh outlook on the world you lived in would be very hard. To explain it to her three aunts and her mother – so proud of her for getting to university – sounded like a test that Hercules would refuse.

After all, her aunts were all so different. Aunt Ima might have gone to university herself if she had been born a few years later. She was a tough woman who held down a demanding job in a large corporation and who seemed to thrive on the grudging respect of colleagues. They respected her because she told them, as she told everyone, the truth, but did not like her because she told it so bluntly.

Aunt Enid was, everyone knew, a champion gossip who was fascinated by people, but they had to have names and addresses, and mothers and spouses (and maybe lovers), and modernity was so abstract Mila was surely going to lose Enid's attention as soon as she started to explain it. Aunt Bee-Bee was the most fastidious of the four sisters – fastidious in matters of cleanliness and good taste (especially where food was concerned). Mila hoped Auntie B would be the one who asked her about her university course. This seemed likely because Bee-Bee had always been the most interested of the three in Mila's progress, but there was a risk in this. Auntie B had a great sense of humour, and this was sometimes exercised at other people's expense. She could never resist making fun where she thought people were being pompous or ridiculous and Mila feared that a lecture on modernity might be both.

At the meal, Mila's aunties took pains to steer the conversation away from the trial and its aftermath. Aunt Bee-Bee asked Mila whether the showers in her block worked and what she was eating. Aunt Enid wanted to know whom she had met. Aunt Ima asked Mila how she was getting on – meaning what sort of results was she getting, was she doing well – and what sort of job she hoped to get when she was finished. Mila did not deal with this well. Even though she had known it was coming, she felt her reply was short and defensive. Aunt Ima gave her a long look and said something tepid in response, and Mila thought that might mean they would be having this conversation every time they met from now on. After that, the conversation somehow steered away from Mila until towards the end of the meal when Aunt Bee-Bee said: 'What is it you are studying? What is it *exactly* – you know my own education was cut short, so it does not help if you tell me the name of the subject. Just tell me the sort of subject you are learning.'

This was it, and with her eyes fixed on Bee-Bee, looking for a stifled yawn or any sign of merriment in her aunt's eyes, Mila began. 'We are learning about human control over the natural world. Modernity meant that we found that nature is not something we need to live by, but something we can control and reshape. Work moved out of fields and into factories, where machines produced much more than could ever have been made by human hands alone. It was called industrialism.'

Bee-Bee was horrified. 'But we know better than that now, don't we, dear? Those factories made people ill and people lived in slums and died young of terrible diseases.'

Mila was surprised by this and her response was hesitant. 'We do it a different way now. But we still make goods and provide services. We think this is the way for our country to get richer. We think we need to do more, and create more jobs for life to get better. That's still industrialism even if we don't have all those horrible factories.'

'Or have put them somewhere out of sight,' put in Aunt Enid.

Mila went on to say that the basic idea had been around for a very long time. Industry expanded from the late eighteenth century onwards – only in a few places like Britain to start with, and then in other countries, and finally nearly everywhere. This meant people had jobs in industry instead of farming. They started making tradeable goods in factories, not in people's homes; then, later on, there was steam power and machinery; then making thousands of the same items and selling them to thousands of people at a time. That was when mass production started.

'So we're doing a history lesson now? I thought you were studying sociology. Are you studying history, then?' said Aunt Ima. Mila turned to face her other aunt while keeping one eye on Aunt Bee-Bee, who could sabotage her with one smirk.

'Well, you've got to know what those big changes were, the ones that put questions in people's heads that led them to start doing sociology. They looked at the new industry and thought: where is all this leading? What might be possible with this kind of power? For the first time it seemed realistic to imagine a world in which everyone might have enough to eat.'

Aunt Enid interjected again. 'So it was all wonderful then? I thought there were bad changes, too, like Bee-Bee said?'

'Yes. Both kinds of changes happen at the same time: everyone is packed together in the new cities, they have no proper sanitation, and disease can spread more easily. Sometimes the food is poorer than it has been in the countryside: bread adulterated with chalk, beer with opium.'

Mila said that living standards, and life expectancy, fell dramatically. Lots of people wondered if these changes were really for the good at all. There were also big social changes, especially when everyone moved to the towns from the countryside. There were lots of places where these changes were still going on today. Whenever they happened, traditional family and religion no longer meant as much, and people no longer paid attention to the authority of family or religious figures.

Aunt Enid frowned to show how disappointed she was that people no longer cared for their families, but Mila said: 'Lots of people thought this kind of development was terrible when it first happened, but then some of them thought it was great because there was more freedom in the cities and new possibilities. People's living standards eventually rose, but improvements in the quality of life were never certain. The towns and cities gave you more possibilities, but they took liberties away too. Freedom could mean breaking old bonds but creating new ones, so people who once deferred to a remote feudal lord now obeyed a very close factory manager.'

Mila's mother had been silent until now. The truth was that Mila had forgotten that she was even there, the big idea test was for her aunts, not her mother, but it seemed that Mila's mother had also been listening to what she had to say. She asked Mila gently why she had not mentioned the people who had got rich while so many went to live in unhealthy squalor. Very carefully not looking at Aunt Ima, Mila said this was what people meant when they started talking about capitalism. They wanted to understand why industry was expanding so fast and what it was all leading to. One important answer was that, as her mother had said, some people were making money out of it. They were not making money to spend and show off, but to *accumulate* more and more. The purpose of money in feudalism was to create works: to build cathedrals, castles, to pay artists to paint you in a flattering light. The purpose of money in capitalism was to generate more capital. Money became more and more about itself. It became a value in itself, as well as a way of buying other values.

Money became the basis for competition between companies and individuals. More and more activities were judged solely on their market value, in money terms. Their 'worth' became their 'price'. So people often say, 'you can't put a price on happiness', but then act the rest of the time as if you can. In one way, this was good. Competition for markets stimulated new technologies, new ways of working, which brought us the railways, steam power, and electricity. Markets that worked required laws that were, if not just, at least fair and transparent. However, this could also lead to a situation where everything was valued in terms of its market value, rather than its moral or social worth.

As with industrialism, capitalism did not simply *happen*, said Mila. People got caught up in it to the extent that they started to believe it was the best way to run all sorts of activities, because it promised so much prosperity and such an improvement in people's living standards. But, again as with industrialism – when people did not like the undermining of traditional authority and the family – there were critics. Critics of capitalism did not like the way that money had replaced God, or faith. They did not understand how a recent human creation could have so much power over so many aspects of life. They pointed out the costs of accumulation. What happened to those who could not compete if everyone's living depended on the market? If accumulation was the be-all and end-all, then wouldn't capitalists work their workers too hard and pay them too little to make sure they accumulated more? It was Aunt Ima who supplied the answers to these questions.

'But those critics were very wrong. We have been able to find ways of living with capitalism which allow us all to benefit from growth. We are all more prosperous and more healthy because of capitalism. You are giving us a history lesson again. Capitalism was harsh years ago. Mistakes were made but people learned from those mistakes.'

For the first time in her self-imposed ordeal by aunties, Mila felt she ought to give up and she was not made to feel any better by Aunt Enid taking her sister's side: 'Life was so different back then, dear. Ordinary people had no say over what happened to them – women had no say at all.' Now Mila gratefully took the chance to change direction.

'I was getting round to that, because it wasn't just the market that changed people's way of thinking about their place in the world. Democracy is part of modernity too. There were big changes already going on when capitalism started to have an impact.'

Mila said the idea that more and more people should have some sort of say in who governed them had been around for hundreds of years, but at the end of the eighteenth century the idea of democracy got its biggest boost with the French Revolution. That revolution, just as much as the industrial one, was part of modernity. It made people think about how far this process might go, how far it *should* go.

Before the French Revolution happened there had been another set of events that made it, *as well as* industrialism and capitalism, possible. The Enlightenment was the time in the first half of the eighteenth century when freethinkers tried to apply reason to all the problems that had, up to that point, either been simply accepted as not needing an explanation, or being a consequence of God's will. It started in France, Scotland, and a few other countries, but then gradually spread to the rest of the world.

In the Enlightenment, people came round to the idea that humans weren't just pawns of fate or divine will. Because human beings mattered, and because they had reason, they didn't just have to wander through life being blindly buffeted by the events that happened to them. They could become authors of their own destiny and seek the answers to what had been hidden. They believed that nothing could really be hidden from human reason, nothing would remain inexplicable for ever. The Enlightenment meant that light could be shone everywhere.

It was not just that there were new situations to ask questions about in modernity. It actually became OK, even compulsory, to ask questions about everything: where humans came from, what it was to be human, to think, to live. This compulsion to ask questions was the result of the Enlightenment. According to Mila, the Enlightenment was so fundamental that it wasn't simply the foundation of democracy and industrialism and capitalism: it set off lots of developments that could not be summarised under any of these headings, like science. When all of these changes started to turn the world upside down, then you got modernity.

Mila spoke. 'If the idea of modernity works for you, then you think there is something that tied all of these major changes together. That's all modernity is. It's the theory that all the major changes that people all over the world have been through are part of an even bigger change, a massive revolution, in which the world was turned into a new kind of place. It's because of this massive change that the subject I am studying, sociology, was invented. It wasn't needed before, but once you get modernity you need sociology to describe and explain the new world that is being created. It is needed to understand the new relationships, ways of working and thinking that are constantly being created by modernity.'

Mila found she was looking at her Aunt Ima for a response, waiting for the next pithy comment that would leave her self-confidence in tatters, but Ima smiled: 'If you ever came to work with me you might find modernity is taking a long time to arrive in some places in this country.' Aunt Bee-Bee saw the room for a joke (how long she had waited!), but this was at her sister's expense, not Mila's: 'But Ima, you are always telling us how modern you are. When our niece tells us modernity is really two or three hundred years old maybe she is talking about your dress sense.' At the end of the laughter, with Bee-Bee, as ever, taking the lead in laughing at her own joke, Mila thought she could even try some summing up. She looked at her Auntie B with gratitude as she went on.

'So, Auntie, we are learning that sociology has a theory that a new kind of world was created from the eighteenth century onwards. It was like the Big Bang in astrophysics that made the stars and the universe. It created lots of different ways of doing what made life work *and* they all fitted together – institutions and habits as different as laws, science, religion, entertainment, work, politics, and the way men and women treated each other.'

Mila smiled at Aunt Enid and carried on.

'The idea of modernity sums up the newness of all this and the kind of feeling it gave people of opportunities and possibilities. The new world was about getting rid of the old life with its superstition and tradition, and everyone living where they were born until they died, and nothing ever really changing for anyone. This is one of sociology's *really* big ideas: there was this great break in history, a new world opened up, good and bad, and set us on tracks that we are following now. Modernity was the short label that summed all of this big idea up. It is such a big idea that it has been taken up by all sorts of people outside sociology.'

All her aunts were beaming at her and Mila could feel herself relaxing. It was beginning to dawn on her that her first big idea had passed the test and this was quite something: sociology even had its own equivalent of the Big Bang! But then her mother spoke. 'What Enid says is not such a joke. Have we really gone forwards so much? If your grandfather was alive today he might tell you otherwise. There are achievements that he fought for all his life that many people don't have, not even here, like good health and a feeling of being valued by others. People used to care about these ideals, but they don't seem to care about them any longer. How can we say we have gone forwards not backwards?'

Here it was again, the misery that you could never escape – surely that was what was behind her mother's negativity? And wasn't that allusion to not 'being valued by others' just self-pity? Yet what her mother said reminded Mila of something she had briefly glimpsed herself when she first heard about modernity. This insight now became much clearer: when you really understood that modernity had changed the world once – because people decided the world could be changed and needed changing – then you realised that it could happen again. The idea of modernity showed us we could have another big revolution in the way we lived. Now Mila remembered something else.

She remembered something Randolph had said about it being possible that life has now changed so much that we are not on those same tracks anymore. Did this mean the world was no longer really modern and modernity was a theory that was becoming out of date? He had said something about families having changed so much recently that they were no longer like the ones created by modernity. Mila looked round the table at her aunts and her mother: were they the sort of family that fitted modernity? Since the trial, she had felt they did not fit in anywhere, but at least her mother and father were loyal to each other, her mother and her sisters were close, and she, Mila, felt her membership of the family was the most important jewel in the world to her. Would these feelings and even these relationships also turn out to be impermanent? Mila could not imagine what her world would be like if this ever happened.

Visit the companion website at **www.palgrave.com/companion/ Bancroft-And-Fevre-Dead-White-Men-2e/** to access additional learning resources, including seminar questions based on the chapter's coverage, a jargon buster that defines key terms used in the text and a timeline which provides an overview of the development of sociological thought.

● ● ● ● ●

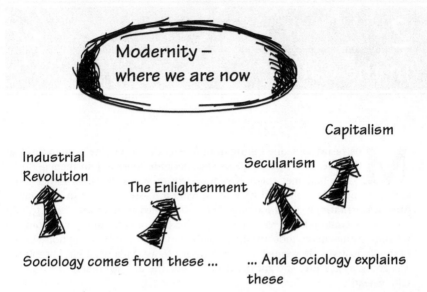

Modernity –
where we are now

Capitalism

Industrial
Revolution

Secularism

The Enlightenment

Sociology comes from these ...

... And sociology explains these

1. Modernity means a constant state of flux. It is a combination of revolutions in economics, society, politics and thought, which created a world very different from that which had existed before. Sociology has a close relationship with modernity because it was created as a way of explaining the many changes wrought in modernity. Modernity brings both new freedoms and new restrictions and forms of social control.

2. Sociology tells us how society can still work without its traditional foundations – so what we thought were the unchanging foundations were just one instance of the type of activity needed to keep society going. For example, it was thought once that the Church bound people to a shared morality, and that feudalism made them do their duty. So when those institutions and ways of life declined it was feared there would be nothing but a chaos of atomised individuals.

3. Sociology has been called the science of democracy since it in part came into existence to study public opinion, mass culture and other aspects of life in modern, democratic societies. It showed why the decline of traditional ways of life and belonging did not lead to social disorder. It was not churches necessarily but associations that kept people together. Not hierarchies but networks make them reliant on others. Sociology showed how new associations and networks came into existence.

4. Many aspects of life that are stereotyped as out of date or backward are modern. Fundamentalist religion, a rigid division of gender roles, and strict racial distinctions came into existence with modernity. So 'modern' does not mean 'free and easy' or 'smart and tolerant'.

2
In the Café

Mila heard someone calling from further down the line as she waited in the café. Two older students were beckoning her to join them.

She had met them already. Garrison was very large, rather loud, and quite objectionable, and he was studying a master's degree in economics. Arun was irritatingly good looking. Garrison seemed to have asked her to join them so he could tell her what a great job his economics training was going to get him in the energy industry (he actually said he would be 'a big noise in the energy industry'). He seemed unlikely to want to ask Mila what kind of job she was going to get after she got her degree – but she did not much like what he said instead.

'Of course you are only here so you can meet a rich husband.' He really looked like he wanted to provoke her.

'It's all about money with everybody, not just you,' he expanded. 'Everybody is out to get the best deal they can. Women know if they come to university they will get the chance to meet someone who is going to be rich. It's costs and benefits: you lose out a bit by not earning money when you are a student, but you make more in the long run. And you don't have to work so hard – you're studying sociology, aren't you? You don't even have to learn much to get to meet your future husband.'

Mila rolled her eyes at this gambit. 'Testing my mettle?'

'What's sociology about anyway? Sociologists always say people are hard done by, "deprived", "exploited"? It's like we're meant to feel sorry for those who are too lazy or stupid to work out how to make good.'

This was one opportunity to test out a big idea that Mila was not going to take. She did not have a theory in her head which she was ready to explain and, more importantly, she would have to be an idiot to put the judgement of it in the hands of someone like Garrison. Arun said that his friend, Garrison, had some classic personality traits – like aggression and narcissism – which were always getting him into trouble. 'It was probably something in his upbringing which had gone wrong. Wasn't that something psychology and sociology could agree on,' he said, 'that the way people are brought up affects the way they think?' Mila felt a vague feeling of unease begin to stir. Anything that made her think about her parents could make her anxious, but this question was even closer to those subjects which Mila felt were dangerous for her.

He added, 'that's what traditional psychologists would have thought – psychodrama in infancy laid down what your personality would be. Cutting-edge psychology thinks that upbringing is marginal to shaping how people think. It's the hardwiring they were born with – the way their brains are put together and the way their brain chemistries work – that make the difference. If sociology is all about nurture against nature then maybe sociology is out of date.'

She replied, 'How do psychologists know how anyone's brain is making them behave in a particular way?' Arun told her in a straightforward way that they did it by looking at scans of brain activity which showed how different parts of the brain were active in different situations.

'It's simply a matter of time before we find out where in the brain the location of each behaviour lies. So it makes little sense at all to ask if variation in brain function is a product of anything on a human scale like upbringing.

Mostly the human scale is way too small. If you want to understand how human behaviour changes, you need to look at a much longer timescale where you can get changes in the shape of our brains. That's why the most interesting psychology is actually about the way evolution has shaped the way we think. Evolution is on the right scale – tens of thousands, hundreds of thousands, of years; not the ten or 20 years it takes to make an adult human being.'

In spite of herself, Mila could understand what he meant. It wasn't anywhere near as long a time as the cosmic scale on which Jasmine described the birth and death of stars, but it was certainly on a completely different scale to the one sociology operated within.

'So how does your kind of psychology explain changes in behaviour that do happen between generations, even during a lifetime?' she asked. He told her that 'as the brain matures, its hardwiring develops in line with the genetic blueprint and that accounts for changes over a lifetime. There aren't any changes between generations, at least not any changes that matter.'

Then Mila kept going. 'So we disagree about what matters, then. You say tomorrow will be the same as today because the sun will come up as it always does, but I want to know what the weather will be like. I need to know if it's going to be hot or raining. I need to know if there is going to be a typhoon. It matters to me, to everyone, what the weather is like. Sociologists are interested in the weather, the smaller timescale, because it matters.

'And sociology is not at all about everything being determined by your upbringing. You couldn't ever change in your lifetime if that was the case. And even if upbringing is crucial, sociology is more interested in how ideas about the right way to bring up kids change. Psychology can show how you get one kind of adult produced by one set of ideas about how you should bring up children, and a different kind of adult from another set of ideas. But sociology can tell you where those different kinds of ideas come from in the first place.'

This was what Mila's lecturers, and the textbooks they made her read, had been teaching her, and she knew enough to be able to repeat it. But it hadn't personally mattered to her in any way until this moment. It was quite a simple connection to make, but, for some reason, she had been very slow to make it.

Garrison had been listening to her defence of sociology with increasing amusement. His smirking reawakened in her the uncomfortable sensation that her unspoken thoughts had been read, but what he said next made her stomach lurch.

'So what is the reason why some people are criminals and parasites? It's not the way parents bring up their children, it's not the chemicals in their brain. Oh, I know, it's all *society's* fault! That's what sociologists say: it's never any individual's fault – an individual parent or an individual lowlife – it's everyone else's fault. Society puts all the wrong ideas in their heads and they can't help what they do.'

Mila almost panicked. It was as if he were quoting some of the columnists' condemnations of her father, particularly those written shortly after the verdict when they put up all the arguments that might be made in defence and mitigation and shot them down to reveal only greed and veniality. She kept talking.

'Yes, you are right,' was what she said, 'the idea that society has a big part to play in the explanation of human behaviour is probably the most fundamental theory in sociology. Well, at least that's what I've been putting in the essay I've got to hand in this week.'

'Why do you need to come up with another theory when we already know that you can explain everything by adding up the actions of rational individuals who are maximising their benefits and minimising their costs? All their individual calculations about what is in their economic interest do most of the job for you. What you call society is an illusion.'

Garrison did not mention crime but 'maximising their benefits' and 'calculations about what is in their economic interest' must have been intended to goad her about her father, Mila thought. Though, if you took him seriously, Mila imagined you would think Garrison was saying he understood rather than condemned her father. This thought at least made Mila's panic subside, but she was still determined she was going to do nothing to acknowledge the hidden identity which they seemed to know all about.

Arun asked Mila to tell them about her essay – after all they were master's students and they might be able to give her some tips, improve her approach a bit. They knew some of her tutors were postgraduates so it was quite possible they might be able to help her. If this was the first university essay she had to hand in, she was probably unsure, and quite nervous, about what was required. Tutors were told to be very careful not to give specific guidance on essays, so that students' abilities could be fairly judged, but these two were not her tutors so, he said, a bit of reassurance that she was on the right lines would be OK.

She remembered she had learned, in the previous week of lectures, that the term 'society' did not exist before modernity. In the nineteenth century, people began to use the term to refer to the object that was being affected by all the changes they saw going on around them: not just the political stuff (democracy), not just how commodities were made (machinery, for instance), not just how people lived (in cities, and so on) but *all of these together* and every other aspect of life, too (for example, dress, religion, sex). All of these were changing, but how could you study this if you did not have a word to sum up all the things that were being affected?

Like astrophysics needed black holes and white dwarfs, sociology needed objects to study and the biggest of them all was society. But, as with modernity, the object of study was wrapped up in a theory. Society was a label for a theory that might, or might not, explain a lot. The short version of the theory was exactly what the economics student had said: society shapes our thinking and our actions.

Mila began to explain her essay to them. 'Sociology is built on the theory that individuals are shaped by something bigger than themselves and that something is called society. It is an idea that has been around since someone came up with the term "sociology" in fact. That was a Frenchman called Auguste Comte who was born two centuries ago.'

Mila went on to tell them how what Comte had said became a kind of slogan for sociologists: sociology had to consider individuals as the products of society, not the other way round. In Comte's time there were plenty of people who said there was no such object as society. In Britain that kind of thinking was in charge and sociology did not catch on at all for more than 100 years. Instead there were people like Herbert Spencer and the utilitarians saying individuals were making decisions on their own according to what they thought was in their best interests.

But life was different in France and, later on, there was another Frenchman, called Émile Durkheim, who wanted to carry on what Comte had been thinking about. He did not dismiss what the people in Britain were saying, but he thought you needed the idea of society too. If you looked at how complicated an industrial country like France or Britain was becoming in the nineteenth century, it did not make sense to think this complexity only happened because people were rational, self-interested individuals. She looked at Garrison at this point and he took his cue (and this time there was much more about economics and sociology and less that seemed to be about her father, so maybe talking about her essay was normalising the conversation).

'Of course it did. People could see it made good sense to specialise in different ways of earning a living (you do this, and I will do that) and then cooperate with each other so they could all make more and live better. If everyone carried on doing everything for themselves, like they still do in some backward villages, everyone stayed poor. Look at this café: if they only sold what they could grow or make here, there would be hardly anything to choose from. They buy stuff from people who specialise and that means we eat better.'

'Not everyone agrees,' said Arun, smiling at Mila, who had touched none of her food. Garrison carried on regardless.

'So some people saw they could make money making clothes for other people to buy and those other people did not have to bother making their own clothes. They could concentrate on farming and producing enough food so that they had plenty left over to sell to give them money to buy clothes and everything else they needed. It's obvious to everyone that it's in all our interests to specialise and get markets going, so that people can buy and sell goods.'

'But you need cooperation too, don't you?' said Mila. She took a breath and explained that the new industrial countries were not about having one individual specialising in making clothes. There had been tailors for hundreds of years, maybe longer. Industrialism meant you had factories where people doing different specialised jobs were gathered together and cooperated in order to produce goods like textiles. Markets needed cooperation. Sometimes you had to trust that other people would provide what you needed in future, and sometimes people had to hand goods over without being paid right away. They also had to trust the people they were dealing with. Durkheim thought specialisation would have been a big risk for people to take if they were just calculating costs and benefits. Would they really have put their futures in other people's hands, just give up self-sufficiency, trust to specialisation and hope others would choose to cooperate (through their own selfish interests) and it would all work out in the end? Mila explained that Durkheim thought the answer to this was definitely no and, working backwards, he said this proved that the isolated individuals who acted according to their own self-interest had never existed.

The division of labour between people doing specialist jobs did not get created by isolated individuals, but by people who were *already* used to thinking about each other in a way that had nothing to do with their own selfish interests. The trust and cooperation you needed for complex industrial societies started off because people already felt a bond with each other. In other words, Durkheim said, they must already have had a *society*. By this he meant that people thought they were part of a group of like-minded men and women, people who shared their feelings and their beliefs. Selfish individual behaviour – behaving as if you weren't bound to everyone else, following your 'own' wants, and so on – would destroy society, because it would break the bonds that tied people to each other.

'So, no selfish individuals until you get the division of labour established?' said Arun.

'Yes, I think that's right, maybe,' replied Mila, hesitantly 'but, anyway, this was the start of the big idea, the sociological theory that said society was an important part of the explanation for why change happened. When you looked at the division of labour you could see that society was necessary for trust and cooperation and you could not have modern industrialised societies without it.'

Mila went on to say that the big idea of society was a theory about how we created the more impersonal way of life that we are now used to. In traditional rural villages everyone knew everyone else and it could be very claustrophobic. Now we were used to a more arm's length way of life, but that only became possible because at one level we were a kind of unit, part of something which we recognised as bigger than us.

'What else is society making happen apart from specialisation and cooperation?' he asked.

Mila smiled a little. 'It makes our feelings.' As she said it, she was thinking 'at least my feelings are under some sort of control now,' and it was true she was no longer in that state of extreme anxiety when she felt she was going to be mocked and, in the very next moment, exposed and condemned.

He smiled too. 'There you go again. Feelings are really all about chemical changes in the brain.'

She told them that, in Durkheim's day, people had thought our feelings were created by our instincts, our ingrained responses. If you needed to bring in anything else, then you said our feelings were affected by the good or bad events that happened to us. But Durkheim said there must be more to it than this: people weren't just animals working on instinct. The difference between ourselves and the animals was our sociability. As societies developed, there was a smaller and smaller role for instinct and our feelings were more likely to come from the beliefs and ideas we had been taught to value.

Mila told them that Durkheim said it was easy to prove that individuals' feelings should be explained by what was happening in society. He asked us to look at the way people were brought up in different places. Mila pressed on, unaware that she was heading back into danger. The Mila who had walked into the café would have been screaming at her: what are you doing showing off like the child you were when you last wore those glasses? But the Mila who was in charge of her mouth, now heard none of this and carried on, into the swamp. She said that Durkheim argued that, in some social groups, children were taken away from their parents when they were young and there was no particular bond between parents and children. In other places parents were supposed to love children very much. The difference was not in people's instincts – or the chemicals in the brain – but in the kind of society they happened to live in. She went on.

'You'll probably tell me that neurotransmitters in the brain generate feelings, but sociologists say that they don't start them off. Obligations start off in society, then get absorbed into our heads and then we act on them. And this means we are making society happen all over again. Like in this café we know we are meant to take our dirty dishes back to the rack over there. So we feel we should do it and, when we act on this feeling that this is the right act to do, then, when other people come in, they see us putting the dirty dishes back and they know everyone is expected to do it. That way it ends up a nice clean café where everyone likes to eat.'

'Except you, apparently,' said Garrison, 'are you going to eat that? If you want to keep talking, I'll eat it, but I won't take your dish back. I never take my dishes back. Let the woman who is paid to do it take them back.'

Mila pushed her plate at him and continued. 'Durkheim would say you haven't learned how to be a member of society. He would say that you had no moral feelings.'

'Yes, that's true,' he said, smirking at his friend, 'no morals at all.'

'He wasn't thinking of the kind of morals you mean, or at least they were only a small part of it. For him, moral feelings were anything that we should or shouldn't do. It might be something like wearing a hat or not murdering people. It was all the actions that you felt in some way that you ought to do, or ought not to do, even things as small as when we change our clothes and the sheets on our beds.'

Both of them grinned at her and she fought for a way out of the treacherous swamp she had driven into.

'OK, I know men are not always so bothered about that sort of thing. My auntie says that's because they have no sense of smell, but it's not really. It's because they think that men can live by different standards to women – the rules about what they should do about keeping clean are not so strict. But there are some rules for men that are much stricter than for women.'

'Like what?'

'Like what you should feel when you think you have been insulted,' said Mila. 'Men usually have stronger feelings about that than women do. That's the same thing again – moral feelings in the wider sense of what you ought to feel, how you should behave, in this situation.'

She was still in jeopardy and, though she sincerely hated Durkheim and his obsession with morality, carrying on with the argument of her essay seemed to be her only route away from danger. Mila explained that Durkheim had said that feelings had to have this moral element otherwise we simply would not take any notice and we would not act on what we felt unless we were somehow forced to do it. This showed just how strong the moral feelings were that society put in our heads. This way society could make us do many more actions than it could do if we were forced by people with guns. Durkheim said that each of us finds these feelings so powerful, so hard to resist, because society is so much bigger than us. This makes us do acts that are against our instincts and might even be uncomfortable or hurt us. Something fired in Mila's brain, the electric trace of authentic insight, and it so took her aback that she hesitated just enough for Garrison to butt in.

'I would never do anything that is not in my interest.'

'Is that really true?' said Mila. 'When you get your big job in the energy industry, I bet you'll have to do all sorts of activities you hate, maybe even dress in clothes that make you uncomfortable, because you know that it's expected of you.'

'Yeah, but I'll only do it if it's in my interest. If it pays me to wear a suit, I'll wear one.'

'Yes, but when you wear a suit, you are recognising that others have expectations of you and you have obligations to them. If you wear a suit, you know you have social bonds.'

Durkheim had written that it was the job of sociology to study what these obligations were, continued Mila, and sociologists must also be ready to study *all* the feelings society put in our heads, even the ones that sociologists found most natural. If parents and children loved each other, you needed to explain where this love came from. If people felt so patriotic that they were prepared to die for their country, sociologists needed to explain that, not just admire it. But, not only that, when you studied these feelings, you had to separate out their content from their effects. Whether it was a feeling that you admired, or one you didn't, you should study the effect that the feeling had on social bonds. Again she felt the electric shock of firing synapses, as an insight was formed and, even in her extremely agitated state, she determined that she would put this feeling (if that was what it was) aside for later investigation.

'Not so long ago, lots of people thought there was no point in sending women to university, because they would only get married and waste their education anyway,' Mila said, looking meaningfully at Garrison. 'I think it was an idea that hurt women and wasted their talents but, as long as people agreed with it, then their feelings about what women should and shouldn't do, helped keep society together.'

He shrugged. 'But what happens to your theory now that lots of women waste everybody's time going to university? Society is not falling apart now, is it? So your theory is wrong.'

'Durkheim wouldn't be so sure. He thought the bonds that held people together were fragile and needed working at. The more industrialised and modern societies got, the harder it was to keep them from falling apart. Today I am talking to two men who I barely know. That would only happen in a modern society, and it's a problem because there are no elders or religious figures around to make sure we behave properly.'

'I haven't got a problem with it if you haven't,' Garrison told her. Mila told him not to be silly and explained that, for Durkheim, this was not a coincidence. People learned their ideas and convictions from interacting with other people – working together, worshipping together, simply living together – and the different ways people interacted produced different kinds of ideas and convictions. The obvious example of this was where you met lots of people on a daily basis, but actually did not know the majority of them very well – that was what life was like in a big modern city. This was bound to give you different ideas about life, the world, everything, than you would have had if you were living in a small settlement, hidden away in the countryside, and only ever saw people who you had known all your life. Big modern cities were exactly the sorts of places where people would find that they didn't all end up with the same ideas and beliefs, because they really did not live the same way. Everyone was more and more of an individual, and they relied less and less on traditional beliefs and customs.

'So, yes, there will be more disagreement – and not just about what ambitions women should have – but Durkheim said that modern societies could come up with solutions to the threat to those fragile social bonds. The solutions kept these societies together so coming up with them was the major problem that faced modern societies.'

If they didn't come up with these solutions, said Durkheim, there were going to be all sorts of problems from soaring suicides to soaring crime rates. High suicide rates showed, for instance, that the social bonds were breaking down: people were missing the intense, personal interaction they got from traditional communities and religious worship. As a result, they didn't really know what to believe in, or what they were meant to do, and this drove some people to despair.

In rural villages you didn't have to think about what was the right act to do, you just followed the customs, kept the traditional life going, and everyone knew how they were meant to act. In the city, Durkheim said, nobody really knew the names of most of the people that they came into contact with. The way that people solved the problem of keeping society going in the city was to come up with abstract rules. These rules about how you should behave towards people could be applied in any of the different situations that arose in an ordinary day.

There were parts of the cities, maybe where the richest people lived or where the manual workers lived, that were a bit like the rural villages. Everybody knew everybody and the social bonds between people were still tight. But in other parts of the city the only ties that held people together were the generalisations they were happy to agree on about how people should behave.

Durkheim said that it was not only in the cities that you would need this kind of thinking, but it was, to start with, only in the cities that people were capable of coming up with it because their lives there were so different from the way people had lived in the past. Now Mila felt she could rest. The swamp had been left miles behind and this was the dry, high ground of sociological theory which could have nothing at all to do with her or her family.

Arun asked Mila: 'But how are people going to have strong *feelings* about abstractions and generalisations? Didn't you tell us that society gave us strong moral feelings? You are telling us that society needs those moral feelings to hold it together – so that people don't commit suicide, whatever – and you think that abstract ideas can give people these feelings?' Mila said 'This was one of the cleverest aspects of the theory: Durkheim thought that if you looked at what went on in modern society carefully, you could see that people really did care about the abstractions and generalizations. Don't you have any strong moral feelings?' She aimed it at Arun, but Garrison butted in.

'I told you, I am only interested in what is good for me.'

'Ah, but remember what Durkheim says about guarding against seeing our feelings as natural, taking them for granted. Maybe you can't see the moral beliefs you have because you can't look at them from the outside. Durkheim said that what aroused people's feelings in modern society was a new kind of morality called "*moral* individualism". I think even you believe in this morality.'

Mila told Garrison that she thought he had more belief in the importance of the individual, and what the individual wanted, than anyone she had ever met. She said Durkheim would have told him he was a prime example of the 'cult of the individual', in which we take ourselves so seriously that 'individual dignity' becomes the guiding principle for everything that happened in society. It might not sound like it, but this was a moral belief which aroused strong feelings.

'That's probably why you say such rude things. It's because you feel so strongly that individuals should be free to get what they want.'

'Don't you think individuals should have autonomy and freedom?'

When he pressed her, she said she believed in freedom of thought and lots of other principles that followed when you accepted every individual's right to self-determination. Then she reminded him again about the provocative remarks he had made about her coming to university to meet a husband, so she said she probably believed in these principles more strongly than he did.

'Maybe your belief in the dignity of the individual does not include the dignity of women? I feel that both men and women should be autonomous but I'm trying to look at my beliefs from outside, so that I can understand how they work for society. Durkheim said that was the sociological way to look at beliefs.'

'OK, so you agree with me. You must see everyone – maybe even women – should be allowed to get on and do whatever they want to: be as rich as they want to be or as poor as they can be bothered to be. Most people I know don't think that's very moral but you can call it a moral belief if you want to.'

Now Arun butted in: 'You think that it's OK for you to get rich while someone else gets poor, but do you think it's OK for you to get rich *because* someone else gets poor?'

'Yes, within reason: if someone's foolish enough to let me take advantage of them, then it's their lookout.'

'So you'd steal from them?'

'No, I said *within reason*. I meant it had to be legal.'

'And, if it was legal, you wouldn't mind if someone took advantage of you in the same way.'

'I can look after myself. I'm not looking for special protection. If they can't play by the same rules, that's their lookout.'

'OK, let's say some people come and live next door to your big mansion – which you buy when you make all that money in energy – and they stay up late every night, and make lots of noise, and they don't look after their house, and the neighbourhood starts to look seedy and your property loses value. Do you still defend their right to do what they want?'

'I said within reason – they can do what they like, as long as it doesn't start to affect other people.'

'Yes, that's right. There have to be the same rules for everyone. You say you will take people's money within the law. You want the same freedom as everyone else. You don't want to have special freedom. And it's the same with the neighbours: you want everyone to play by the rules.'

They both turned to look at Mila. She said that they had come up with a definition of moral individualism. It was called *moral* individualism to show us that it was not the ultra-selfish, competitive individualism the utilitarians assumed we all had but a limited individualism which set standards and expectations of our behaviour. It was a kind of individualism that kept society going and it was also an individualism that we learned *from* society. With a considerable effort, she asked Garrison:

'What would you do if your noisy neighbours wouldn't stop making your life difficult?'

'I would make their lives difficult. They would wake up in the morning to find out I had arranged for their electricity to be cut off. Or maybe I would just pay some heavies to persuade them to go and live somewhere else.'

'OK, here we go: society is breaking down. When you are living next door to people who aren't at all like you, who don't go to bed at the same time as you, and don't have the same interest in keeping up the maintenance of their house, you need moral individualism. Without it, you end up with no social bonds and a little neighbourhood war.'

Then Mila asked them to remember what started this argument. She had wanted to show them how Durkheim's theory could cope with the fact that people did not share opinions or beliefs anymore. The idea of moral individualism was how the theory coped, because it meant people still felt strongly, felt morally, but they did not have to agree all the time. In fact they agreed to disagree. They believed that it was alright, in fact it was morally imperative, that members of society be allowed to have different views.

'So, you don't have to share people's opinions but, along with everyone else in our society, you share the belief that it's right that people should be able to act on their beliefs and opinions as long as they don't threaten or inconvenience others. It's this more fundamental belief that holds society together. It's pretty much the only point we have to agree on. And do you remember the division of labour? That's got to do with this, too.'

Mila went on to say that moral feelings which allow differences of opinion were not needed in traditional societies where everyone thought in the same way because their lives were so *similar*. But, in modern societies, people did different work for a living and it was no surprise they thought differently. Durkheim thought that more specialisation meant more difference. He said modern societies had found a way of holding together despite the differences between individuals. You didn't need this new way of holding together when the division of labour was very simple.

'OK, we've got it,' said Garrison, 'back then, people all did the same work, so you didn't have the same problem.'

'Yes, and this was how Durkheim eventually got back round to agreeing, in a grudging way, with the utilitarians, the people who thought like you.'

Durkheim said that now you had got modern societies going, people could see that they needed each other. This became part of their moral view and perhaps it became the bedrock of moral individualism. Maybe seeing that they needed each other was all tied up with people thinking that individualism was great as long as there was no interfering with, or inconveniencing, other people? Anyway, the division of labour itself – the specialisation and the cooperation it made necessary – then become part of the glue that held society together: 'So, in modern society we feel bonds with other people *because* we know we do such different work!'

Arun asked Mila if there were any exceptions to this. She could barely look at him now. At first she was going to say no, but then she remembered something else she had read: 'Sometimes the social bonds need a special boost. Even in modern societies you sometimes need a boost when everyone in society gets to feel a part of the same fabric. It's OK everyone feeling like an individual, but it's not quite as exciting as the way traditional societies tightened the social bonds with religious ceremonies and other kinds of rituals.'

She explained that Durkheim thought that even in simple communities the social bonds could loosen. Even where everyone did the same as everyone else, there were times when people were off doing their own pursuits and this could lead to self-centred egotism, which might break the bonds between people and the community. So, every so often, people needed to be brought together for a special occasion on which they *would* all do the same ritual, and so would have their common ideas and beliefs reaffirmed. When they were all doing the same activity they became aware that they were a group again.

These special occasions worked best if everyone was feeling intense feelings. This was why they needed *ritual* and lots of singing or chanting or maybe even dancing. Durkheim even said that people kept going to religious rituals when they had lost their belief because it made them feel good. Some modern societies also had other rituals that could serve the same purpose and reinforce people's feeling of belonging while making them feel thrilled to be taking part. Great sporting events could do this, so could political rallies. There were other rituals that continued on a smaller scale. Even where families were not the same as they used to be – when divorce was common for instance – people still tried to keep the sense of belonging going by keeping family rituals going, birthdays, special celebrations and occasion like that. The judgement that had overwhelmed the family after her father's trial could be seen as society acting on the individual: so much bigger than them, getting them to behave in the way society expected. This made Mila proud of her father, the rebel, standing out against these over-whelming, superior forces. It was brave and romantic – as long as he had not done anything wrong. At this point, Mila realised that she was revisiting the first of the electric insights and immediately, the second one hit her.

She thought of Durkheim's instruction that you should make yourself distant from your most deeply held prejudices. This was what she had done, wasn't it? She had looked at herself and her loyalty to her father from outside. Because of sociology, she had actually begun to allow herself to imagine, just for a moment, that there was more than one reasonable way of looking at what he had done. Her father might have taken the 'cult of the individual' too far. Perhaps he was not a romantic rebel, but a dysfunctional example of the individualism which is OK if it does not go to extremes. And where, thought Mila, does that leave me? Still, she was satisfied to have answered Garrison's challenge in full.

Visit the companion website at **www.palgrave.com/companion/ Bancroft-And-Fevre-Dead-White-Men-2e/** to access additional learning resources, including seminar questions based on the chapter's coverage, a jargon buster that defines key terms used in the text and a timeline which provides an overview of the development of sociological thought.

• • • • •

How is society possible?

Are we self-interested individuals?

Or do we act within social constraints?

1. One way of understanding human behaviour is to assume that people act to make the most of their own self-interest. This is often used in economics to model behaviour. However, it reduces the range of human motivations to just one.

2. Durkheim's moral individualism describes the moral sense of obligation that we learn from shared social norms. People act towards society as if it were a thing with power – and in doing so they give it power over them. That might be good or bad. It explains how ordinary men and women can commit very harmful, and very good, acts when it is normal to do so.

3. Durkheim explains this through the division of labour. Every society assigns particular tasks to particular people, usually claiming that they are the ones who are best suited to it, perhaps because of their education, sex, social origin, ethnicity, beliefs or for other reasons. Sociologists want to study that process and those justifications.

4. In a complex society, people are reliant on the activities of many others who they will never know or meet. That allows people to do very specialised activities. Specialisation in the division of labour requires the existence of cooperation, as everyone cannot do everything, and cooperation requires trust. So one person can be a scientist working on a very specific problem because lots of other people are lab technicians, software engineers, cleaners, farmers and so on. That allows the great achievements of modern society to happen, from the postal system to the space programme.

3
In the Picture

The following month, Mila's Aunt Enid was visiting the city and asked Mila to accompany her on a visit to a new exhibition, which gathered together a number of important artefacts which had not been shown to the public before. Enid loved art that told her something about the people who were its subjects. When Mila was younger, she had often taken her to galleries and told her stories about the people in the paintings. 'See this young girl here, the one about your age? She is listening to her mother talking to her friends but they can't see her. She's up to no good. Don't you think she looks mischievous?'

This kind of story had always enchanted Mila, not least because her auntie always tried to find something in the picture with which the little girl could identify. So, now, as they began their walk around the exhibition, Mila was once more encouraging her aunt to tell her tales about the artefacts. Of course it would have been childish for a grown woman to be told made-up stories about them, but these artefacts, though never seen before, were connected to stories that a woman of Enid's age and interests would know by heart. The collection they were now seeing had been amassed by one royal family over many hundreds of years and it recorded all the important events of its dynasty, from the high points of heroism and military conquest to the lows of palace intrigue and betrayal.

Enid had already told her niece the stories behind half a dozen exhibits before they discovered one that told of the tragic events that surrounded the murder of a young princess by her jealous husband. It was a story that even Mila knew vaguely. Enid reminded her about the husband, incapable of restraining his emotions even when his jealousy was utterly baseless. Enid called it: 'An achingly sad story. Look, this panel depicts the end of the story where he comes into the bedchamber, still holding the sword that he murdered the princess with, and realising his terrible mistake, turns the weapon on himself.'

Enid obviously enjoyed the aching sadness and the passions that carried away the young husband and his bride to destruction. Mila thought it must have been such a terrible waste – two young and immensely privileged lives brought to an abrupt end through lack of self-control and good sense – but she kept her counsel. Her inability to respond in an empathetic way brought home to her how little in tune with Enid she was, now that she was no longer a little girl listening to her made-up stories.

Earlier that week, Mila had attended a lecture on the sociology of emotions which took up some of Durkheim's themes about the importance of feelings to social solidarity and sociology's responsibility for reminding other social sciences of this fact. The lecturer had said that Durkheim had written, in a fairly generic way, about parental or 'filial' love, but Durkheim did not contribute all that much to the sociology of the interpersonal feelings that animate us all. Emotions, including enmity and hate, mattered when it came to understanding behaviour (even though there were some sociologists who forgot this), but the discipline was still, apparently, fighting a sort of 'turf war' with psychology over who was best qualified to study them.

This was about as much as Mila took from the lecture. The lecturer had gone on to say what sociology could add to our understanding of emotions, but she had understood little of it. As she might shortly have to take a test on the work covered in lectures so far, she turned to her textbook for help. She had eventually bought a book that the university bookshop had on display at a discount and soon discovered she loathed it. It was by two pompous men called Fussen and Stein and she (in common with many students before and after her) called the book 'Frank 'n' Stein.'

Loathe Frank 'n' Stein as she might, she could not help but be interested in what it told her about the sociology of the emotions. If you got over your instinctive distaste for the writers' habit of using words you did not know when familiar ones would have served just as well, it was a bit like the stuff she actually liked to read in magazines. Or, if it wasn't really like it, it was on the same topic at least.

Once Mila thought that she understood it, she decided she would put the theory of the social origins of emotions to the test of seeing if someone else thought it was a big idea. She was not sure that all the sociologists would agree it was, but this did not matter to Mila. The fact that she found the theory vaguely interesting, and understood it, was enough. And she knew just the person to test it out on to see if they thought it was a big idea. Aunt Enid would serve as a judge again. After all, Enid was more or less an expert on human emotions.

As they continued their visit to the exhibition, Aunt Enid was, predictably, trying to make Mila see that being under the sway of your emotions was a glorious and natural state. She asked Mila if *she* ever got impatient with people, even got angry with them, and regretted it later? Mila said that yes, of course, like everyone else she was not always in control of her emotions.

'I remember being told by mother, *a lot*, "control yourself, stop crying, cheer up, stop looking miserable" and I remember all of my dear aunts saying "smile for your auntie" when I wanted to be disagreeable. It was really irritating being asked to control your emotions when you wanted to let them all out. But then you learn self-control as you grow up, unlike that jealous prince!'

'Well, perhaps we are not all that different to the prince. I don't believe that most people can really control their emotions. They settle for controlling the appearance of emotions rather than the emotions themselves.'

Mila thought, yes, that's you but it's not me. I don't think the emotions are all that important. But where she might now have refused to empathise, even have changed the subject, her self-imposed task of explaining what she understood of the sociology of emotions made empathy more logical. While Mila was trying to recall something from her textbook that might be relevant, they found themselves standing next to a collection of miniature pieces at the centre of which was a very formal family group. For all its small scale, the piece exuded the power and opulence of the ruling family it pictured. But look closely, Enid told her, look how very stiff they were, not one of them was touching the other. They sat or stood far apart and the only objects they touched were the symbols of their power and wealth. Mila found she could see what her aunt meant.

'Even the children are sitting apart, the only living creatures they are touching are those animals which I suppose were their pets, though they look like more symbols which show how rich and powerful the family is. All the emotion seems to be locked up in the family's relationships with objects and their position in society.'

'They were meant to be completely in control of their emotions, weren't they? Poor dears, what a terrible curse they had to live under, never being allowed to let anyone see how they truly felt, maybe not even allowing themselves to feel ordinary human emotions. They could never be themselves, never.'

If it had not been for Frank 'n' Stein, Mila would have had nothing to say, but now she began to draw on what she had learned from her reading. Speaking slowly and carefully as she put the thoughts together, Mila said there might really be two points here: letting out your feelings and being yourself. Letting your emotions out implied that they were already formed within you, and could either be let out or bottled up depending on what you chose. But was this necessarily true, Mila ventured? Maybe the 'letting out' was part of the emotion itself?

As they walked through the part of the exhibition where the smaller pieces were displayed, Mila carried on her explanation. She told her aunt that being yourself implied that there was a ready-made self to be put on display, but the self did not come pre-packaged. Then she returned to the subject she thought she knew a lot about: learning to control your emotions in childhood. Mila said that part of the reason such emphasis was placed, in your early life, on controlling your emotions was that emotions are seen as standing in the way of reason, of being chaotic, barbaric, feminine, animalistic, and so on. Being yourself and expressing your emotions might be in conflict.

Mila explained that being a rational adult involved not giving the world a stream of consciousness about your current emotional state. It required some level of self-censorship, some degree of filtering. Part of this filtering was simply intended to give the best appearance of yourself. For instance, some people were praised for being unflappable and keeping their cool, although this was always a double-edged compliment and the same coolness could be described as 'infuriating' and 'inhuman'. Part of the filtering was also needed because emotions could spell trouble.

Enid could quite see how this fitted the ruling family they had been discussing and, as they pored over other miniatures, she found more examples that seemed to accord with Mila's ideas. Enid said they showed that the ruling family were meant to be on a higher plane than their subjects. They had to give the impression of disinterest and objectivity, other-worldliness, even. The actions of the royal family embodied justice. Their subjects could not be allowed to think that the ruler would ever punish them because they hated them or for any other reason except that they deserved punishment. This was why the subjects must think the same cold formality ruled inside the royal household too.

At this point, although nothing was said, the two women exchanged a glance which might have suggested that this observation could apply to another family they both knew very well. Then Enid ventured that, in her experience, it was not always the case that women were less capable of hiding their emotions. Mila knew well enough who her aunt was thinking of, but she did not want to talk about her mother to her, not now at least. To change the direction of their conversation, she asked her aunt if she thought men tended to bottle up emotions which would eventually explode. Enid could not help but agree and then Mila said that if women were more inclined to display emotion easily you would never be certain that these emotions were totally genuine.

This question set Enid's tongue racing and while her aunt talked, Mila tried hard to recall the next part of Frank 'n' Stein's chapter on emotions. She remembered that Frank 'n' Stein said there was a strong tradition of philosophy that saw emotions as distorting the true way of seeing the world. The Greek philosopher Plato was one example: for him, emotions were like a fog of the mind. They clouded your perception of what was. For a long time emotions were seen in this way, as a hindrance, as part of a primitive legacy that we needed to curb and control in order to behave like civilised human beings.

Frank 'n' Stein said that Sigmund Freud, the Austrian psychoanalyst, thought of the relationship between emotions and reason as more dynamic. He saw civilisation as existing in opposition to instinctive feelings, and in fact as having developed through the historic suppression of some very basic instincts by humanity. Civilisation was built on people repressing their emotions, especially their sexual desires. The crucial difference between Freud and earlier thinkers was that he saw a person's reason and their emotions as being in an inextricable relationship. The conscious mind could not float free from the subconscious, which was the repository of all that emotional gunk. The decisions we made and the words we spoke, while appearing to be the products of our conscious minds, could in fact be the outcome of the murky whirlpool of our subconscious.

Mila thought the higher plane the royal family were meant to inhabit indicated that they were more civilised than their subjects. There was also plenty in what she had remembered that she could draw on to talk about gender differences in emotions. Now Mila said that, in the past, women were often represented as being governed by their emotions, which really meant their conscious, rational minds were under the influence of their unconscious, irrational bodies, which held a hormonal party on a monthly basis. Since emotions were working against reason, against progress, women were called literally 'unreasonable'.

Enid reminded her that it was the jealous prince who was unreasonable, not the princess. 'OK,' said Mila, smiling. 'But don't you think that there is more freedom for both women and men to show their emotions now? People used to be seen as inadequate if they expressed their emotions too readily. When, or maybe if, women were stereotyped as being at the mercy of emotions, they were seen as inadequate. Men were supposed to be stable and governed by reason. Now the tables have turned in many societies around the world and people – especially men – are seen as inadequate if they don't express their emotions enough, or in the right way. There's a compulsion to talk; and "reserve", once the badge of the upper classes in those societies, has been abandoned in favour of letting it all out.'

'You're certainly right, Mila. Displaying your emotions in public – on television for instance – has become the norm in some places, for both men and women.'

The two women found themselves standing before a famous porcelain piece which was decorated with pictures redolent of just the kind of stereotyping they were discussing. It depicted a succession of scenes in a funeral ceremony: a procession and some sort of lying-in-state. The king had died and the images were of women mourning, not in any sober or dignified way but with complete abandon. They were consumed by grief: tearing at their hair and clothes and fainting away at the sight of their dead lord and ruler.

'In those days, they could really enjoy a good funeral,' said Aunt Enid. This caught Mila by surprise and she burst into laughter, causing disapproving looks from other visitors to the exhibition. When she had recovered her composure, Mila suggested that grief went in and out of popularity in different societies, like some sort of fashion craze. There was evidence for different emotions dominating at different points in history and in different societies and there might be sound material reasons for this. It was possible that the rise of grief came as mortality rates fell – people could afford to be psychologically attached to one person, they became more strongly attached, and grieved more on their death.

Now Mila was really getting into her stride. The ideas she had taken from Frank 'n' Stein were dutifully appearing in a logical way in her mind, just as they would have to do if she were to pass a class test on them. Moreover, Aunt Enid looked to be impressed by the big idea. With her confidence increasing, Mila carried on to say that, later in history, a decline of religiosity and the rising importance of private life might have made emotional hygiene the order of the day. Public displays of emotion became intrusions into the 'wrong' sphere of life. Anyway, this showed that emotions had a history, though it was often a history that was hidden from view. Now our emotional landscape was changing again, Mila went on.

Just then her auntie stopped her by putting her hand on her arm. She had seen someone she knew over Mila's shoulder. Mila glanced round. She thought she could see the man her aunt was indicating. He appeared to be making his way through the exhibition at a brisk pace, taking in the exhibits without really breaking stride, and would soon catch up with Mila and Enid and the unhappy piece of porcelain.

A minute later, her aunt was introducing the man as Mr Lee and Mila as her niece, using her real name. This did not come with a jolt to Mila, as her aunt had been calling her by her proper name all day. She imagined her aunt would never be able to learn to use her fake name, but Mila hoped that she was right to be so free and easy with her real identity with this man.

From the way they were talking, it seemed Enid had known Mr Lee for many years. He must therefore know all about the trial, and he was hardly shunning her aunt because of it. That was something positive. There was also something sympathetic about his demeanour towards Mila, which suggested he understood how awkward her life had recently become. As Mr Lee was talking to them, he was joined by his son, who had been trailing several exhibits behind his energetic father. Had Enid happened to glance at her niece at this moment, she would have seen the panic in her expression as Arun, the master's student who had talked to her in the café, ambled up.

Even if Aunt Enid had known that her niece had already met Arun, as Mila, she would not have thought this grounds for the extreme reaction the younger woman was experiencing. Enid believed that there were always going to be unexpected turns of events in life. You could not control the pattern of human relationships, and you just had to enjoy the ride. Maybe such an intriguing point of contact between two young people as a false identity could grow into something. It could be truly romantic, like an initial meeting at a masked ball in some opera or other. At least, now the secret must come out, this young man would be someone her niece could confide in.

Enid was unaware of the emotions her niece was experiencing and was simply delighted to learn that Mila and Arun were attending the same university. Her delight was increased when she learned that Arun was studying psychology when Mila was studying sociology. From here she went on to tell Arun and Mr Lee that they had been talking about emotions and that her niece had said different emotions were socially acceptable at different points in history. She then turned to Mila. 'That's what sociology says, isn't it, dear, and does sociology say anything else about emotion?'

Mila had no faith that Arun and his friends would protect her identity but she had to carry on with this polite conversation, however miserable she felt and however much she focused her annoyance on Arun. All her confidence had disappeared and, with very little conviction, she told them that some sociologists were interested in saying something about the form and purpose of emotions. They needed to do this because they were not going to understand human behaviour if they could not study emotions. Sociologists thought people did not necessarily work out what state of being they desired and the best methods to arrive there. Much of what they did – especially day-to-day activity – involved doing what they felt was right rather than what they thought was right.

Because they were all listening politely, she had to plough on, telling them that emotions were vital for the way society worked at every level. They gave us a shared language, a shared way of understanding that worked on a level other than that of rational thought and calculation. By their very nature they were unthinking. We could be ruled by our emotions rather than our reason and, as Mila had heard from those who knew better than she, anyone who had been in love knew emotions could make you do pretty stupid things, irrational and self-destructive acts, even when you knew you were doing something wrong.

With relief, Mila could now see Arun's father was looking at him, expectantly, waiting to hear his contribution. Dutifully, his son said yes, he could see all this, it rang true on a common-sense level, but psychology had more to bring to the study of emotion. All branches of psychology had been interested in emotion, including those for which Arun personally had little time, and psychology was simply better suited than sociology to understanding emotion: 'after all, it's basically physical stuff: stimulus and response, mediated by perception.'

Enid did not seem convinced by this. She said that the physical symptoms of different emotions could be very similar. If someone angered you, your face flushed, your pulse raced and your heart beat faster. But it was the same set of physical responses you felt with pleasurable excitement: 'your pulse races, your face flushes, and your heart beats faster.' She looked to Mila for confirmation and Mila said, yes, it could not just be a matter of a physical change being registered in the mind. It would have helped Mila if she had been able to remember Frank 'n' Stein:

> There are two explanations sociologists have used for this, both relying on the idea that there are no inherent bodily responses that are not learned or socially mediated or constructed. One is that we put very different interpretations on the same set of bodily responses depending on the situation we are in, and how it is defined. In part, we learn what sort of emotions to have in a given situation. The other one is that, not only are our emotions social constructs, but our bodily reactions are as well; the whole package is a product of society. Emotions are entirely existing in the relations between people. They do not float free on their own.

But only a little of this had gone in, and what Mila actually said was simply that emotions were 'social constructions'. Arun shook his head:

'That's a bit of a leap. What do you mean our physical reactions are socially constructed? It's bizarre. Our physical reactions are physical and not the result of us thinking about them. Sure, social stimuli can contribute to producing them, and culture can have an effect on our perception of them, but the reaction we have is nothing to do with the social. And the reaction is the emotion. It's how we know we have an emotion – by measuring electrical activity in a particular region of the brain or levels of certain chemicals in the blood. In the old days it was sweaty palms and their effect on electrical conductivity.'

'Ah, you mean the polygraph, or lie detector?' said Mr Lee smugly. 'I have seen one in action, you know.'

Arun nodded to show he was impressed, but his father wanted him to carry on. Arun said, 'People have always talked about emotions being experienced as shivers up the spine, tingling, heart palpitations. Emotion is physical reaction based on changes in brain chemistry which you have no conscious control over, so how can social stuff have any effect on it? The words people say and do to each other only affect the production and perception of stimuli and all that happens before the brain generates emotions.'

'We don't decide to have emotions, not consciously at any rate. It feels like they're happening to us,' Mila said.

Then, with a particular emphasis to her voice, she added: 'I suppose emotions must have something to do with how we react to a situation, and what it means to us.'

Mila could not tell if any of this hit home with Arun – perhaps he was too stupid, or too clever, to realise what she was saying between the lines – because his father was quickly on his back again.

'Well, Arun, she agrees with you. If there is going to be any future for the study of emotions, we are obviously going to have to rely on psychology, so tell us a bit more, please.'

Arun just did as he was told. It sounded as if he was recalling one of his psychology books line by line: 'Evolutionary psychology sees emotions as hard-wired possibilities in our brains that are there from the start. We may not each get the chance, the right stimuli, to use the full range of our emotions, but you can see the potential for emotions is built-in. They are pre-existing, a set of emotional states that individuals are born with, but they may or may not get triggered by what then happens in our lives. Evolutionary psychology focuses on how the set of emotional states we are born with played a part in human survival. Evolutionary pressures and competition for resources favoured group cooperation that was facilitated by trust, gratitude, mutual affect, and so on.'

Mr Lee seemed pleased. 'So emotions are simply functional for survival?'

'Yes,' said Arun, 'at its most basic level this includes instinctive reflexes triggered by external stimuli, for example fight-or-flight responses when in danger. Emotions are part of the animal part of being human; the legacy of our evolution, and so have little to do with society at all.'

Arun looked uncomfortable and it crossed Mila's mind that he might actually be embarrassed by having to talk this way under pressure from his father to perform. There is nothing like a taste of your own medicine, Arun, she thought, and she was not going to let him off the hook.

'That doesn't make a lot of sense. You might explain where emotions come from originally in that way, but emotions aren't always functional, like you said they are. They can be destructive too. I don't think they can be all about contributing to the survival of the fittest, because humans need certain instincts to survive. And who cares about their origin at some distant stage in our evolution, anyway? Emotions might have long since lost their original purposes and acquired new causes and new effects.'

By now, they were standing before a glass case containing an exquisite robe. Mila asked Enid to tell them who it was made for. Enid explained how Hania, the crown princess, demanded it be made for her to wear when she succeeded to the throne. It was adorned with priceless jewels and, it was said, had taken the most skilled tailor in the kingdom five years to make. The story, or perhaps it was a legend, told how, on her accession, Hania cast off the robe in the middle of the throning ceremony to show that she was really the same as her subjects. Hania accepted it was her destiny to rule, but she could not cope with the huge gulf that this destiny put between her and other human beings.

Enid said the story showed how we can be confused or mistaken about what we feel, and feel contradictory emotions, such as loving someone and hating them at the same time. Mr Lee agreed that emotions were not straightforward experiences that, as soon as their presence was announced, revealed their meaning instantly and transparently. He couldn't help embellishing this with a philosophical reference and Mila thought she saw Arun flinch a little when he made it, or perhaps it was his father's condescension that made him flinch.

'Psychological perspectives seem to be heavily influenced by Descartes if they see an emotion as a sensation which can be simply classified as soon as it occurs. Enid, you remember Descartes insisted on a complete separation of mind and body.'

Enid admitted she did not really understand all that Mila and Arun were saying, but that any perspective that did not take account of how we could be emotionally conflicted was incomplete. 'When you've lived as long as we have, you know through your own experience that you can have an emotion without feeling it or understanding it.'

This made Mila think about the way she had been trying to second-guess what Arun was feeling.

'Don't we develop a *shared* understanding of emotions? How else can we know what goes on in each other's heads unless we share our understanding of what we are feeling by communicating with each other? I don't mean communicating by talking to each other necessarily.'

Mila hesitated as if she were checking to make sure she had explained herself properly, then she carried on. 'This also means our knowledge of other people's emotions changes. We wouldn't know about all the modern-day Hanias if we relied on the simple emotional displays which are encouraged on television.'

Judging from what he now said, all the subtlety and potential in what Mila had said had gone straight over Arun's head. This made her wonder if there might be something in the gender stereotypes of ways of relating to emotions, after all. What Arun said was that her ideas about emotions were silly, because: 'Experiments, brain imaging, all confirm we have broadly the same responses to stimuli. Or at least that is the way we're set up. Maybe if our brains are damaged in some way this is altered, and of course other physical factors interact so that reactions in the emotional centre vary, but these are very largely pathologies – we aren't meant to be like that.'

Mila could not help but reply with some sarcasm in her voice. 'So, the only shared understanding of emotions that is possible is at second-hand in a laboratory?

'Well, as usual, common sense is not up to the job of understanding science – the answers aren't self-evident, they're maybe even counterintuitive. You are concentrating on all the thoughts and talk *about* emotions, but maybe these are just aftershocks, irrelevant side effects which don't touch on the understanding of real emotion, after all.'

'You mean they are *epiphenomena*, Arun?' said his father, looking very pleased with himself. For the first time, Mila thought that Mr Lee might actually be competing with his son, showing off his superior learning, rather than simply wanting his son to demonstrate the knowledge he had acquired from his master's course.

'Maybe it's time we got him off your back,' Mila thought, 'then you can think about what we are talking about properly instead of quoting phrases from books.' The irony of this thought made her smile, as she remembered she would be struck dumb without the help of Frank 'n' Stein. She did not hold it consciously, but the smile stayed on her lips as she spoke. 'If you see someone you like, you smile. Does smiling make you happy to see them? It does a little bit. You don't have to go along with the idea of mind and body being separate. I know that, without the bodily feelings, emotions would not be emotions at all. We know that emotions have to have a physical part, because of the way people describe them. Yes, fear really does take place in the stomach and love in the heart. The words we use to describe this – heartache, butterflies in the stomach – place emotions in bodies, but I don't think you can say this is all that emotions are about. That would be cutting life down to what psychology alone can explain!'

Arun appeared flustered for a moment, then spoke. 'But you can't prove that thoughts aren't just, literally, afterthoughts, part of how we deal with emotions.'

Then Mila, still smiling, said weren't they going round in circles? 'Didn't we just have anger and excitement being the same physical responses, but different emotions? Your approach reduces them to the same experience. Or maybe they look different in a brain scan – I know I don't know enough about that, but I bet you have a whole big list of emotions which everyone else treats as separate which are collapsed into something you call "arousal".'

At this point Arun appeared to suffer some sort of coughing fit. By the time he had recovered they had reached the next famous artefact (now that Mr Lee was with them they only seemed to pause at the pieces he considered important). Enid asked him what he made of it. He asked if she meant did he *like* it and she said no, what did it tell him, what was its story? Mr Lee looked puzzled.

'The man is dying from an obvious wound in his side – it's presumably painful but he has a serene expression. He might even be happy. Is he in some kind of spiritual state of grace in which he feels no pain? Maybe he's content to die, because he's done some good deed for others.'

'Bravo. He *is* serene and his story tells us why he is. It's because of something which happened a long time before his death. I think that many of these artefacts remind us that states of emotion – serenity but also pride, despair, and confusion – can hold individuals for a long time and have little to do with what is happening to their bodies.'

Mila was very proud of her aunt for the confident way she dealt with this pompous man. Of course Enid then wanted to tell them the full story behind the serene death, and this took a long time. When she had finished, Mr Lee spoke.

'It's the context, isn't it? Emotions have a context – like anger. I frequently get very angry with subordinates at work who are lazy or inefficient but, you know, it's not the same anger as some poor fellow feels who has lost his livelihood because of the laziness and carelessness of others. With me it passes in a moment, with others it lingers and breeds ill-feeling. People who are clinically depressed might have a persistent, irrational feeling of guilt, but it is not the same order of emotion that we would usually expect guilt to be. I have heard that some young people take drugs that result in the temporary manufacture of affection for others. That's not a real emotion either but presumably it is the same chemistry in the brain as genuine affection. In Arun's terms, I suppose that, if all these emotions have exactly the same chemical signature, then they *are* the same.'

Enid added that you might not even experience the same emotion in the same way another person did, even where the emotions were genuinely equivalent. Some people found stress stressful; some found it addictive. We all knew people who loved to moan and who got satisfaction from being dissatisfied. His father asked Arun if there were any psychologists who recognised that this happened, that some people decided to see the glass half full while others saw it as half empty. Arun said that something like this could be read into the simplest form of 'psychological behaviourism'. Emotions were simply different sorts of behaviour and holding an emotion was just behaving in a certain way: 'I behave angrily, therefore I am angry; I behave stupidly, therefore I am in love.' Arun was pleased with his attempt at humour, but Enid was dismayed.

'A robot can be programmed to smile, or to cry. Look at the art that goes into these lovely exhibits, trying to convey deep and complex emotions, and shifts in emotion. Often people only become aware of their feelings at the last minute.'

'When it's too late to do any good,' interrupted Mr Lee, 'judging by all the terrible and tragic ends of the people in the stories you have been telling. Look at this one: these two look as miserable as you can imagine. What happened to them?'

Enid said this was an example of great endurance, of what the Ancient Greeks and Romans used to think of as stoicism: people making the overcoming of their emotions and pain a matter of pride and even the foundation of their claim to human dignity. 'Your behaviourism doesn't take into account the private inner world, how we conceal some emotions,' she told Arun.

Mila took over from her aunt and said yes, you might pretend to be cool about someone you are attracted to. Arun replied that the easy bit could be convincing others – the hard part was convincing yourself. 'Yes,' said Mila, 'for instance, on breaking up with someone you might pretend not to be bothered, even though you are upset.'

Mr Lee cut in to ask Mila what she thought of behaviourism. 'All these theories draw an artificial distinction between body and mind, I suppose. Either the body reacts and the mind interprets, or the mind interprets and the body reacts. Neither feels quite true to me. I know I keep saying the same argument, but sociology suggests we look at emotions as social constructions.'

Mila was calm enough now to think about finishing the test of her big idea. What else did she need to say to find out if the theory of the social construction of emotions stood up to scrutiny? Frank 'n' Stein said that:

> The most that cognitive theories will allow is that emotions are produced in the mind or the body, and then experienced or mediated in terms of social or cultural context. Emotions are inherent, and might be shaped to an extent by the context, social norms, and so on. Social norms might mitigate against expressing strong emotions in some societies and for them in others. So people repress or display their emotions depending on the level of display permitted in that society. This is often the source of culture clash when tourists visit cultures different to theirs.

Mila was explaining this in her own words when Mr Lee interrupted. 'Like the British who think that their famous reserve is a part of good manners, and putting people at their ease, whereas to everyone else the British can appear distant and cold. But surely this is out of date, Mila: "the Japanese and British are cold; people from South America wear their hearts on their sleeves?" These are simply stereotypes. Is that how sociologists think the expression of emotions is controlled, by cultural stereotypes?'

Mila wondered if Mr Lee was the right kind of person to explain a big idea to – he always seemed to be sure he was right, and you could not tell him anything he did not already know. She replied that there were different kinds of sociologists. She preferred the social constructionists who, Frank 'n' Stein said:

> View emotions as they view everything else: as enacted meaning. They are interested in identifying the ways in which norms and expectations about emotions are created and reproduced within society. They take these norms as producing emotions rather than either repressing them or letting them out. This is a very different methodological standpoint from that taken by psychology. In less relativist theories there are a limited number of biologically based emotions independent of social influences and learning. Theodore Kemper identified four physiologically based, primary emotions: fear; anger; depression; and satisfaction/happiness. Other emotions, like love, guilt, shame, pride and nostalgia, were secondary emotions that were learned in a specific society or culture. For instance, some societies were 'shame societies' and some were 'guilt societies'. Shame was a sense of public humiliation. These tended to be more collective societies – we might think of the concept of 'face' in Eastern culture, or Catholic ones like Spain and Italy, or at least like Spain and Italy once were. Guilt was a more internalised feeling, a sense of wrestling with your conscience. Guilt societies were more individualised, more associated with the Protestant or Jewish religions where sin was a matter between the individual and God. These were societies often marked by smaller family structures and weaker social constraints, perhaps with higher social mobility. In each case shame and guilt were manifestations of primary emotions. Shame was *fear* of punishment or being ostracised for inappropriate behaviour; guilt was *anger* within oneself at one's own knowledge of a transgression. Each was based on a primary emotion, the experience and understanding of which had been learned and socialised. The social structure shaped the emotions which were dominant in that society.

Mila explained the difference between primary and secondary emotions, and then she pointed out that the artefacts they had been seeing were specific to a particular culture within a culture, the royal family, and its court and entourage, in a certain time and place. While they might well imagine the primary emotions would be common between the ruling family and the most lowly servant, they had been seeing how the royal-family members were subject to a particular set of emotional rules for their display of secondary emotions because of their place in the social structure. Frank 'n' Stein also said:

> The more strongly relativist theory of social constructionism works in the same vein, but detaches emotions from any inherent biological inheritance. Emotions cannot be seen as separate from the social and cultural context that they occur in. These sociologists draw on cross-cultural anthropological research to claim that emotional expression is not universal across cultures. The terms we use to describe a particular internal state, thought or set of behaviours as a specific emotion are chosen in relation to a particular situation and are used to rationalise or explain the resulting actions. Emotions are never entirely internal. They always occur in relation to other people. Our relationships with others are always social relationships in some sense. Emotions therefore have no reality outside the social context. Emotions are judgements people use to understand the situation they find themselves in and communicate that feeling simply to others.

Mila hoped she was summing this up by telling them that the expression 'I feel sad' was much better than stating the million reasons why you felt a particular way and hoping the other person worked it out for themselves. Emotions did not have an existence outside of that situation. Mr Lee continued to take issue with her, even if Arun seemed quite content to keep his mouth closed.

'Aren't you – forgive me, I mean *they* – reducing emotions to what people think and say about emotions and leaving what really matters entirely out of the account? You complained about psychological reductionism, but this is extreme: you are throwing out what matters altogether because you cannot explain it, whereas psychology can.'

As calmly as she could, Mila replied that you never could tell with social constructionists whether they were making a point about how you ought to go about studying emotions, or whether they really believed that there were no rock-bottom emotions common across different cultures. It was impossible to tell because you could never separate an individual from society. Mr Lee said, rather brutally, that the constructionists would 'expect they would feel pain if their legs were broken.'

Mila said this was a sensation rather than an emotion, but she had already agreed there were definite physical aspects to emotion. And, yes, maybe the constructionists overstated differences between cultures. There were a small number of facial expressions that appeared to be universally recognised in different societies – happy, angry, sad. At this point Enid joined in, perhaps to save Mila from another show of condescension.

'It seems to me that all these psychologists and sociologists oversimplify everything and leave out all the subtlety that provides the inspiration for great art through the ages. It sounds to me as if none of them can come to terms with the fact that emotions are very difficult to understand and interpret, and often contradictory and, very often, have confused and uncertain effects on people's decisions.'

Mila said: 'I think that's true, Auntie, but it's not just social science that does this. It's built into the structure of the society, it's even built into bureaucracies.' Mila said this because she was recalling another point in Frank 'n' Stein:

> One of the reasons why people experience any bureaucracy that is evaluative or judgemental as often producing unfair or unreasonable outcomes, is that they, like much social science, take as their starting point the idea that people have clear and conscious reasons for their actions. For example this applies in the criminal justice system: the courts have great difficulty getting around the fact that two individuals observing the same event may give wildly differing, but individually honest, accounts of what happened based on their feelings about it.

Mr Lee looked pained by her attempt to summarise this and Mila remembered, too late, that, when he had been introduced to her, her aunt had said that he was an important bureaucrat, a senior lawyer in a large public agency. She quickly pressed on and, perhaps because she was anxious for Mr Lee to think that she had simply been making an academic point which had nothing to do with him, she tried to use the kind of language he had been using:

'So in modern society we treat emotions as illusion and reason as reality. Then we subject emotions to reason but this puts many of us in a dilemma. What we feel and what we think can be different, but each is also a product of the other. It is not just a matter of working out what we think is right, and what we feel is right, partly because both can be very different. Reason can't work without emotion and emotions have no meaning without reason.'

This was complicated enough, but Mila knew that Frank 'n' Stein went on to explain that:

> Reflective thought – the ability to reason, to make judgements, and so on – requires that emotions be attached to cognition. Thinking requires emotions to think with. People who have been brain-damaged so that they cannot form or experience emotions seem to find it impossible to reason as well as they once had. Emotions are needed for reason to be effective, in other words for decision making. Judgements are partly instinctive and emotional, or appear to work that way.

So, Mila concluded 'doing the right thing is not a question of weighing up all the alternatives like a computer calculating the odds on a horse race.' Perhaps because he could not fully understand what Mila said, Mr Lee was, apparently, won over at last – the slight to the bureaucracy was forgotten. He had clearly understood the allusion to gambling.

'This I approve of. It is more like choosing which horse to bet on – a combination of reason, experience and instinct, or a feeling for what is happening. So making decisions which are right doesn't just need a set of abstract rules of behaviour. You find in the professions, and in public service, that such rules can inhibit your decision making and prevent you doing what is just.' Arun seemed to recover the power of speech that he had apparently lost fully for 15 minutes (perhaps he found his father's enthusiasm for the gambling analogy amusing).

'Reason sometimes follows emotions – you have a feeling and then think of a reason to justify or explain it. And emotions can get in the way of reason, of rational decision making: an experimental subject in the lab who is subject to a stressor cannot perform complex tasks as well as someone who is unstressed.'

Mila thought this rang a bell with something Frank 'n' Stein said about social science and philosophy having a problem with emotions:

> Social science and philosophy find it hard to accept that emotions can be a force with an existence outside of social constructions, social relations, power relations, representations, and so on, although they are of course interpreted and channelled by these and other aspects of social life. They can be a force that cuts across categories, violates expectations and norms.

Knowing her aunt would agree, Mila said that it was probably a big mistake to seek a single reason or motivation that explains human behaviour. Many theories in sociology – and economics, politics and philosophy and even psychology – tried to do this, but we are a mixed-up collection of emotions, desires and needs.

They were now close to the end of the exhibition. Mila was finding it easier to talk to Arun as a fellow student, rather than an intellectual rival.

'I can only come out with all this sociology stuff because I want to find out if I really belong here at university. It's like putting on a comedy act or something.' Mila laughed at his bemused expression. 'You know, shy people who can pretend to be someone else on stage go back to being shy afterwards. My version of that is talking about sociology when it's the last subject I really want to do.'

Arun was not entirely convinced. 'Why do you put yourself through it?'

'You probably think it's silly, but I've been finding out whether other people think any of sociology's ideas are worthwhile. I was doing it with Aunt Enid when you showed up.'

'And the idea you were putting to the test was the social origins of emotion?'

'Yes – you turning up made it a much tougher test than I was going to get from my aunt. Though maybe that's fair because I probably picked her as I knew she would be on my side.'

'So, did the idea pass the test?'

'I don't know, I didn't really try to explain it to Enid in the end, so I guess it's up to you or your father.'

'Well, I don't know either. I don't believe half of that critical stuff I was saying, though. I don't believe that different academic disciplines should be arguing over which one has the right to explain aspects of life. I think I gave my father the impression that I did back when I was a first year, and he's never let go of the idea. And he thinks coming to university is like being admitted to a secret society where you get given bits of arcane knowledge, one at a time. I think it's not about that at all: it's about changing yourself, self-transformation.'

Mila asked him what he meant. Arun said that he thought it had something to do with her idea of forcing yourself to take on a role you weren't used to in order to find out more about your potential. 'You said you were finding out whether sociology was worthwhile in order to find out whether you belong at university. Well, maybe asking those sorts of questions turns you into the sort of person who will get a lot out of being at university. Try summing up your idea for me. In one line, what is sociology's big idea about emotions?'

'I think the big idea is that my Aunt Enid is right. Emotions are the unsaid bond in society, the invisible knots that tie us to each other.'

'OK, so it's emotions, rather than rational assessments of mutual interests and what we can do for each other?'

'Yes, exactly, it's not all about me doing a favour for you and you doing a favour for me. We don't just do that because it's a fair exchange. Emotion is what ties you together when you are *not* weighing what's in your interests, or what's fair, or when you're being made to act by other people, either because it's your duty or because you're being forced into it, or tricked into it.'

'I understand what you mean about a sense of duty. I think you've got a big idea all right. Emotion keeps us, keeps society, going. When people interact, emotional relationships are created. This emotional stuff is the underpinning of mutual understandings. We can make life together because of our good feelings, our good will. Without this emotion – when we have lost it, lost trust in another person – we are left with trying to reason about what their actions mean.'

Ah, thought Mila, you are capable of subtlety, after all. 'Let's hope we don't lose that trust,' she added.

Visit the companion website at **www.palgrave.com/companion/ Bancroft-And-Fevre-Dead-White-Men-2e/** to access additional learning resources, including seminar questions based on the chapter's coverage, a jargon buster that defines key terms used in the text and a timeline which provides an overview of the development of sociological thought.

● ● ● ● ●

How do you know what you feel?

... or what anyone else feels? #sadface

1. Aspects of life that appear to spring from human nature frequently turn out to be what are called 'social constructs'. A social construct is an idea or way of living that is presented as natural, stemming from the way the world is. It might be so normal and unquestioned that nobody even refers to it. A closer view though shows that it is an agreed upon reality. We all act as if it is true.

2. Emotions are experienced as natural – but like other social constructs they have to be learned, their meaning agreed. Emotions are deeply personal experiences that guide our choices and actions. They are both personal, which gives them their power, and interpersonal, which gives them their meaning.

3. Sociology makes use of the emotions in explaining society. Certain emotions can be required for society to work. For instance, the modern division of labour requires and promotes trust in strangers.

4. Despite that, there is often a desire to rely on un-emotional explanations. Human life is often presented as divided into two – the life of the mind and of the body. The mind is home of reason and cool judgements, the body of emotions and ungoverned instincts. This split is called 'dualism'. It does not reflect reality. In fact, emotions are used to make judgements, and reason becomes impossible without emotion.

5. Social constructs are found throughout society. There are many other 'facts of life' that are social constructs and quite a bit of sociology involves finding out what they are.

4
In our Genes?

Mila awoke that day to find a large parcel on the doormat, addressed to her. She hefted it up and shook it. This action revealed little about the contents. Somewhat put off by the parcel's failure to disclose its true nature, she left it in her room while she made her breakfast. Later, she sat on her bed ripping the brown paper off it with one hand, while eating with the other. Inside was a cardboard box full of yellowing paper. Her mother had put a note on top: 'I know our lives have been difficult sweetheart,' it read.

'Here's a little present to put you in mind of happier times.'

Mila shuffled through the paper in the box. There were old school reports, self-portraits in crayon, essays entitled 'What I Did in My Holidays', drawings entitled 'My Family', and crinkled photographs, collected over her years at school. Mila had assumed, if she thought about it at all, that this old stuff had been consigned to the trash. She left it to go to class during which she mostly daydreamed and thought about the party she hoped to go to that night. When she returned in the evening she had nearly forgotten about the parcel. She started spreading the material out on her bed.

She pulled out an old handwritten essay for her school sociology class. The topic of the essay was feminism. Like many women her age, Mila had thought that feminism did not apply to her. She had grown up in an environment where women were expected to have careers, to be politicians, soldiers, professors, be independent. They lived feminist lives, which meant that feminism often did not appear to matter to them. She scanned the essay, remembering how her schoolteacher had been very keen on feminism.

In the essay Mila had written about what sociologists called the gendered division of labour, which meant the way in which women and men often ended up doing different work inside and outside the home. Women tended to do caring work at home, and when they had careers, these often involved doing much the same activity for other people. Although she made it clear that his ideas were out of date and ripe for criticism, her schoolteacher had taught Mila about Talcott Parsons, who at one time had thought that different roles for men and women 'complemented each other' to produce a stable system. For instance, the way that women adopted caring roles and men 'breadwinning' roles meant that the two sexes did what they were best at. Women got the caring duties because they bore the children and it made sense that they did the emotion work as well. Parsons thought the family worked well to divide what he called men's 'instrumental' functions from women's 'expressive' functions. Women's expressive work in private life provided the succour men needed after a hard day being instrumental in public life.

At school, Mila had been told that the neat set-up Parsons described had never been true for most men and women, and was very quickly challenged by feminists who did not think that biology was destiny. In her essay, Mila had written that these liberal feminists argued that the structures of society itself were gender neutral but that discrimination prevented women's access to the top layers of it. Discrimination was an irrational holdover from past times. They found the source of inequality between men and women in their varying attitudes and expectations, and the legal and institutional barriers that were put in the way of women getting to the top.

Liberal feminists like Mila's own Aunt Ima focused on measures like removing discrimination, training women to give them a helping hand, and raising their expectations. They thought equality required that women developed confidence in their ability to be politicians, business leaders, and so on. She remembered talking with Auntie Ima about her schooldays. Ima had given Mila a very old children's book of hers to show how life should be different for her. It was called *Shari and Sammy*. In Auntie Ima's book, the two young characters, a boy and a girl, went about what appeared to be completely separate lives. Mila read, 'Shari helps mummy do the washing-up.' 'Sammy plays with his chemistry set.' Ima's teachers would have thought this role socialisation thoroughly appropriate. Liberal feminists thought this could be turned around, so that girls and young women could be taught to want much more than to do the washing-up and play with dolls.

Underneath Mila's old essay there was a jotter, bound with blue card and containing sheets of wide-lined paper. She opened it and was struck by the absence of déjà vu at seeing her old, careful handwriting, which seemed to belong to another person. On the first page she had written,

'My Mum And Dad' and her age '7 And One Quarter.' 'My mum putting on her makeup,' she read. 'Dad is working in the garage.' Two stick figures accompanied the story, one with a hat, the other with a skirt. Her father never wore a hat, he did not like machines, and her mother wore a trouser suit most of the time, but they had been transformed into caricatures of male and female. Mila thought to herself how subtle some stereotyping of male and female roles could be. She had picked up these expectations even when much of what liberal feminists wanted had been achieved, and without being force-fed *Shari and Sammy*. She thought this might mean that liberal feminists had a tougher task than they had at first thought, that gender was more deeply ingrained in the structures of society than they had hoped.

She thought of what her schoolteacher had said: assumptions like this illustrated the feminist point that, even if women go into the workplace, they still have a double burden of responsibility. She remembered how her parents had paid for a cleaner to help out, a woman who had somehow become invisible to her childhood eyes. Even when women were successful, they often had to rely on the work of other women, often immigrants and always low paid. The burden of domestic labour appeared to have been shifted, not resolved.

In Mila's experience, men had not got in the way of anything she wanted to do. Her mother had not been a vocal feminist, like her sociology teacher, but she had always encouraged Mila to excel at whatever she chose to do and had never given her any sign that she expected less of her than she did of her brother. She saw very little of her father as she was growing up but Mila could remember nothing to suggest that he had different expectations of his daughter. Her brother had certainly tormented her for being a girl, just as he tormented her for being younger, but Mila understood this as the usual tactics of sibling rivalry. Nobody else who mattered in her life, for example her aunts, had given Mila the slightest inkling that, because she was a woman, she was to play by, and be judged by, different rules.

Aunt Ima, particularly, thought that one of the additional benefits of her own success in the business world was that Mila would have a strong, female role model. Her childhood memories of her aunt suggested she was one of the first liberal feminists, but there were many kinds of feminism, many feminists and many more women who cut their own path in life without being bothered very much by what feminism meant.

If Mila had ever heard from people who suggested that life might be otherwise, they had generally been people who did not matter to her, rather like that student in the café, Garrison, who had goaded her with jibes about coming to university to find a husband. Mila had to admit that this provocation had certainly worked, and it had even crossed her mind that she might just have more in common with her feminist sociology teacher at school than she had imagined. If she was annoyed by this kind of statement when it was pushed in her face, perhaps the reason she had been so unmoved by feminist arguments in the past was that she had been insulated from whatever it was that feminism had been established to combat.

Frank 'n' Stein said that some sociologists were not happy with liberal feminism, since it required women to be like men. These feminists said that equal opportunities as promoted by liberals had benefited only a small number of better-off women, and in a small way. To focus on the individual, they ended up blaming the victim for not making the effort to change. There was no other way of explaining why inequalities persisted when legal barriers had been removed, and the majority of people in public life were in favour of the equality of the sexes. Mila was trying to remember what that viewpoint was called when Circe and Ana, who shared her accommodation, knocked at the door.

'What are you up to?' Circe asked, perching on Mila's bed. Ana retreated to a chair in the corner of the room, as usual. Mila picked up the report and, turning over a page to hide her name, read out loud: 'She is an intelligent pupil but has become rather demanding in her behaviour. She may not be getting enough attention at home as both parents work.'

Mila thought she knew how feminists would explain that. Frank 'n' Stein said some feminists, those influenced by Marxism, looked into the structure of society for the sources of inequality. Women worked unpaid in the home as mothers and carers. Thanks to liberal equality, they also worked outside the home too. They worked a double shift supporting capitalist 'reproduction' (that simply meant bringing up the workers of the future), while having both women and men working supported capitalist production. For these kinds of feminists, the solution was that women should become active in the overthrow of capitalism, and that would also inevitably lead to the disappearance of patriarchy, by which they meant the domination of women by men.

Another group of feminists, radical feminists, thought that this let men off the hook. They applied Marxist class analysis to argue that men as a class exploited and oppressed women as a class. In their view patriarchy was the fundamental organising principle of society, capitalism just being the latest model. Men dominated women by violence and the threat of violence, such as rape and domestic abuse. Women who could not bear the restrictions imposed by feminine roles went slowly mad – and insanity was partly defined as rejecting a female role.

'What was your school like?' Circe asked. 'I went to an all-girls' school.' Ana had nothing to say. She looked as if she had been thoroughly traumatised by the experience of school, but then Ana usually looked glum.

'Mine was boys and girls,' Mila said. She realised then how strange that must have been to someone like Circe. Frank 'n' Stein had mentioned Raewyn Connell, who had written about how every society had a 'gender order'. Every classroom, school playground, street and workplace had a set of expected relations between men and women, and masculinities and femininities. So, in the playground, boys were meant to play rough – push each other around, pull girls' hair – while girls were expected to stand around in groups and gossip about each other. Pupils and teachers enforced this order.

Mila told Circe and Ana about playing football with the boys in her class when she was nine or ten. She had been scolded by her teacher and her mother for being covered in mud and grass stains. Nobody seemed to mind that the boys were in the same state. She inwardly blushed at the thought that maybe she had only played because that meant they had liked her more.

'Everything was pretty calm at my school,' said Circe, 'until we discovered boys. Then it was make-up and backbiting. And the white girls pulling your hair if you went near the white boys.'

It seemed from what Circe said that there was a racial order as well as a gender order. Mila thought about what she had read about black feminism: many black and Asian women writers felt that white feminists had treated *them* as not-women. Some white middle-class feminists had tended to speak for 'women', as if all women were the same and had the same needs and experiences – which surprisingly enough were just like their needs and their experiences. They did not have to suffer racism, and poverty, on top of sexism and they could, without intending to, generalise from their experiences to those of all women. Middle-class women's freedom had been bought with the cheap childcare and housework labour of black, Filipino, Polish, and Mexican women.

Black American feminists wrote in a long tradition of black women activists who campaigned against racism, class prejudice, and sex discrimination. Sojourner Truth, born a slave in the USA, made a famous speech to a women's rights convention in 1851, known as 'Ain't I a woman?' White men did not treat her as a woman, according to their ideal of femininity. Nobody, she said, opened doors for her or put her first. She worked in the fields, harder and better, she said, than any man. She saw first-hand how these forms of oppression linked together, denying black women their humanity, and devaluing their womanhood.

Tuni knocked on Mila's door and stuck her head round it. 'What are you wearing tonight?' she asked in the tone in which one might enquire after a terminally-ill relative. Though they had only known each other a few weeks, Mila knew by now Tuni's response to whatever clothes she pulled out of her wardrobe was likely to be a quick rearrangement of her sentence into 'You are wearing *what* tonight?' Mila made a gesture with her hand to indicate that what she was wearing at the moment, jeans and a t-shirt, would be sufficient. Tuni rolled her eyes.

'I suppose it's because you are a feminist that you don't know anything. Sociologists are all feminists, aren't they, Mila?'

'Yes, and we all look like frumps who don't care how we look.'

Tuni added, laughing: 'You don't wear make-up; you wear those hideous glasses and that ridiculous hairstyle, and you have absolutely no idea how to dress, but you could be absolutely stunning.' Whenever Mila heard people say her face was familiar she did her best to divert the conversation quickly.

'So, people who don't spend hours in front of the mirror each day must be feminists?' Mila asked. Tuni replied.

'Feminists don't approve of paying attention to their appearance. They think if they do it means they are being dominated by men. Of course that's all nonsense. I don't pay attention to how I look for the sake of men: I do it for me. I love looking as good as I can. It's mad not to.'

Mila wasn't sure feminists didn't care about their appearance and she suspected Tuni also wanted to look good to keep up with the other students on her art and design course, but she wasn't going to say so for fear of offending her. When Tuni had mentioned feminism she had, at least, given her and Circe something to talk about and maybe nothing would get Ana to join in. Perhaps Tuni had even engineered this opening for her benefit after seeing her and the other two flounder with every subject she brought up. Maybe Mila should simply start talking about what she had learned about what feminists think.

She still hesitated, not because she would find it a hard subject to talk about (after all, she must have deserved some of those high marks), but because the last thing she wanted was any real discord among the group. They had all been very good humoured up to now, but this was one of those subjects on which people could take offence. Mila decided to proceed with caution, and she adopted a tone which was somewhere between neutral and slightly self-mocking. She started by telling them that sociology tells us people can have different perspectives on the world depending on their experiences and circumstances. Circe butted in straight away. 'That's for sure. Look at the way we can never find a subject we all can talk about.'

They were all grinning at this, except for Ana who seemed to be too nervous to smile and terribly uncomfortable about the whole situation. Mila told them that Jasmine, had she been here, would have been a good person to ask about the cultural differences between people from different countries. They knew so little of each other that it was even news to Tuni that Jasmine was from another country. Circe did not think you had to be from another country to understand what Mila was getting at. After all, she explained, she and Ana were studying languages and students of languages could not help but study different cultures. Half of her courses were about the way these differences were expressed in art and politics and the media: 'If people speak a different language, they might describe the world differently, and if they have different customs and behaviours, they might relate to the world differently. Take film, for instance. Even where countries are quite close together geographically, you find many cultural differences expressed in their films.'

The mention of film got Tuni talking about cultural differences in film design and she soon got onto differences in fashion. Circe and Mila exchanged a glance and Mila cut in.

'Yes, you've got it. People brought up in vastly diverging situations might see their lives differently, but men and women share the same lives, the same existence, live in the same houses, work in the same offices. So how come you have men and women thinking differently, acting differently? You could say that they were different all along because of biology. Or you could say there is something like culture that operates within each society to make them separate and different, even when they seem to be sharing everything.'

Tuni laid down the law.

'I think men and women are just different. They are born different. How can two sets of people who share the same space at the same time appear as if they are occupying two different worlds unless they are different? And I like being different. I don't want to be a man. I like the way I look as a woman. If I was a man, I would look different and have different likes.'

'And men can't have babies,' Circe added.

'But aren't they supposed to stay good-looking longer?' said Tuni.

'Yes,' said Circe, laughing mischievously, 'but they die first.' To which Tuni replied that there was not much point in living longer if your face looked like an old handbag. They both dissolved into laughter. When she had recovered, Tuni said feminism was not about whether women and men were different because of nature or culture.

'It's about whether we live in a man's world or a woman's world.' She said this was all nonsense because in the fashion business you could succeed as a man or a woman if you had the talent. This had been the case in haute couture for nearly a century.

Circe agreed and said that the way feminists went on about men and women all the time was annoying. 'I don't think being a woman should be the one fact about me which matters more than anything else in my life. I think it shouldn't matter at all, but feminism is as bad as the other side. It makes it the be-all and end-all of life.'

Mila was amazed, and slightly worried, by how quickly this subject had produced an animated conversation, and she still feared that the conversation might easily degenerate into bad-tempered squabbling. Again, she picked her words carefully. 'You said sociologists were all feminists. OK, sociology points out that men and women often behave in very different ways, and respond differently to the same situation or set of circumstances. Sociologists point out that women and men have been known to have separate beliefs about the world and ways of relating to it. They sometimes even use language differently. For example, they use the same words in different ways, and often have the greatest trouble making themselves understood to each other. Either we are dealing with two entirely separate species that find it pleasant or convenient to live together, or you are expected to behave very differently depending on whether you are male or female.'

Tuni replayed her theme. 'Because men and women are so obviously biologically separate – just think how we *look,* Mila – then of course they will behave differently and think differently as well. But you are going to tell us that the differences between men and women are in fact socially created.'

'Well, that is what sociology claims,' replied Mila. Then she paraphrased the discussion in Frank 'n' Stein that began with the observation that, when we are growing up, the question of what it meant to be a man or a woman is a pretty vital one.

Becoming an adult is usually taken to mean entering manhood or womanhood. Since, as men or women, we still possess the same biological characteristics we had as boys or girls, we are clearly talking about adopting a socially created identity, but it is important not to dismiss the influence of biology and physiology. We relate to the world through our bodies. Sociology does not claim, for the most part, that biological differences are irrelevant. The male and female aspects of our bodies are a part of our identity as men and women. Sociology suggests that these physical attributes exist in a complex, two-way, relationship with our social selves: the identity as men and women that we have to develop, and live with, and persuade other people is an authentic, worthwhile, acceptable way of behaving.

'I hope that doesn't sound as if I am overcomplicating the explanation,' Mila said. Circe replied. 'It's OK, we can cope. So when did sociology start realising that there were men and women? I mean, when does sociology say people start realising that they are men or women?'

Ignoring that barb, Mila continued. 'It varies: at some time in their early lives children become aware that they are not just people, they are men and women, and this distinction then governs a huge amount of what they do from then on. It can govern your way of speaking, how you sit, walk and run, what sort of games you play and what jobs you get. Every aspect of life is changed by this distinction that we make. If all sexual behaviour were biologically programmed, then we would know all of this stuff from birth. I think sociology often preferred to think of all people as potentially either men or women.'

'Like hermaphrodites?' said Tuni and they heard Ana giggle from her seat in the corner.

Mila said that research had shown there were observable stages in a child's growth at which point he or she began to separate other people by their sex, and think of itself as a boy or a girl. The age at which this happened varied between cultures and societies. Then, at around the time of puberty, there were often very important rituals which admitted boys into manhood and, sometimes, girls into womanhood. Tuni thought she had spotted the weakness in this sociological approach. 'At puberty, you said. That's when the biology starts to make a difference. Society is just making a fuss of the start of the hormones and everything else that starts making men and women so different from that point onwards. It's in their genes to develop in diverging ways from this point on.'

Mila said it was difficult, perhaps pointless, to separate social effects from biological nature. Each one shaped the other.

Tuni pointed out that Mila kept saying girls *might* be this and boys *might* be that and Mila explained that there were wide variations in what was expected of boys and girls between cultures. This had been used by some to suggest that what was considered appropriate male and female behaviour was always ... guess what ... socially constructed. Such interpretations tended to over exaggerate the differences between cultures and to miss a fundamental point: roles and functions might vary, but most societies had ideas of what male and female behaviour was and should be. There were few complex societies in which being male or female did not mean having different lives of some sort. Pretending that it did not matter was rarely an option.

Mila said it was generally accepted in sociology that there were two different facets to being male or female: *sex* and *gender*. Sex meant the biological and physiological differences between male and female. Gender was the term used to describe the learned features of being a man or a woman: the social definitions and psychological behaviours which men and women adopted. New developments in genetics had suggested that the division between the two was not as clear-cut and unchanging as was once thought, and sociology showed our 'gender' was not a fixed identity that we each adopted and tried to fit into as best we could. It was fluid, something that was created in our everyday encounters and relationships with others.

'Being male or female can sometimes be a bit of an act. Isn't that what you were complaining about, Tuni? Didn't you say that I was not very good at being female, at acting like a woman, and wasn't that why you asked if I was a feminist?'

Tuni was sure it wasn't like this in art and design:

'In the industry I want to work in, people treat you how you want to be treated. Men who feel more feminine are not expected to be different on the outside to how they feel inside. I think people choose to behave in a certain way. When they are growing up, boys force themselves to do acts even if they don't like it – like learning to drink revolting alcohol or to endure pain from their friends. Being men or women isn't something that is forced on us, it's something that we want to be.'

Mila could not help but agree with this. She said that gender governs what you do but what you do confirms what gender you are, and remakes and recreates the idea that there are two clearly distinguishable genders. And Mila decided that what a lot of sociologists missed was the extent to which individuals actively wanted to be feminine and masculine, and worked hard to achieve it. She said: 'You think that being a man or a woman is something each of us wants to be. This is true: throughout our growing up, in our adolescence, we go to a lot of effort to show that we are one or the other, to develop the habits and behaviours that make us men or women in the eyes of our peers. So, being a man or a woman isn't just something we want to be, it is also something that we have to do. That doesn't sound as if it's all down to genetic programming, does it?'

Mila really had not meant to score a debating point. She had just been carefully following an argument, being as truthful as she could be, and drawn the logical conclusion. But she wanted this to be a nice friendly chat not a debate and she felt she must do her best to restore the right tenor to the conversation: 'I don't think I'm doing very well at explaining sociology. Tuni, you said feminism was all about whether it is a man's world or a woman's world. And Circe, you said feminists always thought their gender mattered more than anything else. Sociology does have something to say about this.'

'Let me show you something,' Mila said. She picked out two photographs of herself from the parcel her mother had sent her. At eight years old she was a 'tomboy', a girl who behaved like a boy. Her hair was unkempt, she wore shapeless trousers and a top, and glasses which were even more unfashionable than the ones she wore now, and she looked relaxed and happy in her skin. The other photograph she held was from a few years later, around aged 13. Superficially, this was a better photograph. She had posed demurely, her hair and dress were neat and tidy, and she wore a smile but no glasses.

Mila's mother had perhaps intended a message in sending these photographs – look at you, then a mess, and look at you later, the butterfly emerging from its chrysalis. Mila might once have felt the same, but now she looked at the photographs differently. She saw a happy child, and a slightly nervous girl, straining to look like a young woman. Mila said:

'At some point you realise you are male or female, and if you're a girl, that there's a category that doesn't include you.'

Then Mila tried to explain to the others what Frank 'n' Stein had told her about a philosopher, Judith Butler, who had said that gender was a performance. Mila winced inwardly as she told them about the metaphor of the guilty verdict and, to cover up, she said provocatively: 'So, Tuni impersonates femininity as much as anyone in drag.'

Men and women are formed by power. Essentialism is the process of claiming male and female natures as unchanging, rooted in their bodies. Butler argues that anticipating this essentialism is what generates men and women as fixed beings. Gender is performed – as saying 'Go!' at the start of a race creates the race, or 'Guilty' in a trial sends a person to jail. Butler wants that performance to be taken to pieces. She thinks that wearing 'drag' – men dressing as women and women dressing as men – is a way to undermine the gender order. Butler believes feminism should not represent women as a single category – people should not be lumped together in this way. As women are the 'other' to men – the powerless that the powerful define themselves against – and she argues this could be used to point to the pretence at the centre of being male or female. She wants us to fragment identity. Then there is no 'woman' for 'men' to define themselves as different from. Butler wants us to shatter identity in order to disrupt each point in the chain, to create 'gender trouble'.

Tuni was not easily put in her place. 'So not wearing eyeliner is sticking it to The Man?

'I think it's something like that,' Mila said. To Mila this seemed quite practical. Many sociologists wrote as if an ideal society existed where men and women were still different, but basically the same (same jobs, housework, childcare). Well, that was a bit dull and unlikely. Butler seemed to present a way of shaking the status quo up right now, taking apart the binary distinction of male and female on which gender orders depended.

'Remember you said something about men and women speaking a different language sometimes. I don't think that's true either,' Tuni said.

'Well, there's a branch of feminism that says language is actually patriarchal and constructed by men. Women have to translate their thoughts into patriarchal language and back again. Therefore only feminist women can find out about the experiences of women.'

'OK, so they are the lunatic fringe, the feminist extremists. Tell me what they are called, so I can be sure to avoid them.'

And then, at last, Ana spoke. She spoke so softly that neither Circe nor Tuni heard her and were carrying on, talking and laughing. But Mila had heard Ana say something and she asked her to repeat it. Ana said simply:

'There's something missing from all this: men.'

Mila thought for a moment and shook her head. 'Feminists said that was what sociology was all about before feminism. There were a few studies which mentioned women, but from a male point of view. But the rest of sociology was made up of studies of male society and male behaviour.'

'I didn't mean that. I meant sociologists looking at men behaving as men, being masculine,' Ana said.

Now Mila understood.

'Oh, well, I think there have been some sociologists more recently who have done this, but you are right, Ana, it's not an area I heard much about when I was studying sociology at school. Even feminist theories had taken masculinity and maleness to be a given, something that is largely straightforward, constant across times and places, and not a problem for men, provided they oppress women enough. But feminists move with the times. They can see how life has changed for women and men. Now being a woman means living with contradictions. We expect to get jobs after we leave university that reflect our abilities. I know you wouldn't put up with anything less, Tuni. We also love preening and showing off. We also want to have relationships, have families, along with these other ways of living.'

'Some people don't want to be either men or women,' said Circe, but Ana ignored her.

'To understand relations between men and women don't sociologists have to examine both sides of the equation?' Ana said, and Mila thought that Ana was hitting the nail on the head. It was really quite surprising that masculinity had been thought of as unproblematic for all that time, although Frank 'n' Stein had said this was now changing.

Mila felt herself to be very close to the outward boundary of her knowledge now, but she told her friends that masculinity, like femininity, was something created in the acts of men and women. It was a rather one-sided and limited view to assume only men are responsible for masculinity, both of how masculinity was produced and how it was maintained. Masculinity (and femininity) were relational constructs between men and women, as well as between men and men, and women and women. To reject one, was to reject the other: to change one, was to change the other: 'This means that much of it happens in the way men and women relate to each other, how for instance men define themselves as being like some men and not others, and not like women.'

From the end of the last century some sociologists wrote about a crisis of masculinity, particularly in some Western countries, which came about because men were being displaced by women, in areas where they previously had lots of power. For instance, men had to adapt to unemployment where they previously had found their role as worker and supporter of their family the main source of their masculine identity. Masculinity, like femininity, is not just a single set of behaviours or identities that are more or less static. Different masculinities exist. Men have to adopt one or another of them, adapt to them, and then find that the form of masculinity they have taken on has become outdated, and have to adapt again to changing social circumstances.

Circe sounded exasperated. 'When will people stop thinking that male and female is everything? Lots of people who should know better divide the world into male and female. Part of becoming an adult, should be about looking beyond what you might have been taught about what to expect from the opposite sex, and from yourself as a man or a woman.'

Mila was nodding as Circe spoke, and she said there was a tendency in a lot of modern thought, not just sociology, to find slight overall differences between men and women as groups and assume that applied to each and every individual. Functionalists like Talcott Parsons had claimed this was simply because they could see the mutual benefit in splitting emotional and instrumental work. Feminists said it was because men saw their interest in exploiting women. This time it was Ana who sounded exasperated: 'But what about the feelings men and women have for each other? You haven't said a word about happy, loving relationships between men and women.'

Mila said followers of Parsons and the feminists saw emotions, when they acknowledged them at all, as merely instrumental in the social order and she could see why Ana was impatient with this. For example, feminists argued that power inequality made relationships like marriage very important for women. Women were restricted in their career and other opportunities, so marriage was a kind of a career for women: 'Feminists argue that men have vastly more power, so they can lay down the rules for these relationships, including the rules for sexual behaviour. In many places a woman who has sex with a lot of men, or perhaps simply has sex at all, is still stigmatised or persecuted whereas a man who has sex with a lot of women is accepted, even celebrated.'

Mila was aware that they had all become quite animated, and that the barriers between the new friends were coming down quickly, but she wondered if she should have said this. Circe and Tuni asked Mila what *she* thought of all this. Mila said that, while everyone was used to the idea that excessive and uncontrolled emotions caused trouble, she wondered if emotions might be the hidden hand of society, the hand that stopped us (most of the time) from destroying each other, or from spinning off into our own little individual worlds. Men and women were emotional and rational animals at the same time. Maybe relationships between men and women were at their finest when the two were working together, and at their most fascinating when the two were working apart?

'I don't know about you, but it's time to perform,' Tuni said, looking at her watch. 'The party's already started.'

The four of them finished getting ready and left. As they walked down the street, Mila took Tuni's arm. As they waited at a crossing, they heard a song through an open car window. It was an old song about two-faced men who leave you to sing the blues. They started singing along. Behind them, Ana was saying to Circe that it was a shame they were attracting attention to themselves like that. They had been the same earlier on with all that shouting and waving their arms all over the place when they were arguing about feminism. Ana said she just couldn't behave like that and, with a hint of a rather smug smile, she told Circe that Tuni and Mila had ended up 'behaving just like boys.'

Later, lying in bed, it occurred to Mila that she should count this evening as another explanation of one of sociology's big ideas. Until tonight, the idea that feminism was a sociological idea had not occurred to her.

Mila decided gender was a particularly good example of how sociology could be good at explaining the links between the personal and the social, how we can feel as if we make certain decisions out of free choice, but they are not in fact free; or, conversely, how we can feel constrained to make certain decisions, even though we may in fact have the power to say no. It also showed how sociology could easily fall into the trap of assuming that everyone behaved in a particular way, and did so because they were told to. There was really quite a lot of scope for individual men and women to behave in ways that were not traditionally masculine and feminine. When they did so, all those little changes could add up to something quite big, and lead to something really new: a society in which men and women were happy being men and women, and were happy with each other. At least she hoped so.

Visit the companion website at **www.palgrave.com/companion/ Bancroft-And-Fevre-Dead-White-Men-2e/** to access additional learning resources, including seminar questions based on the chapter's coverage, a jargon buster that defines key terms used in the text and a timeline which provides an overview of the development of sociological thought.

● ● ● ● ●

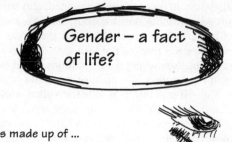

Gender – a fact of life?

Gender is made up of ...

Sexuality – especially heterosexuality

Stuff we have and a whole lot more

1. Gender is what seems to be the most basic and simple fact of life, that humanity is divided into men and women who have different challenges, roles and expectations of life. Sociological research on gender shows that male and female are categories people are put into, which then affects many things that have nothing to do with their biological sex. A frequently used formula is that sex is biological nature and gender is the psychological and sociological identity and sense of self built on it. Gender reaches into the workplace, the home, public and virtual space.

2. The conundrum faced by anyone who thinks gender does not matter or should not matter is explaining why actual inequality between sexes exists alongside legal and formal equality of opportunity. Can a woman be equal in a society where women are not equal?

3. There are many hidden ways in which the burdens of a gender divided society fall on women. One is the division of labour. That term means the distribution and reward of work in society. One of the ways labour is distributed is through paid work. Feminist sociologists showed that unpaid work was just as important – and this is the kind of work women end up doing. Caring for children and working in the home was a 'second shift' that women did – hidden and not remunerated.

4. These influential studies still assume gender is a fact of life in some sense, as it is based on a biological distinction. Queer theory argues that this is the wrong approach, and that gender is a performance, without that fundamental driving factor. Gender roles and identities are socialised and also performed, so we never entirely learn about how to be feminine or masculine, as we constantly recreate what these identities are. Each identity is a copy without an original. It is performed in rituals, habits, conversations and so many facets of life that there is no need for an underlying biological truth. Judith Butler pointed to drag, gender cross-dressing, as an example of gender trouble, where individuals perform gender in a way that highlights how malleable it is.

5

In Cahoots

Now well into her first semester, Mila had made good friends with Ana, Circe, Tuni, and Jasmine. They had established a comforting routine of chatting as a group – in fact usually just as much laughing as chatting – at odd hours of the day. They had all felt lonely and isolated to start with. Now they found that, although it was really not like being home, they had developed a little social network that worked in the same way as the social ties they might have had at home. As Durkheim said, the relations with other people were important for belonging and happiness.

The next big idea she encountered on her course was the relationship between mind and society. She was reluctant to test her friends' patience with it, but Mila decided the chats with her friends were a perfect opportunity to explain this big idea.

Durkheim had thought about the relationship between mind and society, as had two Americans who were writing at about the same time, the end of the nineteenth century. Society was the big new object for study, but they wondered whether there was a place left for human consciousness. The theory said that society shaped our thinking and actions, but where did that leave free will, and, most importantly, where did it leave the idea of thinking for ourselves? The two Americans were called Peirce and Cooley.

Reading Frank 'n' Stein, Mila found that Peirce had come up with a theory which explained exactly how society was shaping the ways in which we thought and communicated and even felt. He suggested that we got our ability to think from society and, indeed, society had already laid out what would make sense to us before we were conscious of the need to make sense.

Cooley came at the same problem from the opposite angle: society might make our sense for us, but it was in our heads that society lived, and only there. What we thought of people shaped our actions, and the ideas that we had about other people were the most important factors in society. Without our imaginations of each other there was no society. Society, he said, was all in the mind.

On the surface the big idea about mind and society was difficult to understand, but it was actually her new-found relationship with her friends that made it easier for Mila to grasp. What she was learning about feeling as if you belonged to a sisterhood made it easier to understand the theory of mind and society. It helped because if you did *not* know that we all take our thoughts, and even feelings, from the same place, it really was inexplicable to Mila how people who had only known each other for such a short time could feel so close. If there was not already something else binding them together, how could they almost immediately have become members of the sisterhood? It would have been a kind of miracle if she and her friends had not already felt part of something much bigger than themselves: society.

But, while having this group of friends might not be quite a miracle, it seemed, at least for now, to be quite a flimsy arrangement to Mila. She thought her new friendships were so fragile, and perhaps ephemeral, that her connection with the others could be blown away by a puff of ill wind. When she was not with her friends, she often doubted that the group really existed. Maybe it was a convenient fiction that would get them all through the first couple of months of university until they made true friendships. Maybe there was one true friendship at the heart of it (Ana and Circe?) and the others were only deluding themselves?

Yet when they were all together the feeling of belonging could be so powerful and it made her feel happy and safe. It was especially wonderful when Mila realised that on those few occasions when she let her guard down and let herself seem less than bright, attentive, and amusing, the connection with her friends did not disappear. Mila could not help but see then that an awful lot of this was in her head. It was as Cooley said: the group came into being despite them, but nevertheless the group only existed in their heads. It seemed to come from outside them but only lived inside their minds.

Mila knew that before too long she would not be able to pass up the opportunity to explain her third big idea to the sisterhood. After all, the chats were all about her and her new friends cementing their friendship, and one of the factors that was central to this process was the way they each told each other stories about who they were. Although Mila knew well enough that her stories were sometimes short on detail, she did know that the way they told stories to each other would be a big help in getting big-idea number three over to them.

Ana had much more to say for herself now. She was the most earnest, and anxious to please, of the new friends, the one who never expressed doubt or even reserve about what the others said. She was always smiling and simply happy to be with them. Her gratitude sometimes brimmed over in a way they found a bit embarrassing, but one night, while the friends sat around talking, she did something so typical of herself it became part of the folklore of their group. Ana and Circe had begun to talk at the same time and had expressed more or less the same idea, word for word, and had apparently expressed the same thought and had the same feeling. Ana was delighted.

'Isn't it amazing how we all seem to be on the same wavelength? You know, like with Circe just now, that isn't meant to happen unless you have known someone for years, but each of us seems to know what the others are thinking all the time. It's just wonderful to be so close. It's like magic.'

Not for the first time, Mila wondered about Ana's home life and why she, more than any of the group, was so grateful for the closeness of their friendships. The entire group, except Ana and Mila, had spoken about the good friends they had at home and their surprise at making just as firm friends, so soon, at university. To Ana it just seemed to be a surprise that she had any friends at all. Mila was not the only one who was curious and Jasmine asked, 'Why do you say it's magic,

Ana? Isn't it just what people do? I know it's nice, but we have been given a big opportunity to blend together. Isn't it natural that we should become friends?'

If this had been a few weeks before, Ana might easily have been a little hurt by what Jasmine had said but now all the friends had learned to expect Jasmine to be a little blunt. They gave her licence to ask questions that were not tailored to take account of each friend's strengths and weaknesses, so Ana said, 'I didn't mean that it was magic to have friends, but that it was like magic that we know what each other is thinking. Anyway, having such a close group of friends may seem natural to you, but I never really felt I fitted in like this before. I thought sometimes I never would and now I've got you four and we get on so well and it's wonderful.'

The stories they told each other about who they had been before they met frequently took on this confessional tone, but Ana was almost always the one who reached this point first. Usually someone would then reciprocate and off they would go into telling each other about their past – key passages, revealing secrets – never tiring of delving deeper and deeper into themselves to reveal the secrets of their own personalities. 'It's still a surprise to me too. How can you be so close to people who you have only known for such a short time? I love the way we know what each other is thinking and anticipate what we are going to say. It makes me feel so safe and appreciated,' said Circe.

Mila could simply not resist the temptation to put her big idea to the test and she began to talk, trying as usual to sound nonchalant and conversational, in other words trying to avoid sounding like one of her lecturers.

'It was a big surprise to me too how close we have all got so quickly. But I guess it's the surprise, and the fact that we are all so happy, and I suppose relieved, to get on so well that leads us to think it's magic that we know what each other is thinking. Sociology has an alternative to the magic explanation of how people can seem to read each other's minds.'

Jasmine wanted to say something, but Mila did not give her the chance.

'The question leads to one of the big contributions sociology has made to human understanding – it's actually not about the special times when we come out with the same words, though this is the best example of it – but about all the times when people are able to share thoughts with each other. If you don't think it's natural,' Mila smiled at Jasmine, 'you start to wonder how it might be possible at all.'

Everyone looked baffled by this and Mila thought she could see Jasmine gearing up for a demolition of what she had just said, but Tuni was nodding at her. 'It's like colours you know. I say something has to be magenta and Harper, our demonstrator, does it in orchid.'

All the women burst out laughing at this but Tuni wasn't to be put off. She was used to being thought a bit lightweight by the others and normally played up to the ditzy stereotype they had made of her.

'I know you think it's silly, but it's a good example of what I mean. You don't care about shades – look at the clothes you wear! – so I'll make it obvious even to my friends who it's clear know nothing about colour design. OK, how do Harper and I know we are seeing the same colour? If he sees a colour as green every time he says red, and I always see it as red, we always agree it's red, but see something entirely different.'

Mila was delighted.

'That's exactly it. Whether it's colours, or anything else, we can never be sure what the other person experiences, but we share the language that allows us to talk to each other. It doesn't really matter if it's green or red because as long as we apply the same name we can talk to each other.'

This now set Tuni off into giggles. 'Well it matters if you let Harper choose the colours for your project. Maybe we really do see different colours, because I think Harper is colour blind!'

Mila carried on regardless. 'We cannot ever see into each other's heads but we manage to interact together all the same. Sometimes in this process we come out with exactly the same thoughts – like Ana and Circe did – but that's only a special case of what happens all the time. We don't ever know what the other person thinks, but it doesn't stop us talking to them, buying presents for them or telling tales about them. If we don't accept that this is magic, we need to find an explanation.'

Mila explained that it was in the 1870s that Charles Sanders Peirce came up with the first piece of the jigsaw that was needed to explain the miracle of human interaction. Peirce was interested in how we go about thinking, especially when we are being logical. He started thinking about where our thoughts came from and wondered if we might all get our thoughts from the same place, a kind of human-thoughts-store. This would be why all people could think like people.

'Start by thinking of language,' Mila said. Everybody knew that little children have to learn to speak and they did it in the languages that people speak in the places they grow up in. Not many kids were going to make up lots of new words and persuade other people to start using them. Mostly they just used the words they had learned and so they ended up speaking the same language as everyone else.

It was the same with thoughts: we got them from a store rather than making them up ourselves. In fact sometimes we got them from exactly the same place as we did our language because for most of the time we used words to think: our thoughts came as words and we thought by stringing words together. In fact our thoughts were made up of the words we had learned from everyone else. 'So they are not our own thoughts at all, but everybody else's,' said Circe. 'We just borrow them?'

'That's what Mila is trying to get us to believe,' Jasmine answered, 'but I don't buy it: because we don't always think in words, though, do we, Mila?' Mila thought she was prepared for this: 'That's true: some people think with numbers or with graphics, colour and sounds, maybe music. But most people don't make up their own numbers or pictures to think with. It's really no different to words because they still come from other people. Words and numbers, and maybe graphics, are what you find on the shelves in the store you go to for your thoughts.'

Mila explained that Peirce called all of them – words, numbers, pictures, sounds – *signs* because they were always pointing towards something else.

'You know how, when you say a word over a lot of times, it loses its meaning and just becomes a sound? Well, that's because the word isn't really the
object it makes you think about; it's just a sign for it. We've just got used to
that set of sounds being the sign for the object we see. It's the same with all
the other signs. There is nothing special about them that ties us to using them
to mean what they do now. Another sign would do as well if we started using
it that way.'

Mila said you could call the human-thoughts-store 'society' – meaning everything we do together: living our lives, learning, working, spending time together.
It's when we are doing all those acts that the words and other signs get made
up, and passed around. Of course lots of the signs were made up a long time
ago but there were new ones coming into being all the time (with science and
technological and social change) and with them you got new thoughts to think.
Circe had a question.

'But isn't a new thought more than a bunch of names for objects, or *signs* like
you call them? When you are working meaning out, you aren't going "this thing,
that thing, another thing over there". When you work things out, you make
connections, you think: "Tuni's shoes got broken *because* Mila borrowed them".'

Everyone laughed at the standing joke about the shoes, including Mila:

'I bought her a new pair, didn't I? But that's right. Thinking is the connections
between words or numbers, whatever, not the words themselves.'

But how did those connections get made? Mila explained that Peirce thought
the signs were already configured, so that they could only be connected to each
other in a limited number of ways. It was as if they were already connected to
other signs in the store, before we took them home. It was this connection of
signs with each other that made up what we called our 'logic'. Each of us was
like a little kid making something out of the sort of building blocks children
use. We went to the box to pick out the blocks, the blocks that fitted together in
predetermined ways. We called this 'thinking logically.'

As long as we could put the blocks together in this way, we would think we
were thinking or speaking the truth. It was like one of those picture books for
children where the children draw in the lines between numbered dots and a
picture emerges. Adults could usually look at most of those dot-pictures and
make the connections in their heads. They could make the picture emerge from
the pattern of dots without using a pencil, and this was what we all did when
we recognised the truth. Truth was simply a matter of joining up the dots in
our heads.

Mila was trying her best to remember what she had heard and read as she
talked, and she decided she had not explained it well enough. She went on to say
there might be even *less* variation in our thinking than she was suggesting. She
said it is as if there were extra rules that said you must only fit together all the
blue blocks and only then the blocks of the same size. Peirce reckoned there were
two sorts of ways the building blocks, the signs, could be connected together.
She said it was easiest to see this if you thought about the way that words could
have links to each other.

There were connections between words that shared meanings, or bits of meanings, with other words: words overlapped with each other. Although they did not always mean exactly the same, 'luck', 'chance', and 'fortune' had a lot in common. According to Peirce these connections were 'semantic links'. There were other kinds of connection called 'syntactic connections', the rules about how you strung words together to make sense. Peirce called his theory about the way we think the 'science of signs', and he was known as the founder of modern 'semiotics' which was pretty much the same as the science of signs.

Mila said the really important conclusion to grasp was that we got all these signs (that connect with each other to make our thinking) from society. We really were like the kids at a playgroup: they did not bring their own building blocks to play with but used the ones they found there to make their little houses and toys. This was us too, only we were making our thoughts instead of little houses.

'So the way that we all feel about being so close, the way we are all surprised at making good friends (or making good friends so quickly), the way that we all feel safe and happy knowing we have such a tight group of friends – all of this can be explained too. We all feel the same way about how friendship has worked out for us because we are all taking our emotional cues and connections from the same place – from society. It's not natural in the sense that it doesn't need to be explained, but it's so common that we hardly ever think to question how it happens.'

'Maybe that's why Jasmine here sometimes disagrees with us,' said Circe, and everyone laughed, including Jasmine who asked her what she meant. Circe replied, 'I mean you have a bit more difficulty with joining up the dots because you come from somewhere else. That's why we thought at first you were a bit unfriendly and critical but then we got used to you. You don't mean to be blunt, that's just what you are used to. We don't join the dots up in that way but, now we understand you, we know that the dots make a different picture for you.'

Mila jumped in almost before Circe had stopped. 'Most of what we know about how to think is shared between societies. Jasmine isn't from Mars, Circe!'

'Mars isn't very far away in astrophysics, Mila,' said Jasmine, and Mila realised the damage had been done. It had not been intended, but Jasmine had been pushed to the margins of the sisterhood. There was an awkward silence and they all felt very grateful to Tuni who broke it by asking them if they thought they were all too young to fall in love with anyone. Tuni went on to say she could see it happening to herself sooner rather than later. Mila said she thought Ana was the one who would fall in love first but none of the other four would say what was in all their heads – that Jasmine would be the least likely to fall in love. They were determined not to make her feel an outsider again.

Tuni said she had been thinking about the ideas Mila told them about that guy Peirce: 'Is that stuff about the way we join thoughts together really meant to be applied to our emotions as well?' Mila said yes and Tuni went on: 'That's really disillusioning, and I hope it's wrong, because, if it applies to our emotions, it's got to apply to *love* too. If he's right, there is no true love, but simply us fitting together the blocks that society has given us, with their predetermined connections.'

'I guess so,' said Mila 'and we eventually decide we are really in love with a person when the connections seem to fit best and our doubts are minimised.'

Tuni continued. 'I never believed that people were made for each other – and only the right person would do, but it makes falling in love sound like working out what you need to do to choose your first car.'

Mila said: 'It's a bit disappointing, maybe, but the next guy who made a huge contribution to theories of mind and society was Charles Horton Cooley and he had plenty to say about how you know whether someone loves you or not.'

Mila explained that Cooley thought that when people relate to each other they do it in their imaginations. 'It is my idea of a man I like that relates to the rest of my mind and a man's idea of me that relates to the rest of my mind. It's the same with all of us and all of our relationships with other people, not just when you fall in love with them.' She told them this was a really important objective for somebody to work out, and it made all the difference to the big idea. Circe seemed to get it and Ana was nodding hard (though you could never be sure if this was simply her urge to be agreeable), but the others were looking a bit confused. Mila pointed over to the pinboard on the wall where she had attached a few photos and some scraps of paper with lists and memorable quotations. She wanted to bring Jasmine back into the conversation.

'Look at that one, Jasmine, third one down, on the yellow paper. Read out Number One please.'

Jasmine read the words that Mila had noted down in a lecture: 'If there is something in you that is wholly beyond this and makes no impression upon me it has no social reality in this situation – Charles Horton Cooley.' As usual, Jasmine was not impressed. 'That's silly. If one of us has a secret that none of us knows, it might make a big difference to how they behave towards the rest of us, even though we know nothing about it. Isn't the secret "socially real", Mila?'

Mila said: 'OK, let's imagine I have a secret' (that shouldn't be too hard, she thought), 'and I don't tell any of you. Let's imagine I am a vampire. If you don't know I have a secret, the secret can have no effect on how you relate to me. Sure, it will affect my behaviour, sleeping in, not being a blood donor, that kind of activity, but what you know of my behaviour has already been processed to form your imagination of me. You just think I am lazy and not very public spirited, because you don't know about my secret life as a vampire. Cooley is trying to get us to think about the situations we create together – our *interaction* – and there is no vampire in the interaction, so we relate to each other as if I'm not one. You all let me hang around with you, you don't try to put a stake through my heart and I don't bite your necks.'

Mila pretended to bear down on Jasmine's neck and Jasmine joined in the general laughter, as she pushed Mila lightly away. Tuni was sure she had spotted a flaw: 'OK, but there are times when the fact that you don't know something about someone becomes socially real. Like if I know you are keeping a big secret and don't know what it is, it's certainly going to change my behaviour a lot.'

'Oh, yes,' said Circe, 'she'll spend every minute of the day trying to worm the secret out of you. There has never been anyone who is less happy with someone keeping secrets – better not to let her know you have one in the first place.'

Tuni was laughing again, but she was determined to make her point. 'In history of art and design they were telling us about the masked balls they used to have in several European countries. That must have been really exciting. You could dance with people who might keep their whole identity secret. The fact that you knew nothing about them was the whole point of the masked ball. You can't say that wasn't "socially real", Mila.'

'You're right,' Mila said, 'but so was Cooley. If you didn't know a person's identity, this would greatly influence what your imagination could do to create an idea of the person. The fact that their identity is a mystery means you start to speculate on who they might be. The same speculation happens when you are going to meet someone you don't know.'

Ana chipped in, but in a quiet voice. 'Like in arranged marriages. You don't know anything about the person other than what you have been told by your parents or your uncles and aunts and you look at their picture and imagine what might be.' The tone of Ana's voice suggested that some of what could be imagined might be less than pleasant, and Circe spoke to Ana just as softly.

'I think it's terrifying – knowing you are going to meet someone who you are meant to make yourself love just because it suits everyone else.'

'But if the connections that society has laid out for you fit together well enough – so that you don't have too many doubts that you are in love – then why can't people in arranged marriages believe they love each other just as much as any other couples can?' Mila asked Circe. Circe looked at her in a meaningful way and almost imperceptibly shook her head, but Mila missed the gesture.

Tuni was simply delighted to realise they had got back to her original question. 'It's like I said at the start: you are never really sure you are in love, you just give up doubting too much.'

Mila smiled broadly. 'You never really get to know the person you love either, only your idea of him, only the picture you make of him in your imagination. No matter how close you get to someone, you are only relating in your imaginations.'

'But what do you mean by "close" to someone, Mila?' asked Tuni. 'If you get close enough to someone you love (or don't love, I suppose) you aren't just relating in your imagination. If you get really close it's more than your minds that meet ...' Tuni broke off, laughing, and the others joined in, but when Mila had collected herself she tried to explain to them that Cooley thought that it did not matter how intimate you were with someone, because you still had to relate to them in your imagination. It was really difficult for her to explain this without setting all of them off laughing again, but Mila eventually got the others to be quiet.

'You remember what we were talking about weeks ago, not long after we met, about what our mothers said about the way it was for their whole generation?

Sometimes men and women were not very close then, but they still had children, didn't they? The difference between couples like that and what we said we want to be like if we get married is not what people do with their bodies, but what they think in their heads.'

They were quiet and thoughtful for a moment, but Tuni could not help herself: 'Maybe we can do some different things with our bodies too?' More laughter followed and Mila gave up altogether. It was not until an hour later, as the friends were beginning to think about going to bed, that they returned to Cooley and the latest of sociology's big ideas.

They had been talking over very familiar ground: what each had thought of the other when they first met and how this first impression had changed in the months since then. For most of them it was an effortless and oddly comforting conversation to repeat again and again. The comfort that they all got, apart from Mila who was too aware of the gaps in their knowledge of her, was like what a child might get from hearing bedtime stories about herself.

Circe was telling Ana, as many times before, that she had thought Ana a bit standoffish at the start, before they became close friends. As ever, Ana needed more reassurance. She wanted to know exactly what it was about her that Circe had liked. But Circe could only say, as ever, 'I don't know. I just decided you were a sympathetic person – you know, loyal, funny, that kind of thing – and I wanted you to be my friend.'

'But what was it that made the difference?' Ana persisted.

Circe was tired and looking like she needed help. Mila stepped in to remind them that Cooley had said we only related to each other in our imaginations. She said this was why people who were friends, or even lovers, have to keep asking each other what they think of the other person in the relationship. You had to ask because there was no other way to know.

'You know how people who are in love are always saying to each other "what are you thinking now?" The point is that they *have to ask*. There is no other way to know.'

Jasmine joined in. 'Even then it probably takes a lot of blind faith to persuade yourself that your lover is being truthful when they answer you.'

Mila continued. 'People can have a quite a lot of faith, can't they? Sometimes they persuade themselves of all sorts of qualities about their lovers that aren't true. Those novels Ana reads are full of women who believe that the men they love are much nicer people than they really are.'

Ana said: 'Exactly! Jasmine is always saying that those books are not like real life, but they are exactly like it.'

Jasmine nearly hissed at her: 'They are an *alternative* to real life.'

Mila did not want to give Jasmine cause for offence again. She said that Cooley thought a fictional character might easily have more of an effect on us, more reality to us, than a thousand physically real people. Perhaps he was thinking of literature, but it could just as easily apply to movies or TV. The physically real people were not socially real; they did not *register*, unless they were imagined by someone else. 'Someone may think they love you but they have no effect on you unless you become aware of their intentions. It's the point about having a secret again.'

Tuni said: 'So there could be lots of men out there who love me but, because I don't imagine it, then it has no effect?'

Mila smiled. 'Of course. If we only relate to each other in our imaginations, then society is all in the mind – that's what everyone remembers that Cooley said. Read the next two quotes underneath the last one, Jasmine.'

Jasmine read: 'In order to have society it is evidently necessary that persons should get together somewhere; and they get together only as personal ideas in the mind. Where else?' 'The imaginations which people have of one another are the *solid facts* of society.'

'So, the big idea sociology has is that we should study what goes on in peoples' heads? I thought it was about how people spent their lives, not how they thought about life,' Jasmine added dismissively.

Well, Mila thought, Jasmine is back in the group – we are all meeting in her imagination again. 'I think it's about both, and the theory Cooley came up with showed that you could not understand how people spent their lives if you did not understand what went on in peoples' heads.'

Mila was sure this was a good place to stop before Jasmine came up with another question and, since Jasmine was back in the group, Mila would have to use her usual defence to get her to stop. 'I guess the idea that is in all your heads now is going to bed.' They all nodded except Jasmine, who never seemed to want to go to bed. 'Thanks for putting up with all this sociology.' They all said no, it was all very interesting. All of them except Jasmine were yawning as they did so, but then, it was very late.

Visit the companion website at **www.palgrave.com/companion/ Bancroft-And-Fevre-Dead-White-Men-2e/** to access additional learning resources, including seminar questions based on the chapter's coverage, a jargon buster that defines key terms used in the text and a timeline which provides an overview of the development of sociological thought.

● ● ● ● ●

**Language and numbers
are abstract**

**Signs are concrete
and immediate**

1. How do people arrive at shared meaning and understanding of a situation?
Signs have been used for communication since prehistory. Petroglyphs were
written on cave walls and cut into wood. Peirce and Cooley wrote about signs
as the basic building block of mind.

2. For Cooley, what was real for each person was to what – and to whom –
they could relate in their imagination. According to Peirce, ideas and
thoughts are constructed by linguistic signs, which have a limited number
of ways in which they can link together meaningfully. Every member of society
shared this sign system.

3. Language and numbers are astonishing cultural achievements. They are
abstract, like advanced computer code. Signs are different – they are
concrete, like the basic instructions for a computer. Signs are immediate,
powerful, shared sources of meaning and understanding. Computer icons
and brands are signs like that – we immediately grasp their meaning without
having to think about it.

4. Semiotics is the study of signs and how societies produce systems of
shared meaning that are powerful because they feel immediate. Many
societies have very well developed ways of doing this. Advertising, political
branding, social media, dating websites – they all rely on shared and largely
unspoken meaning.

6
In Doni's Club

The entrance to the club was not as Mila had imagined, but perhaps this shabby door in a dilapidated neighbourhood was designed to escape attention and safeguard the club's exclusivity. Or maybe it told you the club had been there a long time, and the fashionable heart of the city had moved elsewhere. Inside, it was not as she had imagined it either: there was much more space and air. She had thought it would be dark – she had imagined mirrors and red velvet – but she entered a huge room with the evening light streaming in from open French windows leading to a veranda at the rear.

This was all so pleasant, felt Mila: a very pleasing change from her functional and soulless student residence. By association, this thought reminded her of the feeling of anticlimax that had oppressed her after she and her friends had talked about the big idea of mind and society. She had found herself feeling that the theory which had entertained her friends was, in fact, a recipe for despair because it left so little room for self-expression or surprises. You got your ideas from society, and for the rest of your life you joined up the dots. It was little consolation to say society only lived in the mind if you were condemned to repeat the same clichés as everyone else all your life: all your ideas, all your conversations, all your relationships even, all preordained, just waiting for you make the connections.

It wasn't just that Mila thought that this was a miserable view of life: she felt it was a profoundly misleading view. How could something like her and Arun be about joining up the dots? Not that they had a relationship, but there might be a possibility, mightn't there, in the future? And this was why the miserable view was wrong. Real life was so full of unknowns and so it was exciting and frightening. It didn't feel like there were any dots out there waiting for her join up at all. And there was also another reason Mila was dissatisfied with the theory she had explained to her new friends: she could find no room in this theory for rebels like her father who were punished for standing up to society, for trying to blaze their own trail.

She needed a sociological theory that made room for individuals. It was when she read Frank 'n' Stein's explanation of the theories of George Herbert Mead that Mila found out that, even if life was about joining up the dots, there was still a place for the self in sociology.

Mead believed that we were doing more than just following a script that society gave us. Sociology did not rule out self-expression and surprises, after all. It made room for rebellion. Frank 'n' Stein explained a theory called 'symbolic interactionism' and this seemed to help to lift Mila's mood as well. She had successfully banished the feeling of anticlimax, and her doubts (at least for now), and here she was in this lovely light room sitting down to eat some nice food with her brother, Doni.

'The people I know think father was unlucky, that's all,' said Doni. 'This is where he used to come, you know, to do business. It's going to be useful to me, too. You can socialise with the people you want to do business with and get them to trust you. It makes everything easy for you.'

Mila looked round at the people again. She said she could see it was a different world to her own. 'Absolutely,' said Doni, 'and it's the only one that matters to me.' Something about the smugness of her brother made Mila worry for him. If it wasn't just bad luck that her father had got caught out, maybe it was this kind of complacency. Thinking of her father led Mila to ask her brother how he thought their father was coping with his sentence. Doni said he was sure his father would get by. 'He's a practical man – he will do what's necessary to get by, and I expect he's comfortable enough, even there.'

Mila was shocked by this. 'So you don't think it might break his spirit? I think it must be awful for an individualist like him to have to put up with an institution – unable to make the most basic choices about what he does. He is too old and, well, noble for it. In court he seemed quite romantic to me, stand-ing up against the power of law and the media, but now he is being punished by being treated like a common criminal, as if he is not an important man.'

As was often the case, Doni found his sister's views both naive and bizarre. 'Break his spirit?' he repeated sarcastically, 'you seem to think it's like caging a wild beast. And you think he's romantic? I've never seen him like that, and it's not what the court or the newspapers thought, is it?'

Mila thought her brother was no more capable of curbing his tongue now than he had been when he was a child. She told him that the way people portrayed what her father did afterwards, the way they condemned him again and again, was only explicable if you thought he was doing something to stand up for the individual against society. 'He stood against the crowd and that's why the crowd wanted to crush him.

I can see he wouldn't think of what he did as noble but it doesn't matter, I know it was.'

It was Mead's theory, after all, that she knew proved her father was a romantic rebel, but how was she going to explain it? She would have to take a step or two backwards before going on to make her point. Doni was looking round for the waiter but, as she began to explain, Mila kept her gaze on the pattern of the empty plate in front of her.

'OK, whatever people think is normal has a big influence on them, but you can explain that and, at the same time, make space for people to be individu-als. Symbolic interactionism says we learn what normal is from society. In fact society gives us all our ideas but it does not exist outside us. It's not only that we aren't controlled by society but we have to make society all the time. We make it happen again, and again, every moment of the day. There would be no society if we did not do this. It's a process in which we are all involved, and this means that surprises can happen.'

'You and father chose to join this club and meet with these people. You and all these other people here want to be part of the same club. I don't just mean you are members of the same private club but you are in business: you have the same interests, the same lifestyles. That means society does not control us but in fact we control it. In fact not only is it that society takes place in the mind, but we recreate society all the time, every day. If we did not, there could be no society.'

The waiter arrived and they ordered their food. While Doni took his time over the menu, she tried to organise her thoughts. When she began again, she explained that Mead had wanted to understand how we became adults, by which he meant people who could reason in an adult way. He said this was all about learning to think of *ourselves* in an objective way. Mila said this was the key to being able to join any kind of group and without our ability to see ourselves as others saw us, no kind of society would be possible.

Mead said it was being able to reason objectively about ourselves that made the difference between human society and animal society. But if society was not possible without this way of thinking, you only got to learn to think objectively by *being social*. It was this that gave you the idea of thinking about yourself in this way: as an object. This happened because in social interaction other people treat us objectively. Mila had difficulty finding the words to explain this properly, but Doni had already decided what he thought she meant and he sounded both impatient and condescending.

'But people don't treat each other objectively, little sister. Most of us are very unfair. We have our favourites and we indulge them, forgive their sins, and so on, but with other people we are impersonal and objective and we pretend they have no feelings. Like those hypocrites in the court who you hate because they were vindictive towards father.'

'Mead doesn't mean we treat each other fairly or anything like that. I don't think I am explaining this very well. He means other people treat us as not part of themselves, as something "other". Because they treat us in this way, we get the idea that we can think of ourselves like this.

'You do it all the time: when you remind yourself you need to ring mother, or when you finally tell yourself you must go and see your little sister now that she is living in the same city as you, or when you are planning your next business deal. Not that you see yourself in the same way in each case, of course. You think of yourself as the dutiful son or brother but you also think of yourself as a powerful businessman.'

'Maybe. One day,' said Doni. 'Now, here is the food.' After the waiter had left them alone again, Mila told him that Mead actually thought that since we have all sorts of social relationships with all sorts of different people we have not one idea of how we look to other people, but many.

'So, with my new friends at university, I know that they see me in one particular way and you and mother see me in a different way. Of course I feel a phoney with my friends, knowing there is so much about me that they do not know, but everyone knows that one person's view of them will not be the same as another's. It's not that we put on masks, or put up fronts to hide who we are. It's not about manipulation. It's just how we interact with each other.'

Mila felt slightly uneasy for a moment. The thought passed through her mind that the same could apply to her father: he could be the romantic rebel for her but not for Doni. And why was it taking so long to get to the point? Her feelings seemed to be getting in the way of the argument she wanted to make. She tried hard to focus on explaining why her father was a romantic, not a normal person who could turn out to be in the wrong after all. Doni was still looking over her shoulder, but he said, in a way she hoped was not sarcastic:

'I think I understand this. There are situations in which you have to give people a particular idea of the sort of man you are. It's absolutely necessary in business that there are facts about you that you do not allow other people to know.'

'Yes, the amount of you that goes into each interaction is determined by what kind of interaction it is. This was what Mead thought. We are not trying to deceive anyone. It's just that the person we appear to be changes with the situation we are in.'

Doni caught the eye of the waiter as he showed some new diners to their table and pointed to the empty water pitcher on their table. The waiter nodded as he walked past and a few moments later returned with a full pitcher and asked them if there was anything else they needed. This was an interaction, thought Mila: I can use it to explain the theory to Doni.

'That's something else that Mead said: you find out what a gesture means when you find out what response it gets. You pointed at the pitcher and we got more water. But in another situation pointing at a pitcher might mean something else entirely. If you were in a shop it might mean you want to buy it. If somebody in a thriller did that it might mean, "don't drink this, it's poisoned". It's not just who you seem to be that changes from situation to situation but also the meaning of your gestures.'

Mila thought she was back on track. 'Mead said the meaning of the signals we send to other people was sorted out. We make a gesture to someone and the other person thinks about where this is leading: they work out what you intend by the gesture, what you meant by it. It is their idea of this meaning they respond to.'

'They don't respond directly to your signals, only to what they think those signals mean. This is why the theory is called symbolic interactionism. The way we interact with other people is determined by what we think the other person's actions mean – what they *symbolise*.'

'Hold on, Mila,' said her brother, sitting back from his empty plate. 'One minute you are talking about pointing at a water pitcher and now you are saying the same is true for all our actions.'

'But it's right. When Mead talks about gesturing to other people, or signalling to them, that includes all the ways in which we can signal meaning to people. It could be waving at them, talking to them or hugging them, anything really.'

'And it's always the same – you only find out what the signal means when you find out how people respond to it?' Doni sounded as if he might be genuinely interested now. 'But if the waiter did not bring me more water I would still want him to. That's what I meant when I pointed at it.'

'Mead says that is the very interaction we need to understand: what you want does not lead straight to what your signal means. There is another person's thoughts in between. So the waiter sees you point and thinks: "Table 10 wants more water but it's not my table so I will leave it to someone else". You did not mean him to think this; it isn't what you meant, but it's going to influence how the interaction turns out. That's why you won't get any water.'

'Yes, but he knew what I wanted, he just did not think it was his job to do it.'

'Yes – so that's what your gesture meant: no water. Look, if you go and complain about the waiter ignoring you that will not be what *he* meant you to do either (which was to ask another waiter). But you are right that almost everyone would understand what you meant when you pointed at the pitcher. That's because we share a context that allows us to make sense of signals, not just gestures but everything people do and say, in the same way.'

Mila said that Mead thought we only had this shared context because, as we grew up, we learned to *adopt the attitude of everyone*. She explained that this was what she had been working towards before, talking about people learning to see themselves as other people did. Growing up was about learning from our interactions with other people that we had to be able to think of ourselves objectively. This was quite a difficult thing to do, and it took a long time, because all we had to go on in order to find out about the attitude of everyone was the few people that we actually met. When we met them we thought of the attitudes they took to us as being something individual to them.

'You know: my teacher thinks I am quiet. My mother thinks I am a good girl. My brother thinks I am naive and foolish. Mead says we have to sort these individual attitudes we encounter into a bigger picture that will help us to see what everyone will think of us. He called this bigger picture the "Generalised Other". He had this example to show you what he meant. Remember that he said it was the ability to think of ourselves objectively that was the difference between people and animals? Well his example of the "Generalised Other" was the difference between a man and a dog. If two dogs fight over a bone, they are not bothered what other dogs think of them. If two men dispute over who owns something, they both rely on arguing that the "Generalised Other" is on their side. So when they say it's their property they are saying everyone would recognise their rights to own it.'

'But, Mila, isn't your point that our father did not care about your "Generalised Other?"'

'Yes, this is what I have been trying to tell you. Mead thought of that too. Knowing what the "Generalised Other" might expect of us does not always mean we have to meet those expectations. This is what I have been trying to explain. You may be right that father understood what people's normal expectations were, but he chose to go against those expectations. That was him asserting his individualism, and I think it definitely is romantic to go against a whole society like that.'

Mila said that Mead built in this possibility into his account of the process of growing up and learning to think objectively about ourselves. He made room for rebels and non-conformists and outsiders. As we grew up, we learned what everyone wanted us to do, but some of us chose not to do it. Mead often used children learning to play team games as a way of illustrating this point: we would know that we are called upon to do certain actions, like catching a ball, but then it was up to us to go along with this, or not. And the person who exercised this free will was something different from that objective view of yourself from the point of view of others, the view that you picked up from social interaction when you were growing up. It was something much more spontaneous and, creative which you could not observe directly but could glimpse in situations when people were asked to perform some action.

'It's like the way we were just talking about interaction as a three-stage process. In the game the child knows they are meant to be a catcher. But then the child responds, and everyone finds out who they really are. This determines how everyone else sees them – the kid who won't play the game gets bullied and abused and our father got vilified.'

'You were never any good at team games were you, Mila?' said Doni.

'And father was always a bit ashamed of me, but you were good at games so that was OK – you fulfilled his expectations. You see, there is a place in Mead's theory for choice and self-expression. We learn how to conform – joining up the dots in the way society wants you to – but you don't have to do it.'

'I see the point: when a man finds out whether he is going to give in to temptation, or not, only then will he will find out who he really is. You may be cleverer than I gave you credit for, Mila.'

'I'm glad I have surprised you. In fact I have surprised myself. The picture I had of myself growing up does not really fit how I believe people look at me now. There are some expectations my secret self chooses not to conform to. I don't see the point in pretending to be more stupid than I am anymore. I used to think I wouldn't have had any friends at all if I was too serious, but my friends here seem to like me to explain ideas to them. I also worked out I am going to miss out on the experiences I can learn from if I act dumb, and I do want to learn things. It's like people say: the more you know, the more you *want* to know.'

Mila could tell from his smirk that she had been wrong to take his compliment at face value.

'I bet all that stuck in your head because of the example of the kid who drops the ball. That's you, isn't it? Still the lame duck nobody wants on their team. But now you see yourself as a romantic, like father. That's what all this disguise stuff is about. It excites you to think you're different, an individual standing out against the crowd instead of a lame duck.'

'There was the person that I thought my new friends would want me to be if I was to become part of their group and then there was the person I became after I came to be their friend. But there were three stages to this and what comes in between is my free will: my choice to conform or not. It's the secret and spontaneous self that makes the decision. And when the person finds out what their decision was they also find out who they really are.'

Doni smiled at what he took to be her weakness. 'I didn't mean that,' he said, 'and you are not romantic at all, you know: pretending you are not your father's daughter is doing your hardest to avoid standing out. You are desperate to fit in.' He could tell from Mila's expression that this had hit home and he pressed on to show her, as he had so many times before, how superior his views and opinions were. His tone grew more brutal as he went on.

'You need to grow up, Mila. Only little girls think their fathers are heroes. Even if he made the choice to drop the ball, it doesn't mean he was a romantic rebel.

Your theory says it's up to society to decide what his action meant – you only find out what the signal meant when you find out how people respond to it, remember – and now we have all found out what the action meant. It makes no difference whether you think he is a hero, or I think he is just a normal business-man, society has decided he is a criminal.'

'But it makes a difference to me because I know that he is not a bad man – standing up for the rights of the individual is noble. Doing what the crowd wants is not noble.'

'Listen to yourself. You are still a child. He was just making money for himself.'

'And us.'

He waved away the interruption. 'There was nothing noble in it. Thinking of him as a heroic or romantic figure standing up against the tidal wave of public condemnation is just a highly convenient fantasy for you.'

'So you think what he did was bad?'

'No, *normal*. Normal for people like us,' Doni indicated the club members lounging on their leather sofas. 'Your theory does not concern what is good or bad, does it? Father just did what he did because it was normal. Ethics are irrel-evant. What father did is what we expect of each other. I could give you a dozen examples of similar deals which people here have done in the past year. You say it was our father's secret spontaneous self that would not bow down, would not do what was expected. But it *was* expected, it was expected in his world, this world.' Doni gestured to the others in the room again.

Frank 'n' Stein had told her that Herbert Blumer put the term 'symbolic interactionism' into circulation and popularised the message that when we were interacting we created meanings. We did it when we interpreted (or gave meanings to) each other's acts and we did this by taking on each other's roles. As Blumer put it, the meaning of the interaction was a *process*. It got made in the interaction and it was fluid.

What Blumer said about the process by which meaning got created left open the possibility that the process was open-ended. Not only could she not uni-laterally decide what her father's actions meant, it seemed she could not hold her one opinion in place. Doni had given her a new understanding of what her father's role was and, yes, it was more convincing than the childish stuff about him being a romantic rebel which she had believed before. But she could not be complacent about this – as Doni seemed to be – because right and wrong worried her. They had all along – it was the question of right and wrong that had driven the wedge between her and her mother and forced her into her disguise.

If she accepted that her father was just going along with what he thought was normal, Mila feared that his actions could very well be morally wrong, and what of the tide of judgement then? How could she complain of it being unjust? Now she was remembering one more quotation from Blumer that seemed to ring in her ears in the derisory, ironic way that Doni might speak: a person 'may do a miserable job in constructing his action, but [s]he has to construct it.' Might the force of her own logic be carrying her towards the conclusion that perhaps she ought to share in their judgement? This thought kept coming back to her for the rest of the evening and her spirits sunk lower and lower.

It wasn't until she was in the taxi going home that Mila began to feel better. As it wound its way through the streets near the club, and put more distance between her and Doni, she calmed down. Her father might have made a miserable job of constructing his action but she did not have to do the same thing. What was the ball she was being asked to catch? What was the choice her secret, spontaneous self had to make? The most important decision she could think of was whether or not she was going to carry on with sociology.

Whatever Doni might think, Mila was sure she understood more now than she did a few months ago, more now than even when they had walked into the club. Was this a waste of time? She was learning – it was painful at times, and there were lots of setbacks, and doubts, but she was slowly acquiring more knowledge about this complex and frustrating subject.

She could justly claim that she understood why Blumer said we must never think of interaction as simply the time when we do what we have been meaning to do all along. If this were true then interaction would not be worth studying. It would be the uninteresting bit between the causes of our actions and the effects of our actions. But this wasn't true: interaction was not where we simply read the script we had prepared, it was where we wrote the script, and we wrote it with other people.

The thing to hold onto was the idea that society was a process, not a structure. The meaning of everything we do in society was not meant to be fixed but fluid. Without process there was nothing, for instance no social institutions like marriage or systems of justice or education. All the institutions of society were dead, utterly lifeless unless people were breathing life into them. Symbolic interactionism took sociology off into an entirely different direction. It opened up the possibility of understanding the little elements of life that, despite sometimes being very easy to overlook, matter a great deal. As the taxi wound its way through the unfashionable streets near Doni's club, Mila thought about the way we spent hours and hours interacting, not just when relaxing, at home, but in every circumstance: when we went for a job interview, when we went shopping, and when we met the people with whom we seek to negotiate an international peace agreement or a stock deal. All of this required us to be a human being who was *interacting* – communicating, ignoring, working with, and against – with another human being. In science the equivalent to this big idea might be the discovery of molecules and atoms and then sub-atomic particles: before scientists learned about the very small scale, their knowledge was limited to the big stuff they could see. Symbolic interactionism was a departure like this which made us pay attention to the smaller human scale and opened up a whole new world to understand.

Visit the companion website at **www.palgrave.com/companion/ Bancroft-And-Fevre-Dead-White-Men-2e/** to access additional learning resources, including seminar questions based on the chapter's coverage, a jargon buster that defines key terms used in the text and a timeline which provides an overview of the development of sociological thought.

• • • • •

As you think you appear?

As you really are?

1. Becoming an adult means adopting the ability to think objectively, according to G. H. Mead. That means viewing yourself in relation to how others see you, and in relation to shared norms and judgements, as an 'object'. Mead thought that the process of learning to be an adult involves looking at ourselves as we expect others would. Learning to think of ourselves and others in this way is a key part of becoming competent social beings. That gives people the capacity to act differently and present themselves differently depending on the situation they are in. They can picture themselves from outside.

2. So you see what others see, and you know what you would like them to see. And you interact with them in response to what their actions mean – what they symbolise. So there is no permanent norm or way of behaving. The meaning of your actions is given by what it symbolises to others. That is called symbolic interaction.

3. According to this idea, there is no fixed, certain meaning in any situation. Each encounter with another individual is where meaning and significance are created. Which is why people only find out what they themselves think when they say it out loud – when it becomes meaningful for an interaction.

7

In the Night

A voice from outside Mila's head interrupted her train of thought. It was the taxi driver.

'I know you,' said the taxi driver and Mila thought her heart had stopped working. She caught her breath involuntarily as he went on. 'You're that girl on daytime TV, the one who sings to little blind children.'

Mila almost began to laugh but checked herself as she realised she would have to go along with this. If she didn't, there was just a chance the taxi driver might remember who she really was.

Mila said nothing because she could not think of anything to say just yet. She stared out through the cab window into the night so that the taxi driver could not catch her eye in the mirror. He kept talking all the same. 'You get recognised all the time? Or maybe I surprised you?'

'It almost never happens.'

'Because you wear those glasses? They didn't fool me, though. I could tell it was you as soon as you got in the cab. My wife watches you because our children like you, but she says I watch to see your pretty face.'

Mila had no idea who she was being mistaken for. If she had not been so concerned that the taxi driver might realise his mistake and work out who she really was, her vanity might have led her to wonder whether the TV personality he took her for really was pretty. As it was, telling him he was mistaken would be too big a risk. She had no alternative but to pretend to be this woman in a show she had never seen.

She began to answer his questions and tell him about her life on the show. She told him the children on the show were adorable, and agreed that she shed real tears when that little girl got back her sight after the operation. Mila found there was more in this vein that she could make up and it seemed to satisfy the taxi driver's interest. Mila was actually enjoying imagining herself to be a TV presenter. She guessed that, as far as the taxi driver was concerned, this conversation was probably not all that unusual. He seemed to take a passenger telling him about life on a TV show in his stride. Mila wondered if this kind of conversation might be weird for her but normal for him. But then it was her who was making it seem normal for him, she was pretending.

It's *all* pretence though, she thought to herself when the taxi driver's questions began to dry up and he seemed to lose interest in her.

Mila convinced herself that deciding what people's actions mean was a never-ending process and the meaning you fixed on was just that, the meaning you fixed on – it might as well be a random choice. It just depended when, or who, you asked whether someone was a criminal or not, a bad person or not. There would always be another, different interpretation coming along in a minute, or a year. It was just that people pretended there wasn't going to be one. They acted as if they had already had the last word.

This train of thought was comforting to Mila, because it was allowing her to repair rapidly the damage that had been done to her defences against the tide of public condemnation. But following it through led her into some strange places. She told herself that there was no meaning in anything we did or said to other people, not that we could ever find anyway, so we simply pretended there was some meaning. We all simply pretended we understood what was going on when nobody really knew. You pretended you liked your brother, pretended you were dumb, pretended you were a sociologist, but it didn't matter whichever way.

Hadn't Doni gone on and on about her father as just behaving normally? She asked herself if all we ever did, all we ever could do, was just pretend that things were normal. It didn't matter what you actually did, so long as you just told yourself, and everyone else, that it was normal. Though we could never admit it, we were all playacting as we conspired together to pretend that we agreed on what something meant, for example whether something was good or bad. Doni was right after all, and the condemnation of her father was more playacting, part of the big pretence of normality. The tide of public judgement was just the quick fix which was needed to repair the appearance of normality: to make it seem as if there were normal patterns of behaviour against which her father's actions could be judged and found wanting.

Frank 'n' Stein would have informed Mila that 'ethnomethodology' was the label for the sociologists who worked on ideas like these. But Mila hadn't read the right chapter – like her classmates, she only read the parts of her textbook that she needed to pass her assessment tasks – and she had no plans to read it. Frank 'n' Stein would have told her that ethnomethodology says we have to work at making things seem real and normal. The appearance of reality does not simply happen. We don't just come along and recognise it. Instead, we all have to conspire together to make reality. Reality and normality are like a task that we accomplish together.

Alfred Schutz was one of the sociologists Frank 'n' Stein talked about. Schutz was influenced by symbolic interactionism. He concluded that we all have to assert meaning, and do so continuously, otherwise there is no meaning. Symbolic interactionism had said people were always engaged in giving meaning to life, but now Schutz said sociology should *only* study how it happens that people manage to do this. He said it wasn't just sociologists going round saying this bit of social life means this or that, because everybody does it. They had to, otherwise we wouldn't have human lives at all. People acted like unselfconscious sociologists all the time, according to Schutz, but we never talked about it and we took it all for granted. So it was this stuff that we all knew, but didn't talk about, that should be studied along with the fact that we almost never questioned its taken-for-grantedness.

The cab had stopped at some traffic lights. The taxi driver's questions had dried up completely and Mila was free to gaze out of the window again. A man and woman were walking up the intersecting road towards them. The woman was walking a little in front of the man, and she was walking quickly, not running but walking more quickly than people did on city streets. They were together, though – the man was looking at her. Then Mila thought, is she trying to get away from him? Is she on her own and this man is bothering her? But why is she on her own? Is she a prostitute? Perhaps the man had said something to the woman because she slowed and turned round while still taking a step or two backwards. She seemed to be shouting. Mila could not hear her shout but the angle of her body suggested it – Mila guessed that she must be frightened or perhaps angry. It seemed she had something in her hand (money?) because she then threw something at the man.

The traffic lights changed and the car began to move forwards away from the couple who were now quite near to Mila. Now she had to look out of the rear window to see them. No – it had not been money because the man turned to see whatever it was spin down the street past him. And the woman was crying now, standing still with her hands in her hair, crying and still apparently shouting but now up into the night air and not at the man. The man walked up to her and slapped her across the face, at least so Mila thought, but the pair were receding fast as the taxi sped away. She thought she could see the man now had both hands on the woman, maybe he was strangling her? 'Did you see that? That man attacking that woman?' Mila sounded lost. She did not know what to do, but she thought the taxi driver might know.

'Yeah, sure I saw them.'

'Can we stop and help her?'

'What for? It was a couple having a disagreement. Anyway they made it up. Tiffs like that happen out here at night.'

Mila was no longer so sure what she had seen. After all, it was dark and she was overtired. Perhaps there had not been a blow, perhaps the man had been bringing both hands to the woman's face to hold her head and calm her down. Anyway, what could she do about it if the taxi driver had no intention of helping her. What could she do on her own?

'You see a lot worse when you drive around here in the night,' he was saying, 'you see all sorts of things. Last month I saw two young women fighting in the middle of the thoroughfare. There was nobody else there, well, nobody on foot. One woman was kneeling on top of the other, smashing her head on the road. She was holding her hair in two hands and banging her head down. It didn't seem that the other woman could fight back. Maybe she was unconscious, maybe she didn't want to fight. It was weird to see a woman doing that but the weirdest thing was that the traffic was all moving over into one lane to avoid them. It was like it was cordoned off for some works in the road. People did not even look when they passed them. When it's an accident everyone looks, but they all looked the other way.'

'And nobody stopped?'

'Nobody stopped. Maybe we all thought the other drivers would do something, call the police, maybe. I told my control about it but I don't think they did anything at all. They thought it was funny when I told them two women were fighting in the road. That was wrong, but we were all wrong for driving past.'

Mila was sure that the fight the taxi driver had described wouldn't have happened in the daylight. Maybe the fighting women, just like the couple she had just seen arguing or whatever they were doing, would not have behaved that way in the daylight. Mila was deciding that there appeared to be no rules, or maybe fewer or different rules, at night. All people had to do to make the fighting women fit into their version of reality was to treat them as an obstruction in the road. Nobody stopped, nobody even looked at them. They just treated them like roadworks! But if people do not work quite as hard at creating the appearance of normality at night, this made it easier to see how reality got more thoroughly, and successfully, made up during the day. In the night the holes in the fabric of reality were much easier to see because people did not go to any great lengths to mend them.

The idea that a violent assault could be treated like any obstruction in the road got Mila thinking about the way sociology might try to uncover the common knowledge that people draw on to understand their experiences. Frank 'n' Stein could have told her this was what Schutz had in mind when he said we should discover the 'typifications' people have to use even before they can start the job of ordering their experiences. For example, if it was just another road obstruction you treated it like one: you changed lane and that was it. According to Schutz, it was these typifications that made the world meaningful to us – for all practical purposes, in fact, they were our world.

For Mila, the world was appearing to be a more frightening and senseless place than she had imagined, and what she now saw in the streets they sped through did nothing to allay her anxiety. She saw several people who had apparently been sleeping in a doorway being bundled into the back of a plain van by some men with batons. A couple of blocks further on, several streets had been cordoned off for no apparent reason and then, down a side street, she saw something which she could not, at first, understand at all. Parked in long lines, with lights dimmed but engines running, were dozens of the vehicles used by riot police. A few policemen were standing next to the vehicles in full riot gear but there must have been many more waiting in the vehicles. 'Did you see that?' Mila asked.

'I think there is one of the energy summit meetings here tomorrow, or maybe it's one of those meetings about water. Anyway, there'll be lots of VIPs. The precautions are normal.'

Clearing undesirables from the streets, overwhelming armed force in side streets – all of this was normal because precautions had to be taken to protect the visiting dignitaries against protesters or terrorists. For a moment Mila's mind took all this in her stride, she settled into the 'typification' and almost began to think she had been foolish to point out the riot police. But then, with some effort, she managed the intellectual equivalent of slapping her own face. What was normal about having people bundled in vans – what was going to happen to them? And why *should* we take it as normal to have so many hundreds of police on the streets? It is only normal if you don't think about it; and that's the problem, Mila thought. This is not just something that happens under cover of night. If they care to listen, people will learn all about the riot police tomorrow (although maybe not about the way the homeless people were removed) but they just won't think about it and so it will be normal.

The chapter in Frank 'n' Stein on ethnomethodology said Harold Garfinkel taught that the knowledge we all had was not as solid and reliable as Schutz imagined. In fact, there was nothing there at all in the sense of something that existed all the time, whether we thought about it or not. What made society possible was not so much our common understandings but simply our reluctance to question the normality of things. Most of the time we did not even have to guess what the other person was thinking – we did not even have to understand each other, in fact – but we assumed instead that things were normal and that our usual, ordinary, way of making sense of what was going on would do.

Mila was thinking that, with a few words from the taxi driver about a summit and VIPs, she had been ready to join in the usual conspiracy to make the world seem normal. For some reason the threshold at which she was going to start questioning normality was lowered when it came to the riot police, but Mila was thinking that most of the time she was as happy as everyone else to pretend. It happened every time you encountered someone else: you conspired with each other to create the illusion of a reliable stock of shared knowledge. This was making Mila's head spin. Did this mean that there was no society after all, just a tacit agreement between people to make believe that society really exists?

The chapter in Frank 'n' Stein said Garfinkel thought sociologists should study the work people did to create the illusion of society. In fact they had to study people's methods for making the appearance of social order. Sociology should definitely not treat what people said about their actions and thoughts as resources from which sociologists could build explanations which would tell them what was really going on. All sociologists could ever find out when they studied what people said about things was 'talk' and not the stuff that we imagined the talk was about. It was talk that gives us our sense of order and it was only the talk that sociology could get at.

Garfinkel thought that there was no point in trying to make generalisations about this talk. It was always peculiar to the local situation that produced it. Meaning was always open to dispute, but we pretended that it wasn't by operating taken-for-granted rules to establish what things meant. What anyone could say about these practices was either very vague or very detailed and tied to a particular example. It seemed that there were no set rules for the everyday 'practical sociological reasoning' we got up to and it turned out to be very difficult to say anything which was both general and interesting about the way we did that reasoning. The rules were all a matter of what Garfinkel called 'local production'.

The only topic sociology could study was how people do their own, everyday sort of 'sociology,' meaning the ways in which people came up with enough sense of things around them to keep going, getting things done. So, Frank 'n' Stein asked: what was so different about the sociology they taught you in universities, then? Wasn't that just the same thing: more 'talk'? Then you would get sociologists studying their own talk and going round and round in ever decreasing circles while fewer and fewer people found any reason to listen to them.

Of course Mila did not know any of this but, if she had read the chapter, it would certainly have brought her doubts about sociology back up to the surface. In fact, she was struggling with the idea that society was an illusion. If it were, there would be no point in trying to change it for the better, and Mila knew, from the way she had felt when she saw the homeless people being bundled into vans, and the police in the side streets, that she did want to make things better.

An image came into Mila's mind, a picture she thought she might have seen once of a woman protester placing a flower in the barrel of a soldier's gun. The protesters were squeezed up close against the line of soldiers and the gun was aimed at the woman's throat. Mila thought that, with this gesture, the woman was trying to show to the world how absurd we should find the definition of reality (the protesters as the enemies of the state?) that was being suggested by the presence of the soldiers. The flower was a symbol of an alternative reality and an act of resistance, but what was so remarkable about the image was the stony face of the soldier. He was looking at a spot in the middle of the woman's forehead, not into her eyes at all, and in his eyes you could see no sign that his version of reality was breaking down. He remained a soldier who was ready to do whatever was necessary in defence of the state.

But then Mila found herself thinking of TV shows where things that were a little bit similar to this were shown as entertainment. There was the show where people disguised themselves as vegetables and arranged themselves on a stall in a street market. There was no political or social purpose to it of course. It was just meant to create a sense of the absurd and then we were meant to laugh at the way that people pretended that everything was normal even when they found people's heads and limbs among the fruit and vegetables. No matter how silly it was, it proved the same point as the image of the woman and the soldier and the flower in the gun: it showed the lengths people would go to in order to keep their definition of reality going.

Mila would have needed to see the unread chapter in Frank 'n' Stein to find out that Garfinkel used to ask his students to try out *breaching experiments* which demonstrated the same process. He wanted them to get a glimpse of the nothing (or nothing we could ever understand) that would be there if we weren't always conspiring to make the appearance of normality. Garfinkel told his students to pick a time and place to choose to stop joining in the task of creating normality and see how upset everybody around them got.

For Garfinkel and his students, that was the end of the experiment but Mila was wondering about acts of resistance and whether it would be possible to start to make things better if you used them to jolt people out of their complacency. Mila decided she would try an experiment right now. She had, after all, been keeping up a pretence of normality for the benefit of the taxi driver who had believed she was someone else all along. Well, Mila thought, it was time to stop making this so normal for him. 'Has there been a summit in the city before?'

'Yes, many times.'

'Has there ever been violent protest?'

'No, not like in some other places.'

'So, why the riot police and the other preparations? I think our leaders *want* to have protests. They feel left out. The riot police are like a challenge: come on protesters, let's not be left out. You know, like a tourist brochure: "Come on in, the water cannons are lovely; the CS gas will have you laughing until you cry". Our leaders don't want to be shown up in front of the other leaders from countries where they can rely on lots of headlines about violent protest. They *want* people to come along tomorrow and have their heads broken so the rest of us can hold our heads up.'

Mila was not sure she believed any of this but she was delighted by the look on the taxi driver's face. He looked as if the pretty TV presenter in the back of his cab might just as easily have been telling him about her powers of telekinesis or the proof she had that reptile aliens had infiltrated government and were taking over the world. Mila knew what he would do now, after all she knew what she would do: treat what she said as an obstacle in the road and simply change lanes to avoid it.

'What is the address you want to go to?'

Yes, Mila thought, we ignore what threatens our illusion of normality as far as politeness allows and change the subject as quickly as possible. This was what our 'reality' depended on – it depended on us manufacturing it. But Mila had little time to reflect on the easy success of her breaching experiment. The taxi driver repeated his question about the address and Mila realised that they must now be in the part of the city where she lived, although none of the streets through which they were driving were familiar. Then it dawned on Mila that she was not completely confident of her address.

Mila's mail was all delivered to her at the university and she had never had cause to check the address of her residence. She thought she remembered most of it but was hazy about the street name. She told the taxi driver what she remembered and made up the rest so that it sounded more convincing. If she had made a mistake, surely he would know the right address anyway? He would think he had misheard and it would all be OK. The taxi driver nodded to show he had heard her, but the next thing he did was to ask her for directions.

Mila had only ever walked to where she lived from the university, or had been dropped at her door by someone who knew the way. She had no idea how to get there from wherever they were now. At the next intersection there was a gang of street cleaners. The taxi driver lowered his window to talk to them. He asked them for directions to the address that Mila was now almost sure was a fiction. How could they give directions to a fictional address? But they did, one was even correcting the other when he thought of a better route. The taxi driver thanked them and raised the window just as the intersection lights changed. The cab turned right, in the direction the street cleaners were still pointing.

For a moment Mila thought that perhaps the street cleaners had been able to translate the muddled address into the real one, but then she had to consider the possibility that being given directions to a place that did not exist was much more common than she might have supposed. Perhaps it was only the most extreme example of the way that people confidently gave inaccurate directions to places. They felt obliged to help, felt that they *ought* to know, and so they offered directions when they had only a vague idea, or no idea at all, of how to get there.

The desperate need to make sense of things, to make reality, was clearly going to have effects like this sometimes. It was also clear that it could produce some pretty irrational results. Everyone might feel that they needed to keep making reality but there was no guarantee that they were thinking reasonably when they did it. So people gave you totally useless instructions to get somewhere that did not even exist, because they wanted to help. They were trying to be good people but they could send you off in entirely the wrong direction. And Mila was now feeling quite strongly that this *was* the wrong direction but then, with some relief, she realised they were passing the university.

The taxi pulled up at a walkway between two tall university buildings. The walk was well lit and safe. Mila opened the cab door, stumbled awkwardly, flailed her arms and and pitched out headlong onto the road.

The taxi driver stooped to retrieve Mila's bag. The strap was broken and he was holding the broken ends in the way that people do – offering them up to each other to make sure of the damage.

'Is it alligator?'

'Yes, no, I suppose so.'

She was wondering if her knees were bleeding but she could not examine them now. She would have to wait until he was gone. The bag? The bag was probably faux, it was Tuni's bag after all. Mila groaned involuntarily. Tuni was the sort of person who would have the right bag if you go out to dinner in a place like that club so Mila had asked her and Tuni had gladly lent it to her. Here was another cause for shame – she had broken first Tuni's shoes and now the bag. Now she was going to cry. To make it worse, the taxi driver was now very obviously smiling at her.

'Alligator,' he repeated, and then paused, 'so the reptiles are out to get you after all.'

Oh, yes, very funny, thought Mila, but it *was* funny and soon she was smiling too. 'I don't think it's real though – it's just pretending.'

Now they both laughed and he helped her to her feet. She might look a mess but she had regained some composure. She paid him and then the taxi driver stood at the cab door to watch her cross the street. Mila looked back when she reached the other side and he was still looking at her. She shouted across 'What was the name of that music you were listening to?'

'It's by some guy called Bernard Herrmann, but it doesn't have a name.' She waved and the taxi driver turned round and got back into his cab. Mila could just make out the sound of the blaring brass starting up once more as he closed the door.

According to Frank 'n' Stein, Aaron Cicourel was perhaps the most profound thinker associated with ethnomethodology. He pointed out that we experienced the world in a very rich way. We received information from all of our five senses at once and our feelings were being stimulated in all sorts of ways (even feeling the wind on your face could make you feel good or even miserable). Yet when we had to talk about all this richness of experience, including the way it made us feel, we were stuck with the limitations of language.

Cicourel thought language was simply not up to the task of conveying this richness. Our 'talk' could only ever capture a tiny part of our experience and this was why every time you talked about something it really was like an act of creation. We *were* creating a reality because it was actually a thinner, paler, simplified version of our experience. We had to simplify like this in order to be able to put any of our experience into words and talk about it with other people. Cicourel said there were deeply buried (possibly even innate) rules for how we created these simplified versions of our experience. It was these deep rules that allowed us to cope with the fact that meaning depended on context.

If only she had read about them, Cicourel's ideas might have meant something to Mila as, half an hour after she left the taxi driver, she lay safe in her own bed, drifting off to sleep. She was wondering about what made things funny. Was humour all to do with reality being breached? She had gone sprawling across the road and all her pretence of dignity (and political speech-making) had been undermined. Perhaps the more flagrant the breach was, the funnier the situation was. If she had known about Cicourel, Mila might have wondered whether these situations give us a glimpse of those deeply buried rules which help us to create simplified versions of our experience. Perhaps whenever anyone laughed it showed a rule had been broken: someone had failed to apply a rule properly either by accident (like her taxi fall) or on purpose (as in a funny story).

She thought about the taxi driver's joke about Tuni's fake alligator bag, but just as sleep took her, half a thought stirred deep in Mila's mind. Had she actually told him the alien reptiles were taking over the world as part of her experiment? Surely she had just thought it? Then how could he have known what she was thinking in order to make that joke? Mila decided the taxi driver must have meant something else – they had just laughed together even though they were laughing at different things. And so, like all of us almost always do, Mila simply papered over the cracks in reality and went off to sleep.

Visit the companion website at **www.palgrave.com/companion/ Bancroft-And-Fevre-Dead-White-Men-2e/** to access additional learning resources, including seminar questions based on the chapter's coverage, a jargon buster that defines key terms used in the text and a timeline which provides an overview of the development of sociological thought.

● ● ● ● ●

How do you make things happen?

Persuade people that you are right? (It's a carrot)

Just act as if you are in the right? (It's a stick)

1. Ethnomethodology says that it is not just meaning which we create in everyday interaction, but all things that matter to us. Institutions, laws, society itself, only matter to the extent that people make them matter in every situation they are in. A law is just scribbling on paper unless there are people who agree what it is and apply it – judges, jurors, lawyers and even lawbreakers.

2. In contrast to many other sociologists who look at how these big structures make us do stuff, ethnomethodology looks at how people make things happen in every situation. They argue that those institutions have no persistent existence otherwise, which makes many people wrong to talk about 'the government did this' or 'a change in the law has made people do that'. They argue that those things are not independent powers in this way. Instead you could see it as 'a jury reached this decision about what the law meant'.

3. Ethnomethodologists study the 'deep grammar' of situations, the taken for granted reality that everyone acts towards as if it was permanent. Schutz called these 'typifications', commonly accepted meanings and interpretations that are the basic groundwork made before meaning is created. Harold Garfinkel argued that it was our tendency not to question normality that made it continue. To show this he conducted 'breaching experiments' where his students broke the taken for granted rules of interactions – cheating at a game, or haggling over the price of a shopping basket. What happened was not that the situation broke down, but that everyone else tried to incorporate their behaviour into the taken for granted activity. So acting as if you are in the right is a powerful way of making people assume that you must be right.

8
In the Morning

Mila had thought that all we ever did was to pretend that what was happening was normal, then it didn't matter whether the people who judged you were in the majority or not.

Now she wondered if all this might have been her twisting on the hook she seemed to be impaled on, trying to arrange the truth to suit herself again. The next time she turned to her copy of Frank 'n' Stein, she wanted to find some validation for her journey into relativism and nihilism, but her tutor still hadn't told her to read the chapter on ethnomethodology. As her eye slid down the contents page, she gave silent thanks that she did not have to read that chapter with its pompous-sounding title.

She might not know exactly how, but Mila fully expected that Frank 'n' Stein would be able to get her off the hook. She did not think sociology was meant to make you doubt yourself, and question your own behaviour. Wasn't this what Garrison had meant when he said sociology told you that, if you did anything wrong, it wasn't really your fault but society's? She was pretty sure that sociology was not known for being moralistic and she desperately wanted help to shore up her defences against the tide of moral judgement. The chapter she had been told to read next was the one on Erving Goffman.

Mila thought there was a good chance Goffman might help her out. The little that she had picked up in lectures suggested he was the champion of people who had a rough deal. He seemed to care about the ones who were pushed out to the margins or picked on by everyone else. By late morning Mila had finished the chapter on Goffman, and she thought her expectations had been met in a highly satisfactory way.

Circe arrived home as Mila was getting ready to go out. Her face was drawn and she seemed tired and tense. She barely spoke to Mila as she came in, and so Mila followed Circe through to the kitchen, where she was getting a glass of water. Without turning round, and in between sips of water, she told Mila that Ana had been taken into hospital last night, before Mila got home. It had been some sort of an accident but Circe was very vague about what actually happened.

Mila found this was very hard to take in and she could barely think of what she ought to say. She managed to ask how Ana was now. 'Stable now, fine, I think. I've just been trying to find out but they wouldn't tell me much. She may be allowed visitors between 1 and 2 p.m., so we can find out more then.' Mila volunteered to come with Circe, expecting her to say there was no need, after all, she was much closer to Ana. But Circe said, 'I've got an examination this afternoon. I am not in any state to take it but I have to. Can you go to the hospital on your own?'

Of course Mila had to agree to go to the hospital to find out how Ana was, but, knowing full well she was delaying her when she needed to get ready for her examination, she asked Circe to give her directions to the hospital and tell her where she needed to go once she got there. She kept Circe there as long as she could, following her around pointlessly, as Circe grabbed her things. But then Circe was leaving, thrusting a tattered paperback into her hands, as she left. 'Take her this, I think it's the one she was reading – there will be nothing for her to read there.'

By 1.30 p.m. she was standing by Ana's bed, feeling nauseous as she always did in hospitals. There had been no problem getting in to see Ana, and she looked fine, maybe a bit sleepy, with no visible signs of injury. There was no chair, so Mila sat on the bed – it felt awkward and intrusive but she couldn't stand there for an hour, could she? She asked Ana what happened. 'I had an accident.'

Mila had prepared something to say while she had been on her way there, something to cheer up a person in hospital. That was what you did, wasn't it? You made them laugh, made them forget about themselves for a bit. So Mila launched into what she hoped was a funny, self-deprecating story which showed how clumsy and disorganised she was. It included a reprise of her undignified fall out of the taxi a week ago and one or two other minor events, including getting lost on the way to the hospital today. Ana didn't laugh at any of it, she barely smiled, and simply asked if Tuni's bag had been fixed now.

Mila thought she could not bear a serious conversation about getting Tuni's bag mended, and ploughed on regardless. 'Not long ago, I'd have shrivelled up and died if I had fallen out of the taxi like that. I was always terrified about what other people would think. You know, I'd plan the whole night in my head before I went out so I could be sure I wouldn't show myself up.'

Again, there was no reaction from Ana, not even an encouraging smile, so Mila asked Ana why she thought we went to great lengths to create and manage other people's expectations, and experienced embarrassment when we fell short of them. 'I don't know – I'm not worried about embarrassment anymore, not lying here wearing this thing,' she said, pulling at her disposable hospital gown. 'And the people in the ward, they don't worry about it – look at her.'

A woman, quite infirm, was leaning over as she stood next to her bed, perhaps searching for something she had lost in the bedclothes. She seemed unconcerned that the hospital gown did such a poor job of covering her. 'Why don't you go and help her?' Ana said.

Mila was clearly embarrassed at the thought of it. 'Oh no, I couldn't interfere, she wouldn't want me to.'

'Embarrassment is a luxury in here, like saying you can't stand the smell of hospitals.'

Mila hadn't said she hated the smell. Maybe Ana had been able to tell by her wrinkled nose, in any case Mila felt she was being made to feel defensive – why was Ana being so disagreeable? Ana usually agreed with everything you said. Mila tried again. 'Don't you feel that you have to manage other people's expectations?'

'No, I've given up. That's probably why I'm here.'

Mila was sure there was a challenge in Ana's eyes – go on, ask me again, ask me again why I am here. Though she did not know what would happen next, Mila went ahead and asked: 'Did you do something silly?'

'You mean, did I try to kill myself?' Mila nodded.

'Yes, well, I tried to hurt myself, anyway. The girls stopped me. Circe and Jasmine shouted a lot and they brought me here in a taxi.'

Then Ana smiled. The smile seemed to have nothing to do with what she had just said, and it made Mila feel very uneasy. She knew she ought to ask Ana why she had given up on managing expectations. That was what Ana wanted her to do, wasn't it, to tell her what the expectations were, why they were so hard to bear. 'I know. Sometimes it can feel as if you are the only person who has to make an effort to behave like a normal human being, whereas to everyone else it just seems to come naturally.'

Now Mila was all at sea. She had completely forgotten what she had thought she ought to say and was left with a choice between some platitudes she might have remembered from a TV show, or silence, or sociology.

So Mila told Ana that there was a sociologist who wrote about this feeling of going through life pretending to be yourself. He thought the fact that we apparently had to make an effort to give out the appearance of being a normal human being signified an important feature of modern life and society. Goffman described the effort we put into giving the appearance of who we think we are, but Mila said he was especially interested in what happens when that ability is lost. This might happen because of our circumstances or the constraints that institutions or other people imposed on us. The labels for his big idea included 'the presentation of the self' and 'impression management' and 'the dramaturgical analogy' but these different labels added up to more or less the same thing: we were all acting. Sometimes we had to put on more of an act than at other times, and sometimes we had to act in some very difficult circumstances, but we are *all* acting. Mila asked Ana about the example Frank 'n' Stein had given to explain this: 'You know when you see a woman in a public space who is looking at her watch frequently, pacing up and down. What is she doing?'

Ana seemed to have to make a great effort to answer. 'That's obvious – waiting for someone.'

'OK, but why not just stand still and wait? Why all the signals?'

'She doesn't want other people to wonder why she is hanging around. They might think she is a loner, or a lunatic.'

Frank 'n' Stein had said the woman wants other people to understand why she is standing there but not what else people might think she was doing. It had never occurred to Mila, and it was completely out of character for Ana to say something like this. Mila chose to ignore it and carried on. 'Right, everyone does this. Everyone does their own public relations, trying to give off good impressions about themselves and hiding bad ones.'

Ana seemed to take a bit of interest in this. She sounded sour, but at least showed some animation when she spoke. 'OK, so, *you* get embarrassed when you fall out of a taxi but with *me* it's much more extreme. I smile at people even when they are rude. I always apologise when someone barges into me. I seem to be more concerned about what everyone else thinks of me than normal people are. It's an obsession, apparently.'

Ana seemed to be squirming a little as she said this. Mila asked her to explain and Ana said that it was because of the childhood she had, that she felt she had to work hard to be accepted. Since it was all she had to keep her afloat, Mila stuck doggedly to her theme. She told Ana everyone was like that really and, when we presented ourselves to others, it was as who we would like to be. Ana shrugged as if to say, have it your way, but Mila ignored her and pressed on. 'How do you know other people don't have to work as hard at presenting themselves as you do? Impressions are always something you need to work at, but want people to believe you haven't. People who seem to you to be effortlessly cool and stylish are actually working just as hard as you.'

'That would be a relief!' said Ana. To Mila it sounded like sarcasm. It didn't occur to her that Ana was thinking she wouldn't wish her feelings on anyone, Mila found it hard to keep the increasing irritation she felt out of her voice.

'It's hard work making it seem like you have not made any effort at all. We can never let on that we are doing this kind of impression management, or people will see through the whole thing. There are lots of us who learn to do it automatically and hardly notice we are doing it, but there are also plenty of us who live in fear of being found out.'

'I bet Tuni isn't scared of being found out. She's a natural at everything. She's naturally funny and attractive, and naturally happy, she doesn't have to try.'

This was new to Mila. She had never heard Ana voice an envious thought before and yet she sounded embittered. Mila had no inkling that Ana's belief that she had to work harder than anyone to make herself acceptable usually kept at bay her suspicion that other people did not want her friendship, but were merely taking pity on her. Mila's sociological explanation was making Ana wonder if the friends she had found at university really saw her as a kind of charity case. Ana said: 'If everyone's trying to manage people's impressions of them, how do I know – I mean, how does anyone know – who they really are?'

'Remember that sociologist called Mead? He also asked that question: am I what other people think of me, or am I what I think of myself? Mead's answer was a bit of both. With this other sociologist, Goffman, for most of the time you are what other people make of you, which is why impression management is so important to us.'

Mila went on to explain that there were several parts to impression management, the 'front' and the 'role' being the most important, but Ana gave her very little encouragement. Mila said: 'OK, imagine you are going on a flight abroad. The plane is a big one. You get strapped in, along with all the other passengers, ready for take-off. The plane taxis onto the runway. Then, as it is waiting to take off, the pilot makes an announcement. He says that he is excited to be flying you today, as he has never flown a plane this big before, and he has been up all night practising on the simulator, and he's sure it's going to be fun.'

It was another of Frank 'n' Stein's examples and Mila had liked this one too but all Ana had to say in response was: 'Nobody would do that.'

'Absolutely,' said Mila, and continued.

'The front he puts on fits the role of pilot. It's OK to do certain things in some situations and not in others. For instance, if my sociology professor is scruffy and disorganised this is what students expect. It's taken as a sign that she devotes so much time to the intellectual life that she is out of touch with everyday life. The same sort of behaviour would mean something completely different if she was playing a different role, like a business executive or an army officer.'

Mila explained that Goffman thought it wasn't really about always giving the *best* impression, in the sense of the impression that puts us in the best light. Instead people might be working very hard to give the *right* impression – the most appropriate impression for their role. It was extremely hard to resist being put in a role, not only by institutions but by people. If people expected you to be stupid, you would find yourself being stupid unless you made a great effort and had strong self-belief.

Ana was nodding now. 'Which is why first impressions count for so much – people judge you as a person within two minutes of your first meeting and then treat you as that person for the rest of the time.'

Mila agreed. 'Yes, the more they treat you as that person, the more you find yourself behaving like that person. This is fine if, when they meet you, you're at your brightest, but not if you are feeling tense or anxious. And there are all sorts of handicaps and obstacles to cope with when you are doing your impression management, not just feeling ill or tired. Goffman says managing the *setting* is a big problem.'

Mila paused, she could hear a distant alarm bell in her head, and she had to work out why. It was something to do with what Goffman said about settings – in fact he talked about hospitals as settings. Then she remembered: it wasn't any old hospitals he wrote about, it was asylums for people who were mentally ill. This was far too close for comfort. Mila was gripping the bag on her lap hard and then she felt the book inside it, the book Circe had given her to take to Ana.

She pulled out the book and passed it to Ana. It was more of the romantic fiction she read constantly. She told her Circe picked it up but she wasn't sure it was the one Ana was reading. Ana nodded but just let it drop on the bed next to her hand. Mila thought the book might not interest Ana just now, but she had a use for it. It would give her a way of explaining what Goffman meant by setting while keeping hospitals right out of the conversation.

'I suppose setting is everything in books like these. You know, the people are always rich and they visit spectacular locations. Like maybe they have a candle-light dinner in a ski lodge looking out over the mountains in the moonlight. They never end up going to a lodge that has been double-booked or one that is falling down and they never find out there is no snow when they get there.'

Ana did not seem to be listening again.

'What I mean is that you are always telling us that these books are like real life, but in real life the setting always gives you problems. There's always going to be something that will spoil the atmosphere. But these romantic writers can control all that: they make sure the moonlight is perfect and the snow falls right on cue, and the couple are left alone at just the right moment, and they make really sure nobody falls headlong out of a taxi.'

Ana was annoyed at this. 'You haven't read any of these books, Mila. You are making it up. If you had read any of them, you'd know that sometimes the people do look silly and the person they love just happens to come along and sees them looking undignified. It makes you empathise with them, and then it's even better when it all works out for them in the end. And stop going on about the taxi. It's not a big deal.'

'OK, but you see what I mean, Ana' said Mila, trying to recover her thread, and pointedly not taking offence.

'These novelists do try to manage the setting. None of the characters in their books prepare to meet the love of their life by putting on last week's clothes pulled from the laundry basket and laying out their collection of interesting stamps. Not only do they make an effort to make the atmosphere romantic, they do what they can to make sure that there isn't unexpected interference. They hide away things, and people, that might spoil the impression.'

'People?' said Ana curtly.

'Yes,' said Mila 'why do you think so many people are very reluctant to introduce their boy or girlfriends to their friends and family?' Ana's expression quickly changed from contempt to profound unhappiness. Mila felt the bad temper had been Ana's form of defence, but now her guard was completely down. It was hardly something Mila had engineered – she had been trying very hard to keep the tone light. Maybe Ana had just got tired of fighting, but then Mila's intuition finally kicked in. *What had she just said to make Ana so unhappy?* Stupid, stupid, stupid! Of course, Ana was just like her: she was extremely reticent about her family.

Ana had almost never mentioned her family to Mila and the others, and they had wondered more than once if Ana's relationship with them was a painful one. Perhaps this relationship even had something to do with her 'accident' – maybe she did it because of her parents. Mila might have been insensitive but she did not intend to harm, and now she felt she was walking in a minefield. She was ill-equipped for the kind of conversation this was turning into. What would she do if Ana started to make a scene, if things got out of control? And why wouldn't they get out of control? They already had, last night, and Ana was clearly still highly volatile emotionally. What would her doctors be saying about the way she was speaking to Ana? Would they blame her for bringing all this up? Would it be her fault if Ana's condition deteriorated? And this was what was happening now: Ana seemed to be crumbling before her eyes – in fact she looked as if she was in physical pain.

Mila was now looking round for someone to help, but there were no doctors to be seen and the two nurses on duty seemed busy with the woman who had been leaning over the side of her bed. There was nothing for it but to blunder on and all Mila could think of was to tell Ana how she felt.

'I'm really sorry, Ana. I've made you miserable and I didn't mean to. I just meant that the role mothers and fathers put their children in sometimes does not fit with the role those children want to play as they grow up. Their parents still insist on treating them as children when they want to play the roles of grown-ups deciding on their own future. They don't take their boyfriends or girlfriends home with them because they try to avoid having to play two different roles at once.'

'It would never occur to me to take any friend home, never mind a boyfriend. What you are saying fits me and my parents, but the role they want me to play isn't at all like the role I played here with you and the others. I really was a different person here.'

Mila heard the past tense: what did it mean? That Ana had given up the struggle to get away from whatever role her parents put her in? Did she think that you have to choose one role only, and she had realised she could never escape her parents' influence? Mila had the remedy for that misconception.

'We all have many roles, like daughter, sister, girlfriend, flatmate. Goffman is asking us if we think we are the same person in each of them, but simply happen to be with different people, or are we a different person in each role? I think we are different. It's certainly how I feel,' said Mila, trying very hard. 'If anybody tells you otherwise I wouldn't believe them. Multiple roles are really common in modern life – we really are multiple personalities inhabiting one body.'

Mila wondered if Ana might think she was trying to say something about mental illness and she carried quickly on to talk about 'role conflict'.

'It's when you have to play two contradictory roles at the same time. It isn't a problem as long as the two roles are kept well apart. If they aren't, then you have to decide which role to play: who do you "betray" by showing them that the person they thought they knew is not the real you?'

Now the tears started to run down Ana's face, and she was making no attempt to dry them. The tears were just running in little channels by her nose and the corners of her mouth. Mila could even see big teardrops hanging off her chin waiting to fall on the bed cover and the tears were catching in Ana's throat as she spoke. 'I'll always have to keep my roles apart. But it *is* madness, isn't it, if you haven't got a stable personality. And you can't help but go mad if you are being forced to split yourself in two.'

'I don't know, not if you think of yourself as a house with many rooms for visitors. You parents get to see one room, your friends another. Very few, if any, people get to see all the rooms in the house.'

This was Frank 'n' Stein again, but Ana seemed not to mind this time.

'You certainly wouldn't want to see all the rooms in my house, Mila. Some of them are very dark and cluttered with all sorts of horrible baggage I don't even want to look at.'

Was this a cue to go on? Ana would not meet her eye and Mila's intuition was weak. She would have to guess, but she knew she was taking a big risk and she was also aware that she was asking Ana to be more honest than she, Mila, was prepared to be. Mila had a feeling of stepping out on a high shaky wire with no safety harness or net. She knew she had no right to be out here in clear air, pretending she was a wise grown-up. 'So this is why you don't trust friendship, then, Ana, because you don't think we would still be your friends if we saw into those rooms?'

'Yes.'

'Have you thought that some of us might have things to hide as well? Why not take a risk and see if we stay friends after I have seen into one of those rooms you keep locked.'

Ana began to talk without prompting, looking straight in front of her at a blank wall decorated only with an old poster about hospital hygiene.

'I hated school. It's different at university because people don't know about my family. I was singled out at school because my parents are not like anybody else's. They're really religious. They're members of a religious sect. The sect doesn't have any schools, so all the children have to go to the same schools as everyone else but they stand out because of all the sect's rules. The rules don't just tell you what to wear, they tell you everything about how to behave. It's not so much of a problem when you are little but when you get to be about nine or ten everyone starts to notice you are different and they start picking on you.'

Mila believed they had more in common than Ana could imagine. To keep at bay the temptation to tell all, she turned again to sociology. She told Ana again about how people were forced to employ impression management just to get by from day to day. She said Goffman wanted to draw our attention to what happens to people when they can't manage impressions in this way.

'Because of how your parents were, they made it impossible for you to fit in. So you got the same treatment as other kids who looked different, for example because of their looks or their ethnic background. Anything that marks you out as different will get you bullied at school.'

Ana made it clear that Mila had not understood. She told Mila that, at school, she saw people being bullied for being too tall, too short, too thin, wearing glasses, being ugly, stupid, smart, awkward, and all of the other stages adolescents went through. She even saw people being bullied for wearing the wrong socks. She saw lots of other children being bullied, humiliated, pushed around, called names, beaten up, shown up, sent up, but none of it was as bad as her situation, because they all got some respite. In all other respects each of these kids could fit in (the fat kid could fight back, the one with thick glasses could tell really funny jokes) but nothing about Ana fitted in because she was allowed no leeway at all by her parents. This made her a complete social outcast.

Mila thought she understood now. Ana did not have the identity the other children were expecting and her 'spoiled identity' made her, as Goffman said, 'discredited'. There had been no chance of Ana managing her spoiled identity, by becoming more like the other children, because her parents would not allow this. There was no chance that the children might have given her a different, but nonetheless acceptable, identity to the one they expected of their classmates, because she was so completely alien to them. So she remained discredited and stigmatised.

It seemed a long time ago now, but it was what Mila had read about stigma in Frank 'n' Stein that morning that had been so satisfying. She thought that, because of her father's actions, she had been stigmatised and she was convinced this was the perfect defence against the tide of moral judgement. Other people's condemnation of her father was doing nothing more or less than stigmatising her, and Goffman showed how damaging this was.

'I think it's because they don't understand about stigma that people don't do what's needed to stop this kind of thing happening. Goffman said that people who were stuck in a situation where they couldn't manage people's impressions of them were often stigmatised. When schools are coming up with policies on bullying, they always accept stigma as a fact. So they either consider how the person being stigmatised, or the people doing the stigmatising, can be changed to make it easier to live with the stigma. The victims are encouraged to be more sociable, or more upfront about "their problem". The bullies are encouraged to be more tolerant. In both cases the authorities assume that the stigma exists as a thing, as an unavoidable fact. You are fat, so you have a stigma, you have an impairment, so you have a stigma. But Goffman teaches us that stigmatising behaviour is a choice. If people found it a more painful choice, perhaps they wouldn't do it.'

Ana was still not looking at her. Mila desperately wanted to say something that might make her friend feel better and she found herself straying onto dangerous ground.

'I haven't had the same experience as you at all, but I have desperately wanted to fit in. I know what it's like to have to cover something up about yourself that you know other people might see as a stigma. Goffman said that was a common way of dealing with it. He called it "passing" like some black people used to do in the USA when they had lighter skin and so people might think they were white. They passed as white people, they became part of the racially segregated system.'

She tried to force herself to think as a sociologist would again. Yes, the sociologist in Mila said, stigma develops from society itself and a society of perfect people would still find something to stigmatise. Mila recalled Frank 'n' Stein saying that Goffman was agreeing with Durkheim's idea that at a certain level society needed crime, and would invent criminals if there weren't any. The boundaries of the normal would be redrawn to define previously acceptable behaviour as criminal. Then Mila was thinking of her own situation again: her father, the trial and the newspapers. Ana was still talking but Mila's tired mind was tuning out. It seemed to Mila that, if crime was normal because it defined the limits of the acceptable, then she might find a way back to her idealised view of her father after all. To define the normal in society, the abnormal needed to be defined, and stigmatised. Not only was she being stigmatised for what he had done, so was he.

Ana was telling Mila how little kids used to come right up close to her and stare at her when she was sitting on her own. Usually, they did not come to taunt her but simply to stare at her as if she were a freak. 'You can't believe how weird they thought I looked in that religious get-up. It was fascinating to them.'

In spite of herself, of how shallow it was, Mila actually felt pleased. What Ana said confirmed she was right to think of the newspapers and the way they returned to her father's case time after time. She thought that what Ana had said confirmed stigma and crime were the same in some sense. People were horrified by crime and wanted it shut away, separated from the normal or law-abiding part of society they assumed they were members of. Yet people also had a morbid fascination with the sort of stigma Ana was describing and the crime Mila's father was supposed to have committed. The way that the newspapers had treated his case was like circus 'freak shows' which exhibited peoples' physical abnormalities. We used to call people who had physical abnormalities 'freaks' but now we stigmatised people who we thought were abnormal in some other way. Part of being 'normal' was being fascinated and a bit scared by what wasn't, Mila thought.

Mila realised that Ana was looking at her, expecting a response, but she had been so preoccupied with the route her own thoughts had taken that Mila was not sure what response would do. She remembered something that had come into her mind when Ana had been talking about how children could be bullied because of their weight. Mila suggested that Goffman's work on stigma alerted us to the way that norms are constructed, and also to how that 'norm' may have little to do with the actual average of individuals in a society. So, in lots of societies, body weight was seen as a measure of normality but most people were fatter or thinner than whatever the 'normal' weight was supposed to be. Frank 'n' Stein said that, as being thin became the norm, and as diet products became ever more widespread, the actual incidence of obesity and the number of overweight individuals rose. Or was it the other way round, wondered Mila: as more people become overweight, did the obsession with being thin grow? Mila told Ana that she was coming to the conclusion that when sociologists talked about 'the norm' they were seldom talking about something that actually applied to the majority of people at any one time.

'Remember what we were saying about the feeling we have of going through life giving out the appearance of normality? Goffman thought that this feeling was a constant feature of life in modern society and, perhaps, stigmatising some people, making *them* abnormal, might be a way of helping us reassure ourselves that we are normal, after all. You know, they always say that bullies are very insecure people, but maybe it's true.'

'Are you saying we are all potential bullies of one kind or another?' asked Ana.

Because she had tuned out when Ana had begun to talk freely, Mila had got herself into trouble again. She was simply exhausted by now, because she was so unused to making the kind of effort you needed to make to really listen to another person. Mila could not see that Ana might think she was being insensitive, and now she made matters worse. She said that if we were all responsible for creating stigma, then we could all decide to do something about it. If the rules of what was normal were enforced by individuals in day-to-day interaction, then it was within our grasp to alter them. The schools did not always have to throw up their hands and say that this has always happened when children bullied each other. They could do something about it. Goffman had thought the same applied to all relations of power and inequality. It was our choice to live with them, and it was a choice we could make differently, Mila decided.

'I think school bullying policies are so useless because schools have to be dishonest about how children can behave, in order to keep pretending that normal behaviour in school is nice: all the children treat each other with respect, everyone learns about commitment to the community, everyone tries as hard as they can to learn what the school is meant to teach them. Dealing with bullying would force schools to change their definition of normality.'

Mila imagined she was applying sociology to everyday life, but Ana felt that Mila had done her best to minimise the significance of her experience again – that experience that Mila had coaxed her to reveal, even though it was painful to do so. Now Ana thought Mila had said that she might just as easily have been a bully as a victim and that the solution to her problem had been in her own hands all along. Even now, Ana managed to hold onto her temper and her common sense.

'But maybe schools can't afford to do anything else. If they admit the truth, then parents will make life difficult for them or there might be government inspectors who would shut them down.'

'Yes, but schools do control some behaviour, don't they? They do try to make sure that for some of the time the pupils behave in the way that they are meant to. Bullying can be swept under the carpet, so they choose to do nothing, but if some kid who would never hurt a fly says something that someone might think was a challenge to a teacher's authority, then they are humiliated.'

For Mila, this was another example of what Goffman had to say about the places where the self cannot construct its own image, cannot manage itself. These happened most acutely in two situations: when people were stigmatised and when they were in an institution. Both things happened at schools, but there were other institutions that had even more power over individuals. Goffman had shown how your sense of selfhood can be violated by institutions by preventing self-presentation and impression management. For example, he took instances when individuals' freedom to practise their own public relations was curtailed. As she had remembered earlier on when the alarm bells had gone off in Mila's head, Goffman's best-known example was psychiatric hospitals where patients could expect to have their intimate space, their idea of self, violated and degraded in a routine, mundane manner. In the hospital that Goffman described, patients weren't allowed to decide for themselves what clothes to wear, when to eat, when to go to the toilet, what way to speak to people in charge, and so on. Mila had read how, in its control over practices of the self, the institution asserted its power over the individual, ensuring the individual's pliability and obedience.

As insensitive as she had once again proved she could be, especially when she was tired, Mila knew that to talk about any of this might make Ana believe that she was minimising the importance of what was happening to her. And, in any case, for all the superficial similarities, Mila didn't think the hospital they were in was at all like the one Goffman described. Here the effort at control was pretty haphazard and done with the best intentions for Ana's safety. It seemed more like benign neglect than the degradation of the self. But Frank 'n' Stein had said Goffman had lots of other examples of 'total institutions' in which every aspect of an individual's life was controlled – like a military training camp, a naval ship, a boarding school, or a prison – and Mila told Ana what Goffman had written about them.

She said many other institutions had some of the characteristics of total institutions, such as day schools, some workplaces, some political parties. But in the real total institution there was no separation between work, play, and sleep. Everything you did was in close company with others, and everyone was treated alike and required to do the same thing together. All aspects of your life were under the same authority and everything was tightly scheduled by the authority and there were lots of rules. Ana interrupted her.

'There were lots of rules in my family. In fact it was like a total institution. I never had a private life when I was at home. I had no space of my own and no real belongings of my own. Because of their religious beliefs, my parents tried very hard to make sure I was thinking the right thing all the time. If I showed signs of thinking differently, they would take away the little freedom or privacy I had. There was once ...'

Ana broke off in some distress as her frustration got the better of her. She was trying, for one last time, to get her friend to understand what she had been through. Ana carried on.

'They found a book I was reading. You were not supposed to bring any other reading matter into the house except schoolbooks and, even then, they used to say lots of those were trash. Anyway, they found this book I had hidden under my bed. It was the first romantic fiction I had ever read and I thought it was exciting and, just so different, so different to everything in my life. They found it and then they made me tear it up in front of them, and then they made me tell a meeting of the sect how awful I had been, and then they all shouted at me. It was horrible: they all looked at me – my parents, even other children – as if they thought I did not deserve to live. Nobody talked to me for a long time.'

When Ana's voice cracked as she said the words 'tear it up' Ana's experiences finally became fully real to Mila. At last she managed to pull her consciousness away from her own self-obsessions. She did not know what she should say yet, but her demeanour and expression changed immediately. She put her hand on Ana's shoulder and Ana carried on, and now that she had some validation for her feelings, however muted, there was a new hint of bitterness in Ana's voice.

She told Mila about how she tried to get away and that the sect, and her family, was like prison. Mila remembered Goffman had said 'what is prison-like about prisons is found in institutions whose members have broken no laws' but she simply pressed Ana's shoulder and nodded to encourage her to say more. Then Ana told Mila that her mother and father had refused to change the rules to account for the fact that she was an adolescent and then a teenager. She still had no privacy, not even in the bathroom, and she was not even allowed a mirror to check how she looked before leaving for school in the morning. Ana could not stop talking now.

'Even though I was being bullied at school, there was always a minute, maybe even a shorter time than that, every day at school, when I got a sense of becoming another Ana, different to the one that had to keep my parents' rules. But when I got home there was nothing there to back up this feeling. I felt like I was going slowly mad.'

Mila remembered that Frank 'n' Stein said Goffman thought that psychiatric hospitals had the same effect. A patient found the 'symbolic meaning of events in the inmate's immediate presence dramatically fails to corroborate his prior conception of self.' Ana still had more to say.

'I became so brainwashed into thinking their way, I got so used to living that way, that when I finally got away from them it was impossible to adapt. I still haven't got used to having my own hairbrush and mirror. I still check shop windows and car mirrors when I go outside. Sometimes you don't know what to do because you haven't got the rules anymore – there is too much choice – and quite often I don't have much of a sense of what Ana wants, or who Ana is.'

Mila thought this sounded like something Frank 'n' Stein had said about the 'institutionalisation' that lots of people who had been in total institutions went through. They could not escape or resist so they learned the rules. The official reason for the rules was that they made the institution run more smoothly but this was not true. Rules were in fact the heart and soul of the institution. Learning the rules, and learning to play them, was a large part of progressing through any institution, towards whatever goal it had set for you. If you did it thoroughly, you could become 'institutionalised' and find it difficult to live outside the institution. Mila wanted to know how common this was and if her father would be affected by it. She needed reassurance, even from her friend who was so distressed (but who else would know the answer to her question better than Ana?) so she asked:

'I have heard that some long-term prisoners deliberately reoffend so that they are put back inside. They are dependent on the institution to give meaning and structure to them, and everyone finds it very difficult to live without meaning and structure. Do you think that's true? How long would you have to be in an institution to become like that?'

Ana looked intently at Mila, holding her gaze, and spoke very firmly.

'I wouldn't go back, ever. I never see my parents and I don't want to see them again. The sect won't let them contact me anyway. I was meant to marry another sect member and I refused. You are not allowed to refuse. It makes me a non-person, even for my mother and father. They would be treated in the same way if the sect knew they had tried to contact me.'

'How did you manage to refuse, Ana? How did you find the strength when you had been abused for so long?'

'I went a bit mad for a while. I didn't do it on purpose, I just began behaving very oddly and a teacher noticed and then the authorities were called in and I had to see some doctors. They put me in a hospital for a while – not a general hospital like this one, a special one for people with problems like mine. I think it was so that I could escape, but I did have a breakdown when I was in there. Half the time I kept saying I wanted to go home. It must have been very difficult for the doctors and nurses, but the medication helped. I don't tell anyone about it, because, well, you don't want people to think you are mentally ill. Anyway, going to a psychiatric hospital was my escape route.'

Unbelievably, Ana was laughing by the end of this. There was nothing deranged about the laughter. She was just enjoying the irony of what she had just told Mila. Mila clearly didn't get the joke. She was thinking she had asked Ana to take the kind of risk that she was not prepared to take herself. Then she had not been paying enough attention when Ana shared her secret. She had failed Ana through lack of empathy and intuition.

Mila didn't think she could cope with being a grown-up. She did not really want to be part of an all-too-real, unpleasant world where friends had led awful lives and your father might turn out to be a really bad person. Ana squeezed Mila's arm and said: 'I'm the only person I know who had to go mad to get to university. Everyone else just had to pass exams.'

This time Mila got the joke, then she said: 'But what happened last night, Ana?'

'I think I just lost my sense of humour.' Mila looked at her intently. 'Not really, I think I just lost my sense of who Ana was again.'

'But it's back now.'

'Yes, for now.'

Visit the companion website at **www.palgrave.com/companion/ Bancroft-And-Fevre-Dead-White-Men-2e/** to access additional learning resources, including seminar questions based on the chapter's coverage, a jargon buster that defines key terms used in the text and a timeline which provides an overview of the development of sociological thought.

• • • • •

Who do you pretend to be?

Star: YoU
In: Your
Life

... or performers

Are we puppets ...

1. Social life can be understood as a series of impressions by which others judge us. Erving Goffman studied these and how people maintained what he called 'impression management'. He used the analogy of the theatre, where people perform their roles through front and back stage work. A lot of work is put into the 'front', the presentation of self that is prepared backstage. Then people perform – they give the signals and do the activities that present themselves as that self.

2. There are situations when the self cannot be performed as we might like or where it is systematically violated. Goffman called places like this 'total institutions', where the character of the inmate is wholly defined by the needs of the institution. Prisons, residential schools and mental asylums are total institutions. The people within them are totally exposed to the power and the gaze of the institution – which is why they often become obsessed with protecting the small amount of privacy and the tiny freedoms they do have.

3. People who are inmates of institutions become profoundly affected by them. They may adopt its outlook and values. They may end up preferring life on the inside, with its certainty and predictability, to life outside. That process is called institutionalisation.

4. Stigma is another case where a person's self is impaired in ways they cannot control. It is where someone has a characteristic used to mark them as less than a full member of society. Stigma applies often to disability, mental health problems, some kinds of ethnicity and other 'impairment characteristics'. In these cases people can feel a profound powerlessness between who they are to themselves, and who they appear to be to hostile others.

9
In Control

A few days later Ana came home. It was surprising how quickly things returned to normal, but Mila was very grateful for it. She realised that it was not so much hearing about Ana's terrible parents and the bullies that bothered her, as the feeling of responsibility this gave her. She had not minded listening to Ana's revelations, what she minded very much was realising she was expected to act like an adult. She was meant to respond as sensibly as she could and take responsibility for the effect of her words or deeds.

It seemed that growing up also meant sometimes having some control over how things turned out for other people. You could not pretend to yourself that you did not have this power when you coaxed people into revelations they might not have said. You were taking control of a bit of their lives and you had to be held accountable for what you did. It wasn't just the day with Ana: there were other things at the back of Mila's mind that touched the same raw nerve. Shouldn't she have made the taxi driver stop when she thought that woman was being attacked in the street? Was that an adult response? And then there was her father: what was an adult response to what had happened to him?

Now Mila was coming to understand that her lack of conviction that she had the right, or perhaps it was the *duty*, to make decisions that would actually affect other people might be a problem. In time she would work out that she had no special reason for refusing to be in control of other people. She had to grow up and join in and take her share of the burden of control and, just for once, she actually learned this lesson in a sociology class.

Along with her lectures on sociological theory, Mila also attended a seminar group in which students were meant to take the opportunity to explain to the seminar tutor how much they understood of the ideas they were hearing about in the lectures and reading about in the textbooks. The role of the seminar tutors, most of whom were postgraduate students, was to cajole or provoke them into saying what they understood, so that the tutors could criticise it. Some tutors did more coaxing than provoking but not Mila's.

When the names of their seminar tutors were posted Mila found out that her tutor, Bertrand, had a reputation for being both extremely provocative and very odd. Half of the students seemed to have heard that he was a ridiculous character who dressed like a matador, even though he was more than a little bit lacking in the build for it. The others seemed to find him a bit frightening and one student even told her that he had been investigated for some sort of offence, perhaps a sexual one. Apart from rumours, Mila learned that Bertrand was finishing his PhD on a French thinker called Foucault and everything they talked about in seminars always ended up coming back to this man. But it was in the seminar that was meant to be about Goffman that Bertrand really let rip.

Bertrand was supposed to be teasing out of the group what they knew about Goffman's ideas on impression management. Unsurprisingly, most of the students seemed to have done little or no preparation, probably because they found Bertrand so rude they were intent on keeping quiet for the whole seminar. As usual, it was a very serious and earnest woman called Coni who bore the brunt of the burden of answering Bertrand's questions.

Mila sometimes felt sorry for her, and joined in, but Coni was taking on Bertrand single-handedly this time: 'Of all these different personas, these different masks, that I adopt, which one is the real me?'

Bertrand was yawning. He simply could not help showing them when he found their ideas naive and boring and his responses were usually spiteful.

'*Obviously*, you are a combination of what you think you are, what you say you are, and perhaps most importantly, what you *do*. This Goffman stuff is trivial – word games for adolescents who have never done anything in their lives. You have nothing to talk about but me, me, me.'

As Bertrand looked around the seminar table with contempt, Mila was, as usual, amazed that anyone spoke up when they were going to get this kind of treatment. She thought Goffman had said serious things about people getting hurt and damaged. Bertrand's spite brought to mind all of the confusion and shame she felt because of her own failure of empathy and understanding of her friend, Ana. Dismissing Goffman like this just made it worse, so, in spite of Bertrand's bullying, she spoke up.

'There is more to Goffman than impression management. He places it within the context of the power that institutions, or social expectations, have over the individual. In *Asylums* he investigated how the rules of the mental hospitals of the time constructed a person as an inmate.'

Bertrand cut in with characteristic sarcasm.

'Yes, we know, "from a person into a category", well done. If you were being very generous, you could say the self-consciousness highlighted by Goffman prefigures Foucault's idea of the panopticon. We behave as if other people are watching us even when they aren't. We imagine that there are a set of judges outside us, watching and giving out points, scoring our performance. But Foucault did all this much better.'

Coni joined in on Mila's side. 'In *Stigma* Goffman relates personal identification to state surveillance. This was long before it was fashionable to chatter endlessly about these things but he anticipated all of the ways in which we are increasingly monitored and our personal histories, tastes, wants, opinions, get recorded in all sorts of databases.'

The other students were nodding at this. They liked the idea of Coni giving Bertrand some of his own medicine. One of them said: 'Once you've got a store loyalty card, the supermarkets know more about your weekly shopping than you do. You are never anonymous online. This all adds information about us to their databases.'

This was getting a bit off the point for Mila. It was too trivial and it was leaving behind the stuff she thought mattered in Goffman: the way he helped us understand that people could be made to feel worthless and marginalised. She wanted the group, and Bertrand, to realise this. 'Coni is right. Goffman's work on stigmatisation is unfairly neglected. It ties in with racism, sexism, homophobia, in fact any form of social exclusion or rejection. The development of social norms and the stigmatisation of individuals who don't come up to scratch is important, especially for anyone who has felt out of place or out of order because of what they wear, what they look like or who they are.'

It had not occurred to Mila that somebody who was considered as odd as Bertrand was would have their own reasons for getting this message. Even if you just took the point about being stigmatised for what you wore, Bertrand would be a perfect example of someone being out of place (he really should not have tried to squeeze his broad frame into that little jacket). Most of the group thought that Mila had been well aware of what she was doing and they were trying to hide their laughter. Although Mila was not above poking fun at her tutor, she was really thinking about herself, about her own feeling of being out of place. The disguised laughter confused her for a moment (had she said something silly?) and then, with a wave of embarrassment, she realised what she had said. She started speaking again. She wanted to get off the subject and onto something less personal. 'Goffman's argument about impression management says something fundamental about the status of the individual in modern society. As individuals who have many interactions with complete strangers every day we have to behave like this: we have to make first impressions count. We no longer live in tight-knit communities where everyone is known to everyone else. We're all strangers to each other and we have to assess each other within minutes or seconds of meeting. Don't most job interviews last half an hour, in which time both parties have to assess someone they will be working with for years? It's really odd, if you think about it.'

Coni quickly added her own, thoughtful contribution. 'Goffman's observations fit a world in which appearance and surface are valued over substance. Isn't it true that postmodernists were later to adopt his understanding that perception had come to replace substance?' Coni explained that the idea here was that there was no longer a division between surface appearance and reality, rather there was nothing but surface appearance, and the notion that there was a real you below the appearance you project was false.

Bertrand leaned forward towards Coni. 'So you're saying everyday life in modern society gives us enormous freedom, the freedom to make ourselves who we want to be. Maybe you think we should guiltlessly embrace the presentationalism Goffman identifies. Maybe you think it's fun?'

It was Mila who replied. 'Goffman isn't just about making us feel OK by showing how society makes us put up fronts for other people.' She said that Goffman alerted us to the way identity and the self were socially related and constructed, and how society could violate this self for the purposes of social control.

Bertrand was derisive. 'Goffman doesn't have the first idea about social control. We may think we have freedoms but we have none at all – we are *disciplined* at all times and at every turn. Foucault shows that it's not asylums and prisons that do the disciplining. It's us – we do it ourselves!'

Bertrand had apparently decided they knew enough about Goffman and he started to tell them about Michel Foucault. His attitude changed from supercilious boredom and contempt to a kind of wild enthusiasm which was scary in its own way. He told them that the modern world seemed to be full of freedom and choice – sexual liberty, self-therapy, and extreme individualism – but it did not always feel like this. Apparently Bertrand himself did not feel free and he believed they must feel the same way. 'But can we just do what want? Why in the midst of this apparent freedom do we not feel free? Why does massive choice actually feel ever more constraining? Is there some way in which the individual freedom of contemporary life can be oppressive? Are we are being compelled to behave in certain ways without noticing it?'

Bertrand was trying to keep eye contact with each of them in turn as he said this, leaning across the table and speaking very quickly. He pressed on, hardly pausing to take a breath. 'We have to start by pulling apart the question of "can I do what I want?": what is "I" and what is "want"? These both seem very simple and certain facts but they aren't. Foucault was concerned with power: why do people do some things and not others, why do they obey some people and not others, and why do they behave in certain ways at one time and in a completely different way at another time?'

He jumped up and started writing on the flipchart in the corner of the room. Over his shoulder he told them to write this down, and, at the top of the sheet he wrote, in a barely legible scrawl:

Sex and the Body

What explains the obsession with physical appearance in many societies?

One or two of the students appeared to be a bit taken aback by the unexpected and sudden appearance of the word 'sex'. Mila could sense that she was not the only one who had heard the rumour about the investigation into Bertrand. There was now a sense of uneasy anticipation around the table; what on earth was he going to say to them? At first Bertrand appeared to have decided on discretion. He told them that they were all (but especially the women) bombarded with a huge array of advice and instruction on how to become something – how to be thin, diet, look good, have great skin, get a man, be beautiful.

'Foucault reminded us all that you are both a mind and a body. What goes on in and around the body is as much a subject of sociological study as what affects the mind. Power works on both to change how they are. OK, it's not a novel concept, but Foucault argued that the central way in which power works in the modern world is by getting us as individuals to manage our bodies. No one is making you follow the advice about looking good but, nevertheless, it becomes an obsession for millions of people.'

Mila thought this was all tame stuff, and not all that new either. It was the kind of thing she had heard in sociology classes before she came to university. Then Bertrand started talking about sex.

'Sex is a prime example of how power works by getting individuals to manage their own bodies. Foucault was writing in the second half of the twentieth century. He argued that, in the nineteenth century, when attitudes towards sex were apparently a lot more traditional, people actually talked about sex a lot. Indeed they were obsessed with it, publishing medical treatises on all aspects of it. There were manuals for parents that described how to control the sexual behaviour of a child, with advice given on what to do if it is caught masturbating.'

Now he did pause, to see what effect this had had on them. In fact the only thing that happened was that the student next to Mila whispered in her ear: 'Don't you think he is the one who is obsessed with sex?'

Bertrand carried on as if he had been given a vote of confidence. He went on to say that it was true that, in the nineteenth century, European sexual morality was about controlling some aspects of sexuality, and even more about controlling certain people's sexuality, especially women and members of the working class, however: 'It did not apply a blanket "repression" – in fact its vast *scientia sexualis* cultivated and directed sexuality. Only "wasteful" or unproductive desire was condemned – such as masturbation. A range of ways of talking about sex, and techniques relating to sexuality, were produced. They amounted to what Foucault called *bio-power*, regulation and management of the physical, biological body and of the population as a "body".'

Bertrand told them that Foucault thought the supposedly sexually liberated Europeans of the second half of the twentieth century were not so different from their nineteenth-century predecessors. Especially since the 1960s, many societies discussed sex obsessively: there were thousands of magazine articles and television programmes about what was good sex, what was bad sex, and how to have more of the first kind and less of the second. Foucault said this was not a sign of freedom. The more we talked about sex, the more we engaged in reproducing a dominant image of what we should look like, talk like, act like, and think like. In the 1960s and 1970s people thought those in the nineteenth century, and even the 1950s, were repressed and prudish about sex. Yet our choices about sex were just as constrained. Foucault called the power that constrained us the 'discourse of power–knowledge', meaning the way we talked about and categorised things tended to frame how we did things.

According to Foucault, your sexuality was not a well which was either tapped or blocked up depending on how well balanced or repressed you were. Sexuality was constructed within and by 'bio-power.' Sexuality was measured, examined, pored over, discussed, and dissected. One feature of the network of bio-power was the confessional where the individual poured out his or her innermost desires to an objective, distanced professional figure. Society had created a whole class of such emotional bureaucrats – including doctors, therapists, priests, and teachers – who could take this role. Bertrand added that he had his own ideas about this. 'A development of the late twentieth century was the public confessional which started in the US and spread across the world. You know, the TV show in which some hapless set of individuals told the world about their experiences. Foucault would take this pornographic overexposure to be part of a totalitarian "discourse of bio-power", in which any aspect of the individual's life could be exposed in public and judged on by a self-appointed citizens' jury. It's what I am writing my thesis on.'

Bertrand stopped, as if he expected a barrage of questions or maybe just admiring murmurs from his audience but, as there was no response, he changed tack and told them that Foucault's study of sexuality began with the regulation of sexuality in Ancient Greece. What later societies would term homosexuality was accepted and even promoted as the ideal form of love among privileged classes of men. This could be taken to mean that the Greeks did not repress this part of sexual desire but Foucault dug up a far more interesting story. Man–boy love was a part of the development of a young man: an older mentor would adopt a young man to whom he would teach wisdom, and part of their relationship would be sexual. Although condoned, the Greeks condemned this love when it led to one party becoming effeminate. It was only permitted as part of masculine development.

'Some modern all-male groupings still use homosexuality as part of initiation and bonding rites. But the point is that there was no rigorous category of "abnormal" individuals who were considered different to those who were "normal". That distinction only emerged in Europe in the nineteenth century. In Ancient Greece it was up to the free citizen to make his own choices and avoid either excess or passivity. One had to "love properly".'

Unexpectedly, one of the male students, Pallo, spoke up. He spoke slowly as if he were explaining something quite simple to a child or a person with below-average intelligence. 'But if male citizens were all having sex with each other, then they were not normal. They were homosexuals. That's what the word means.'

Bertrand smiled in an indulgent way. 'Foucault emphasises how sex and sexuality are very separate things. Having sex with young men didn't make one a homosexual. This was a category that only came into being in the Victorian era, just like that of insanity.'

Pallo replied: 'Foucault sounds pretty insane to me,' but Bertrand ignored him. He said Foucault suggested the development of both our science of sexuality and our science of sanity were related and he wrote another heading on the flipchart together with a question:

Madness

Were people in previous periods in history more tolerant of madness?

Apparently Goffman was not the only one who did research on mental asylums. Foucault began his work on insanity by examining how society divided the mad from the sane. Taking some historical examples of what would now be considered insanity – Diogenes masturbating in public, Jesus driving out 'demons' from people – it became clear that behaviour which would later have you placed in some form of care or custody had been treated very differently in the past. Was it the case that people in previous periods were simply more tolerant of madness? Foucault said no – what happened was that the institutions of modern society had created a science of regulatory behaviour, a science at which, as individuals, we were required to be experts. Bertrand quickly wrote another heading on the chart and two questions:

Power

Who gets to do what to whom, who tells other people what to do?
Why do some people always do what they are required to, even when they don't have to?

He added 'I'm an adult, nobody is holding a gun to my head. Why do I do as I am told?' There was an uncomfortable silence until the other student, Coni, who had spoken earlier, answered.

'Don't some sociologists argue that there are different sets of rules?' She said that our adherence to certain rules – such as no shoplifting – was in fear of getting caught. Our adherence to other rules – crossing the street at traffic lights – was for survival, since just to walk across might end up in us getting killed. There were still other rules – such as paying taxes – which we obeyed because of our recognition that there needed to be such a thing as society and common services paid for by all.

For once, Bertrand might even have been pleased.

'Good, now Foucault argues that there is a big gap in the study of power. Marx, Weber, and so on were all concerned about power in the form of people being made to do things that they don't want to, or shouldn't want to. For feminists, power forces women into subservient roles. For Marxists it keeps the working class voting for capitalist politicians. Most theories of power up to Foucault, and many since, take it that power is something which lies outside the individual, a tangible entity that hangs over us, like a bully or a dictatorial father, directing us to do things we wouldn't otherwise do. In a sentence, Foucault argued that power doesn't work by making people do what they don't want; it more often works by making people do what they do want. Or rather, their wants, their resistance to power, their desires, are a part of that power. Power is like a web or a network, rather than a pyramid.'

In her mind, Mila was turning over an idea about her father making her do what he wanted when it seemed as if it was what she wanted. It was too confusing for her and, looking around the room, she thought other people felt the same way. In spite of his enthusiasm for Foucault, Bertrand at least had the awareness to notice that this had been too much for the group to take in at one go, so he gave them an example. He asked them to remember where they had started, with all those magazines and TV programmes telling people how to become their ideal, giving them advice on how to get what you want – how to have the perfect body, career, and so on. This industry asked: what do you want, and who do you want to be? Foucault would say that our answers to these questions – our desires, such as sexual desire – were constructed through discourses of power–knowledge. Power was not a resource one group of people had and another one didn't. And that meant 'it cannot be seized, smashed, overthrown, stormed, or defeated. Power does not sit in a locked safe in the bastions of the state.'

Coni said: 'I don't feel powerless at all. I am in charge of my own life. I can make my own decisions.' That's right, thought Mila, I can make my own decisions, I just don't want to make any decisions on behalf of other people. But Bertrand was telling Coni that she made her decisions within constraints set by 'discourses of power–knowledge' and 'technologies of the self' that impelled people to take an active role in managing their selves and their bodies.

'It feels like it is we who are in charge, but in fact we are being constrained to follow a certain path. Foucault wants us to understand that power is practical, local, networked, and peer to peer. It isn't a property possessed by one homogenous group of individuals – men, the middle class, capitalists, whites – and exercised over another homogenous group of individuals – women, the working class, and so on. Foucault's power is both more powerful and weaker than the power conceived of by feminists and Marxists, who take power to be a rather brittle thing towering over the dominated group in society waiting to be smashed down and overthrown.'

'So how is anything to change?' asked Coni.

'Feminists and Marxists think that Foucault endorses a pessimistic view of society in which individuals are so bound up with the processes of power and domination that there is nothing they can do about it, or worse, anything they try and do about it ends up reinforcing the status quo. But Foucault felt quite strongly that his theory of power should not lead people to be pessimistic, and especially should not pull the rug out from under progressive politics. In fact, he'd argue the opposite of the above perspective. Marxism leads people up a blind alley which is why almost all Marxist revolutions have ended up making the societies in which they happened far more repressive than they were to start with.'

Now, for the first time since Bertrand started his impromptu lecture on Foucault, Mila found she was fully alert. There was something in what he had just said that had hit a nerve and she had a question to ask: 'Are you saying people don't take power; they have it given to them?'

'Yes, sociologists like to follow the "top-down" understanding of power that Marx and others introduced because it reassures us that when those in power – politicians, bureaucrats, whoever – do things we don't like, it's not our fault. Foucault makes us feel uncomfortable when he says this is not what really goes on.'

'Does he say these people and organisations really only have the power that we let them have?' Mila wanted to know.

Pallo, the student who had talked to Bertrand as if he were an idiot, joined in, and he was using the same condescending tone again. 'Look, if I say: "My boss is more powerful than I am, so I must do what he says", it's a simple recognition of reality. Someone is more powerful than me; I must obey him.'

Bertrand replied with uncharacteristic patience. 'Foucault gets underneath this statement to point out how that very statement is part of the constitution of power. You say "the boss is powerful", but he is only powerful because we all agree on this statement.'

'So why don't all those who don't want to be under the control of their bosses simply agree that their bosses are not powerful?' Again, Bertrand seemed to allow Pallo licence that the others might not be able to rely on.

'Actually, Foucault's view of power shows that it is *harder* to get out of this situation than Marxists imagine. It's easier to opt out of power in the Marxist sense – if someone is holding a gun to your head you can always pull out a bigger gun. But because we are active agents of power it is much harder to opt out. Power is not a thing, which stands outside ourselves, above us, which we can attack and either destroy or seize for ourselves. We can't storm the Bastille because our Bastille is the fabric of our existence. We can no more take hold of it than an ant can take over the ants' nest.'

Pallo shook his head as if to show the group it should be quite obvious to everyone that either Bertrand or Foucault, or probably both, were idiots. Bertrand was smiling at Pallo and seemed not to notice. He put up another heading and a series of questions:

Discipline

Why are there rules?
Why do people obey rules?
Why do people do what they are told?
What makes people do what they are told,
even when nobody is telling them?

'Let me try to make it simple enough for you. You can understand why people do what they are meant to when other people are watching them. There are social rules, and so on, which we've discussed earlier. Above all, people try to avoid embarrassing themselves. What this doesn't explain is why people generally behave the same way when they are in private. Why don't people just cut loose, go completely crazy, when they are by themselves?'

This time Bertrand answered his own questions. According to the tradition started by Weber (and Marx), power was the ability to get someone to do something that they otherwise would not have done. Your teacher's power to make you stay behind after school was one example. But people stuck to the rules even when no one was standing over them telling them to. They largely obeyed the rules even if there was a very minor risk of them being found out for disobeying them.

'Some sociologists, like Talcott Parsons, taught that we learn to do this through socialisation – a system of rewards and punishments, social sanctions, which we internalise and come to reinforce as strongly as if we were the ones who had made the rules in the first place. Foucault argued that the techniques of surveillance make us behave as if someone is watching us, even when there is no way that they could be.'

Mila was still alert. She had learned about socialisation before she came to university and had always thought it made sense. She could not help intervening again. 'Of course you have to learn how to control yourself, your wants and desires, as you get older. The baby just cries and screams until it gets everything it wants, even teenagers behave like that sometimes. But, as they get older, they learn to control themselves.' The rest of the group were laughing at this. The woman who had whispered that Bertrand was obsessed with sex said pointedly that some people would always be unable to control themselves. Bertrand seemed to be oblivious to all of this and carried on with a very straight face.

'It's not something that naturally comes with age. Little children in orphanages soon shut up, neglected teenagers don't throw tantrums. It's only where caregivers give credence to this behaviour, and give children power, that they carry on like this. If the babies (and the more grown-up babies) get their way, they carry on behaving like this. If they are systematically unable to achieve their wants and desires, these are rapidly scaled down – they don't expect attention and hope simply not to be beaten – and they learn to control themselves. Or, rather, it's not learning to control at all: the situation they are in takes the control away from them. The spoilt Western teenager was given the control, had it thrust upon them.'

Mila was unable to pass up the chance to get the group to laugh again. She suggested that perhaps the happy medium lay somewhere between Western teenagers and what happened in orphanages. Bertrand just took it as a serious question.

'But the point is Foucault's: we don't naturally learn to control ourselves. This control is a two-way process and it depends, crucially, on what other people do. Foucault is concerned with two things: how *discipline* operates in modern society, and what type of society produces this discipline.' Bertrand explained that this was where Foucault's research on prisons came in. He investigated this through his favoured method of an 'archaeology' of the development of an institution.

His *Discipline and Punish* isn't strictly a work of criminology, just as his *History of Sexuality* wasn't about sex. It's about what type of society produces prisons and the sets of rules and disciplines that go along with them. It's about how the structures of society that we all occupy share some common features of the prison. In the creation of the prison, sets of techniques were produced which can be found in almost any institution – school, hospital, workplace.

Bertrand said Foucault examined the creation and application of 'disciplinary power', and its place in the emergence of the disciplinary society, a society characterised by specific techniques of power which created and disciplined bodies. A convict was a subject produced by the prison system, not just a person in prison, but a person made by that system to behave in a certain way and made incapable of imagining another way of behaving. These 'subjects' were produced by the discourse of power–knowledge. Convicts were subjects created in the discourse of punishment, just as the insane were subjects produced by the discourse of psychiatry. In both cases a subject was a person behaving in a way defined by the network of power–knowledge, and the discourse of punishment had changed over time. In eighteenth-century Europe punishment was a spectacle. Public hanging and flogging made it clear that the purpose was the punishment of the body. From the nineteenth century, the purpose of punishment became the regulation of the self.

Pallo butted in. 'That's just like Durkheim's distinction between retributive and restitutive law, and we have been taught that distinction did not fit the facts either. There are plenty of examples of pre-modern law which were about getting people to make good for their crimes rather than taking revenge or retribution on them.' Bertrand had an answer.

'Neither Durkheim nor Foucault were legal historians. They were less concerned to excavate what this says about the legal and penal systems, than what it says about society. Foucault's most famous example of nineteenth-century punishment never actually got made into a reality until much later – and then only a few examples were built – but it shows you what kind of society was coming into being at the time.'

Bertrand told them about the British philosopher and reformer, Jeremy Bentham, who had come up with the idea of a 'panopticon' in the late eighteenth century. This was a plan for a new kind of prison building that was designed in such a way that prisoners would always be in view and this constant surveillance would be the key to their control. Prisons in the eighteenth century were apparently very different from what we would recognise as prisons.

For instance, prisoners were not treated equally: depending on his social status and wealth, a prisoner could buy privileges, such as a private room, prostitutes and even his freedom. Torture was used both to extract information and as punishment. But society underwent rapid change as feudalism was displaced by capitalism. Huge numbers of people were uprooted, removed from the traditional relationships of obligation and loyalty which in the past had served to keep the population obedient. Urban centres grew, the new proletariat did not have much loyalty to an employer whose sole relationship with them was expressed in monetary terms. Society's elite were terrified at the potential for anarchy represented by these *uncontrolled bodies* and also at the amount it would cost to control them.

Bentham worked out how you might ensure, with limited resources, that these bodies were controlled, made to obey the rules and kept out of trouble, and especially to not cause trouble for their rulers. Over time, new structures were to emerge to cope with this situation, such as a standing army, a civil service bureaucracy and a national police force, and according to Foucault, all of which absorbed and employed the techniques of discipline and surveillance that Bentham came up with. These all flowed from the architecture of a panopticon. The basic design was a central tower surrounded by a circular arrangement of cells. A person in the tower could see into any of the cells, but occupants of the cells could not see into the tower and would not be aware if they were being watched or not. In Bentham's time this involved a lot of clever architectural design but now video surveillance made it very easy to see what he was after.

'The eye tracks you in every supermarket, in the street, in the elevator. Is anyone watching the CCTV pictures? We never know for sure. A camera and a panopticon allow a lot of people to be controlled with the application of relatively few resources *because* the uncertainty of not knowing if you are being watched is the key to discipline. Foucault thought a panopticon would make power function automatically. The guard never had to watch if people always thought they might be subject to surveillance. So who was exercising the power? As with social media, was not the guard but the inmates themselves!'

Foucault thought the prison system that actually emerged in the nineteenth century produced a lot of novelties. Inmates were to be treated equally, with access to the same services and facilities. Later on, libraries and chapels were built inside prisons – they became places where inmates were meant to emerge as docile and useful members of society. We told ourselves that prisons were reformed as society became more humanitarian, but Foucault disputed this. In the past the prison extracted punishment from the body of the inmate, often with a display of severe pain. Doing away with the pain and the display did not mean that society could do without the benefits of punishment.

Prisons were reformed as society became more disciplinary. Bertrand said the importance of the panopticon was not so much in the contribution it made to prison design. It introduced into society the crucial principle of discipline, and a feature of discipline was that an individual was meant to discipline *him or herself*. Discipline was something to be internalised and applied to oneself and one's body. 'The prisoners in the panopticon would not know when they were being watched and when they weren't. They would have to behave as if they were being watched all the time. Likewise in modern society we learn to behave as if somebody is watching us even when they aren't. The panopticon is the all-seeing eye: it renders its occupants seen but unseeing. The many are watched by the few, and, being unable to perceive when they are being watched or not, must behave all the time as if they are under constant surveillance. Their bodies are rendered docile, and the panoptic regime of correction renders them as civilised subjects.'

Bertrand said that civilised subjects got through each day in the same docile and predictable manner. Just as prisoners followed the same monotonous daily schedule in the prison, and within specific locations, so we followed our own rigorous schedules at work, in places of learning, even in our leisure time. In many of these situations opportunities for interaction with others are limited, just as they are for prison inmates. But in both situations it is we, the civilised subjects, who carry out the orders and it all depends on us being in:

a state of conscious and permanent visibility that assures the automatic functioning of power.

As Bertrand was writing this on the board, the student who had mentioned surveillance earlier in the seminar spoke up: 'It's what I said before when Coni was talking about Goffman. Everything we do, especially online, is available to be monitored by organisations and governments. Like the guard in the panopticon, the institution looks into you, but you cannot look into it.' Mila was thinking of the institution that accommodated her father. Was there anything about it that resembled a panopticon? Bernard was continuing his impromptu lecture.

'Power in society does not work by force. *We* operate power, we "bear" power. The principles encapsulated in the disciplinary system can be found in many areas of society. Interestingly, schools were the last bastion of the use of physical violence as exemplary punishment, corporal punishment only being abandoned at the end of the twentieth century in many countries. Perhaps children were felt not to be capable of absorbing discipline through the sanctioning system applied elsewhere.'

Bertrand told them Foucault thought self-regulation became general when it became less important to punish people, and more important to make them sorry. He said repressive power was the control of death, but bio-power was the management of 'life'. He meant that repressive state power held the power of death over its living subjects. Society *was* dominated by blood – both the bloodline of the aristocracy and the blood of the condemned person on the scaffold – but now it was dominated by sexuality, by the bio-power. Bio-power managed their lives, intimately constructing their wants and desires and ensuring that they all became little micro-managers of the system.

Coni interjected. 'Isn't he just misusing the term "power"? Power is about exercising your authority over other people, even threatening them with force. But what Foucault is talking about here is people managing their own lives, and being socialised. It's not the same thing.'

'This was his point,' Bertrand sounded as if his patience might be running out, 'our idea of power is wrong. It misleads us. Power is less often repressive and negative than it is productive and positive. Power is developmental, power is creative, power is most powerful when it is most active and involved. It neither sits above society nor the individual, but is productively inserted into our everyday actions, no matter how apparently minor, private, or insignificant.'

According to Foucault, everyday practices form nodes in a network of power–knowledge in which we all participate. Bertrand said an example of this was that ever fewer people in Western society did hard manual labour anymore, yet they spent ever increasing amounts of time punishing their bodies in a variety of ways, seemingly entirely of their own volition. For Foucault this was one illustration of the fact that the body – absent from most social theory – was in fact central to power relations. It was the place in which 'technologies of the self' operated, technologies which were constituted in our everyday behaviour.

The student who had been trying to patronise Bertrand, Pallo, made one more attempt at sarcasm. 'Power is everywhere and resistance is futile. It's all very sad. But people enjoy much more personal freedom nowadays than they ever did. And how are we meant to get out of the "network", or was it "discourse", of "power–knowledge" anyway?'

Bertrand paused, perhaps for effect, and then replied. 'Foucault liked to say that alternative sexual practices subverted the discourse.' Most of the group looked as if they were having difficulty containing their urge to laugh.

Pallo was smirking from ear to ear as he said, 'Well, he would, wouldn't he? This may have had more to with his personal preferences than his concern for maintaining theoretical consistency.'

Bertrand ploughed on. 'Foucault suggested that, because of the pervasiveness of bio-power, important resistance occurs at transitory and mobile points, so acts which change society are far more likely to be at the level of mundane, everyday choices than in the form of mass movements.' Mila knew Coni liked to think of herself as a bit of an environmental activist and wasn't surprised when she joined in again.

'Well, that's right. We change society by resisting at the local level, by fighting against unsustainable development. You don't try to take on the whole system at once. You pick your tactics carefully so that you maximise your chances of winning.'

Bertrand looked as if he wasn't sure he wanted Coni's approval. 'Resistance can be directed by the individual at a technique of power. Because power operates locally, resistance can be local – indeed perhaps the only effective resistance can be local.'

Pallo weighed in again. He said Foucault was over concerned with maintaining the consistency of his theory and not interested enough in the actual evidence. It was a bit strange that he should be so certain when the evidence seemed to point in the opposite direction. '*You* said hardly any panopticons were ever built. There are retributive elements in modern law, like the use of the death penalty in the United States. Not everyone is monitored, not all the time anyway. Some individuals are simply left to their own devices, until they become an embarrassment or something. Other people, like those of us who join the professions for instance, will engage in the maximum level of self-monitoring and self-regulation. But isn't that our choice? We could go and live on the margins, out of sight and out of mind, if we wanted to.'

Mila was thinking of the people she had seen being cleared off the streets in the middle of the night.

Bertrand responded. 'Don't forget the basic point. Social control is not about us being puppets on strings pulled this way and that by social forces much bigger than ourselves. That's what Goffman and the other sociologists thought, but Foucault shows there is no one else to blame. Power is not a thing outside of people that weighs down on them. Traditional theories of power from Plato to Marx had society divided into the powerful and the powerless. Foucault's concept of power as a web, a net, had it that the powerful were as much bound by power as those without it were: they were as much constrained by it as the powerless, as much defined by and inside it as anyone. The most powerful cannot leave the restraining web of power any more than the rest of us can.'

***

As they walked out of the class, some of the students were still sniggering about Bertrand and his alternative sexual practices, but Mila found herself walking out next to Coni. Mila said: 'Did you understand all of that?'

Coni said she thought she did because, 'The idea of power as a network made me think of the Internet.' She said the Internet was a network of nodes, some of which were more reliable and stronger than the others. None of the nodes could exercise domination outside of that net and all of them had to play by a set of rules.

The student who had wanted to talk about surveillance in the seminar was listening and butted in. 'You can't step outside power – or throw it off. That would be like one of the nodes switching the Internet off. It is impossible, since such a command would negate itself: the command to switch off would be lost as computers switched off.' The metaphor confused Mila a little but she understood that you couldn't escape having some power over other people. You could pretend you didn't have it but that now seemed not just childish but, being completely honest, cowardly.

Visit the companion website at **www.palgrave.com/companion/ Bancroft-And-Fevre-Dead-White-Men-2e/** to access additional learning resources, including seminar questions based on the chapter's coverage, a jargon buster that defines key terms used in the text and a timeline which provides an overview of the development of sociological thought.

● ● ● ● ●

How to get people to do what you want

Instructions:
1. Read instructions
2. Follow instructions
3. For problems, see 1

Power makes us be   **More than it makes us do**

1. A big part of sociology is the study of power – the ability to get people to act in ways that they would not have done otherwise. Some think it is a quality or a resource; the ability to get others to do what you want; or the ability to define 'want'. Many theories of power are slightly conspiratorial, or dictatorial. Power is often described as being top-down, people 'in the know' arranging things to benefit themselves and forcing the less powerful to act in ways that are not in their interest.

2. Michel Foucault thought that this did not describe how power worked much of the time. Power was not located in a place, or a group of people, but was everywhere in society. It works in creating identities for people to fit into, to be defined and disciplined by. His studies of sexuality and madness showed how categories of identity and illness were formed by professionals to give coherent identities to human activity. They discipline people within and outwith those categories.

3. Foucault pointed to systems which spread power throughout society. He thought the surveillance that is ubiquitous in modern society, the panopticon, made us act as if we were being watched and judged. It is far more effective to get people to behave in an ordered, disciplined way by making them do it to themselves.

4. The way to resist these 'disciplinary imperatives' was to disrupt these ordered categories. So you might avoid surveillance by using encryption and anonymity on the internet, or create multiple identities and avatars for yourself.

10
In Doubt

The following week, Mila found herself sitting next to Coni in a lecture. The lecturer was late and they filled in time by telling each other Bertrand horror stories. A student sitting in front of them chipped in to say that she had originally been assigned to a tutor she did not like and had simply changed groups. By the time they were walking out of the lecture together, Coni and Mila had decided to give this strategy a try.

Mila and Coni were in luck and found places in a seminar run by a new lecturer called Dalina. As soon as her seminar began, Mila could feel that the atmosphere was totally different. In Bertrand's seminar the students had spent their hour avoiding eye contact with him. Nobody wanted to participate and, from what Mila had seen of the scanty notes people brought with them, nobody did much of the reading they were meant to do in order to take part in the discussion. The only contribution that many of the members of the group had made was to make fun of Bertrand in whispered asides. Bertrand took his revenge by being patronising, dismissive, and sarcastic in equal measure.

Mila could tell all of the students in Dalina's group had done the required reading, because they each had sheets of notes in front of them. Before the seminar started there was an animated discussion between four or five of them. It had nothing to do with sociology, but it showed that they were not going to pretend that they were mute for the next hour. When Dalina asked for quiet she did so in a tactful and humorous way and the conversation subsided, but only for a few moments. Dalina asked if anyone in the group regularly used therapies that were not recognised by Western medicine. If this had been Bertrand's group, nobody would have dared to agree that they did for fear of the withering sarcasm that would have followed, but Dalina's group obviously trusted her and several hands were raised.

Dalina chose a student, Lian, who then explained she had used a herbal remedy before exams to help with stress and improve her memory. This alternative remedy had supposedly been in use for generations in a particular village renowned for the longevity of its inhabitants and was now marketed to anyone with a high-pressure career or degree course. Dalina asked the group for comments and, Mila noticed, quietly moved her chair back a little from the table, perhaps to make the students less aware of her presence.

The other students were then asking Lian to explain why she thought it worth 'wasting her money' on this remedy. 'I don't see what your objection is. You can't just dismiss knowledge that has been around for hundreds of years,' she said.

A student called Jinsong told her that he could easily dismiss this 'knowledge' if the remedy did not work: 'that means it's not knowledge at all.' Mila thought there was something about the way the other students reacted to this that suggested Jinsong was used to doing a lot of the talking in this group.

Lian replied to Jinsong. 'How do you know it doesn't work? Lots of people have used it and say it's helped them. It's not just superstition.'

'Lots of people said that the sun had to be raised in the morning by their holy men, otherwise it wouldn't come up. Then they found that it would come up, holy men or not. Nobody has proved it works, scientifically.'

'Ah! But nobody has proved it doesn't work scientifically and I know it works for me. And, anyways, thousands of people use the same remedy and clearly they all think it works for them.'

'The placebo effect is a wonderful thing.'

'The what?'

Mila was wondering if Lian was feeling harassed (she certainly looked a bit uncomfortable) and at just this point Dalina leaned back into the table, making eye contact with Lian. Mila could see she was taking any heat out of the exchange but Dalina was also taking the opportunity to teach them something. She said: 'The placebo effect is the difference between the clinical properties of a treatment and its actual effectiveness. During the Second World War, an American doctor was so short of morphine that in desperation he injected wounded soldiers with salt water. It worked. People felt less pain because they thought they had been given a painkiller. That's why you have to test medicines with scientific trials. You give the remedy to a group of people; to another group of people you give a placebo; and to another you don't give anything. Then you see what the outcome is. Do the people who were given the real treatment get better than those who were given nothing or the placebo?'

Jinsong might have treated this as a real question, rather than a rhetorical one, and gone back on the attack but Dalina was looking at Lian and encouraging her to respond, which she did.

'Right, but what about where lots of people have used the thing and have become better over generations, scientific evidence or not,' Lian said.

Dalina was now looking round the room trying to encourage the rest of the group to join in. Mila realised that Dalina was looking at her, smiling. This was enough for Mila to realise that she was not going to be allowed to join this group and remain passive.

'You've also got to account for the way we tend to note positive examples and ignore negatives,' Mila said.

Coni, sitting next to Mila, guessed her turn would be next and decided to speak before the tutor turned to her. 'If we already believe something to be the case. For instance, I don't believe in astrology, but astrology columns often sound scarily plausible.'

Dalina said; 'Yes, it's because of the Forer effect. Psychologist B. R. Forer gave his students a personality test to complete. He then discarded their answers, and gave each one the "results"; in fact a paragraph from an astrology column in a popular magazine.'

At this point Mila saw that Coni was scrabbling around in her bag for a pen or pencil and Mila realised that all the other students were writing notes on what Dalina said. They had not been asked to do so, no bullet points had been scrawled on the flip chart, yet here they all were writing notes.

Dalina was saying that Forer's students all rated the findings as being extremely accurate. This was due to the 'subjective validation effect.' We discarded what did not fit in favour of what did, particularly if the outcome was flattering to ourselves or our beliefs, or was in our interests. So we looked for cases where the treatment we had decided to favour was successful, and ignored all those where it was not. This was why clinical trials had to be conducted blind – the people running the trial could not know who was getting the real thing or not. So Lian's remedy might work only because the people who did use it and died the next day were not around to report the fact. The group, including Lian, laughed. Now Dalina turned to Jinsong, the student who had given Lian a hard time. She asked him to tell the group a bit more about placebos and medical trials. In particular, Dalina wanted him to summarise one of the readings they were required to look at before the seminar, a reading about psychotherapy.

Jinsong said that there were trials that apparently showed that psychotherapy did not work. Not only didn't it work, in fact, people who had it were worse off than before. Those trials that had a placebo involved a one-hour conversation with a university professor instead of a therapist. The people that had one hour talking to the professor turned out better than the group that had the real therapy. This resulted in much smugness among non-psychotherapists, but psychotherapists did not just pack up and go home. They said the trials had been too brief, or were not testing for the right outcomes. Dalina said: 'That's right. There are lots of medical interventions that haven't been proved by double-blind trials. There are some that could not be put through these trials or some which have come out with inconclusive results when they have. Obviously Lian would not take something that might have killed lots of people. She knows that thousands of other people have taken the remedy and does not think any of them has suffered as a result. But we sometimes take claims on trust because someone in a white coat said so rather than because we know that there have been successful medical trials.'

Now Coni joined in again. She said that she thought it must be bad science to carry on promoting a therapy which science had not been able to demonstrate was successful. It did not take long for her to find her feet, Mila thought. 'If this process is enough to tell someone if what they are doing works or not – they should stop doing what they are doing if it is not working,' Coni added.

She was immediately answered by a woman called Ubanwa. 'Yes, but that's because they are human like anybody else. They aren't going to give up their jobs and professorships just because a paper was published that says that what they do isn't very good, any more than a politician will quit because the economy is getting worse. They just find somebody else to blame.'

Dalina was still focused on Jinsong. She wanted to know what Jinsong thought of Ubanwa's point.

'OK – it should work like that, but it often doesn't,' Jinsong conceded, 'but what would a sociology professor do if she found out she was wrong about social class or gender, or whatever. Does she just quit her job and take up gardening?'

'Not when there's one-click and a teenage kid with a taste for expensive technology. But I don't think you can ever be proved wrong in social theory' said Dalina, amidst some laughter.

'Sounds like Lian's idea of heaven,' Jinsong smirked.

'You won't admit anything works if it hasn't been created in a laboratory. I've got an exam in a week and I'm prepared to try anything,' Lian replied.

'You might as well put a tooth under your pillow and summon the tooth fairy' said Jinsong.

'Do you think she should sit my exam for me, then?' Lian asked Dalina, and there was more laughter, but Jinsong had found another target.

'You are right about social theory, though. There's always a hundred books in the library that say the opposite to what you've just read. How can you say your opinion is any better than anyone else's? How do you know this is true?'

'Well, what is truth after all? How do we really *know* anything?' said Lian. 'I'm not asking if we are all dreams in the mind of somebody else, or how I know that this room still exists when I walk out if it. I'm asking whether or not sociology can show that what it says is correct; or is it just about who has the most popular point of view? This is what I don't like about social theory. It's that every conclusion seems to fit. You start with an idea you like, and then you think of some more ideas that fit with that one. Nobody can ever prove anything. There's nothing scientific about it.'

Now this rang several bells in Mila's head. It was the point that Jasmine had been making for several months. Jasmine was always trying to get Mila to see how inferior sociology was to a 'proper science'. She called it 'quoteology', because she said Mila quoted books that said one thing, and then books that refuted them, and books that refuted those books. It was all books about books about books. Sometimes authors seemed to be locked in mortal combat with others, in blood feuds stretching over years, each summoning the ghost of a dead German or Frenchman in support. There was no way of resolving these arguments one way or the other – no way of *proving* that one was right and one was wrong – so that everybody could move on. To Mila it seemed that clinical trials were one method of arriving at a final answer about some questions – although perhaps scientists did not take as much notice of them as they should. Maybe something like this approach could work for sociology too.

Dalina said: 'I suppose I was being a bit glib, Jinsong. You're asking if social theory is like scientific theories. I say no it isn't, because of the nature of the object of study – human beings in society – and the kind of raw data we build theories on.'

'You're saying the people we read for this seminar actually involve facts in their theories?' Jinsong asked incredulously.

'Data, but not always facts. The raw data is what you could call common sense, meaning everyday beliefs. Sociology's starting point ideally should be how people get by – what they do and how they understand what they do, their common sense. Common sense is the form of knowledge we use to live our everyday lives – the set of unspoken assumptions, past experiences, knowledge shared with other people – the thinking that we use both to guide our behaviour, make choices, and understand what is happening to us. It's a non-systematic, hence non-academic, sort of knowledge. Most social sciences simply ignore it for that reason.'

Dalina told them that sociology had a peculiar relationship with common sense; it was both a starting point and something from which to move beyond. Sociology often showed that one sort of common sense, 'what everybody knew', was wrong. This might mean it was wrong as an overarching system of thought, as an objective set of facts, but it could not be 'wrong' on an everyday level because it was what people used to get by. Sociology differed from philosophy, economics, and so on because it took as its starting point this sort of common sense. Dalina concluded: 'The basic difference between sociology and common sense is that common sense descriptions are usually justifications. I choose an action then justify it with common sense, whereas sociology tries to offer an explanation, an objective account that involves the often contradictory justifications people offer for what they do. It tries also to explain the many things people do that they don't offer justifications for because they never think about them.'

Coni was nodding at this. 'So you're saying that sociology has to be different from the natural sciences because physics and chemistry don't have to bother about how people make sense of their experiences at all. The raw material of the natural sciences is nothing to do with people's experiences and that makes it, in a way, much cleaner, and maybe even easier, when you are trying to find out the truth.'

Now Mila could not help joining in. She had rehearsed this conversation with Jasmine several times but the previous discussion had given her something new to think about. 'Is that true, Coni? Wasn't what we were saying earlier about scientists not doing proper trials, or ignoring results, not so far away from using common sense, or the knowledge scientists need to get by? And when they ignore results because it would be bad for their careers, aren't they using self-justifying knowledge? What if scientific knowledge is also social knowledge?'

Dalina told them that they had to start with a few basic assumptions about knowledge and she reminded them where they would have come across material on this in the required reading for the seminar. At this point, most of the students began leafing through their notes. Dalina said the first assumption, and the most important for everything else, was that knowledge was a human creation. This was the case on a basic level: we learned to interpret our sensory data – a baby learned to differentiate shapes, sounds, and so on. Some of these abilities were inherited, and then developed in different environments.

In one of the readings, Noam Chomsky argued that children had an innate ability to understand some fundamental rules of language. Again there was more sifting and the group tried to find Chomsky in their notes. According to Chomsky, said Dalina, we were born with a universal grammar which consisted of certain assumptions, or learning biases, that guided us in the acquisition of language. These biases allowed us to acquire language relatively easily – without, for instance, being told the explicit rules of that language. One of these was the *taxonomic assumption* which Dalina asked Coni to explain. Coni was happy to oblige.

'When my baby sister points to a black horse and I say, "horse", she knows I mean a category of objects, rather than the name of that individual animal, or a particular quality of that horse – she doesn't think that I mean that all animals that are black are horses.'

Dalina then carried on. 'Good. Now, on a deeper level, the terms we use to understand the world, the way we talk, the instruments we use to gather data, are all human creations. To some extent, they must reflect or embody the creator. For instance, the number zero has not always existed. It only came into being in the early Middle Ages, in Indian and then Arabic maths.'

'Yes, but that doesn't mean that zero didn't exist before then,' Jinsong said. 'It didn't just come into being when they invented it. The laws of nature are mathematical, and zero was discovered, not created.'

'But there's the question of *what* is discovered. What this means is that knowledge does not lie around like gold nuggets in the riverbed waiting for a prospector to sift it out of the silt,' the tutor continued. 'What we know is a factor of what we look for, and how we look for it, and how we classify it when we find it, which is partly based on what we know, or think we know, already. We are talking here about epistemology – the way knowledge is acquired and assessed. The way you evaluate competing explanations of the same event, or competing claims. To some extent we all have an epistemology without knowing that we do, such as that taxonomic assumption that Coni explained with her black horse.'

'Natural sciences have the best epistemology: experimental observation, comparison of results, replicating experiments,' Jinsong said. 'Compare this to sociology and what do you have? People digging up the same old corpses, zapping them with electricity and seeing if they walk. It's only concerned with what people think rather than what they know.'

Dalina asked for other members of the group to contribute ideas based on their reading and another student, Sam, said: 'Weren't there, I think, some ideas about society's general attitudes to rationalism and objectivity and the way science fitted into this?' he said, scanning his notes. 'There were examples of feminists and environmentalists arguing for science to be sensitive to cultural difference, environmentally aware and anti-sexist. Don't they call for scientists to abandon claims to objectivity and the idea that there's an external material world about which facts can be gathered by investigation?'

Another student, Assumpta, chipped in. 'Yes, I came across that too,' she said. And then she read from her notes. 'They argue that science, along with any truth claims it makes, are social constructs. And there is something here that says the boundary between science and pseudo-science is no less socially constructed than that between high and low culture. We should be no more obliged to accept the authority of science than we should have to accept the judgements of our schoolteacher about what is good and bad literature, apparently.'

Sam added, 'I think some of the extracts I looked at were saying that a lot of what Jinsong criticises in sociology is present in other fields of study: arguments from authority, categorisation of findings by expectations, discarding unwanted results, and so on.'

'Yes, but that's just science done badly,' Jinsong replied.

'It strikes me,' Lian added, 'that there are plenty of problems with knowledge in the natural sciences as well, and especially in those which most closely involve human beings as subjects, like medicine. Science asks, what do we know? Epistemology asks, how do we know? But how do we know what we know?'

'That neatly brings us to scientific knowledge as an object of sociological study in itself,' Dalina said, chuckling to herself, 'which we may all have forgotten is supposed to be the main focus of the seminar today! It's taken a long time to get there because I've had you chasing off at all sorts of tangents. Anyway, we have got here at last. Who is going to tell us about the two versions of the sociology of scientific knowledge, the weak and the strong programme?'

Using her notes, Ubanwa explained that in the weak programme, society shaped scientific knowledge quantitatively. Scientists were humans, and responded to the same incentives that other people did. For instance, some branches of science progressed quicker than others, because they were more fashionable, or more economic, or had better rewards, or attracted better funding and better scientists for any number of reasons. So more work would be carried out in some areas than others and, although lone geniuses might continue to make discoveries in unfashionable fields, simple resources would count. In some countries, the state might place limits on what could be studied for ethical, ideological, moral or religious reasons. For instance, in medical research the greatest return in pharmaceuticals might be in lifestyle drugs that modified moods or combated impotence. These products had the richest set of consumers and market advantage could be very profitable, so far more effort went into research and development of these products than did into, say, anti-malarial drugs whose consumers were likely to be poor.

Dalina stopped Ubanwa, so that Assumpta could say something.

'Jinsong just said that when scientists are discarding unwanted results, and so on, that's bad science, but there're a few other effects that aren't just doing it badly.' Assumpta looked down at her notes.

'These effects are down to identifiable institutional and cultural constraints and pressures. And there is something here called the "desk drawer" effect where studies that do not prove something tend not to be published, so skewing studies towards outcomes which show a positive outcome, and against those which do not show anything. Nobody wants to read a boring scientific paper that comes to the conclusion that nothing happened.'

'This works in sociology too, by the way,' said Dalina. 'Histories of science show that science often did not work in a scientific way but the guiding principle was that we were moving towards a better form of science, so problems like these were treated as side issues or temporary hiccups. David Bloor said that we should not just try and explain why knowledge went wrong, but how it went "right".'

Dalina said this was part of the strong programme in the sociology of scientific knowledge and asked Ubanwa to explain that for them. She said it could also be called social constructionism or constructivism. The idea was that society shaped scientific knowledge *qualitatively* and this idea relied on 'epistemic relativism.'

For the weak programme, science developed largely according to an internal process of reasoned discovery, which was channelled or distorted, or sometimes held up, by social forces (as when astronomers used to be burned at the stake). For the strong programme, this was an error, called teleology, which accepted science's claim to be different from other forms of knowledge in the way it developed. Several members of the group said they had problems understanding 'epistemic relativism' and Coni asked what it meant and what was it relative to.

Ubanwa rifled through her notes again and began reading a passage to them. 'Relative to the society, or subculture or subgroup in which it was developed, relative to the local culture. Rather than looking at how closely it reflects some underlying truth, science is treated only as a truth game with a particular claim to authority. Or rather, its claim to authority is that which scientists have been able to achieve through establishing intellectual dominance as part of the Enlightenment revolution. It is not only the limits or boundaries of knowledge that are socially constructed, but the content of it.'

Jinsong cut in to say he could see the argument that debates between rival scientists, or scientific schools of thought, or people who support competing theories, were played out as a truth game. Science was a human activity, and it shouldn't be too surprising – though people here seemed to be surprised by it all the same – that it was affected by the same greasy-pole climbing, backbiting, empire building, accepting of received wisdom, kissing up to those in power, that you saw in any other sphere of human activity that ended up making statements about things.

'Religion, politics, art, you see it anywhere. But there is one small problem with the postmodernist view of science as a truth game and reason as one dis- course among many. And that is: that it is completely wrong.' Jinsong said you could not say that science was simply one cultural discourse, because reality was always going to bite back. If you believed, like the Han emperors, that ingesting powdered jade would guarantee you eternal life, sooner or later you would find out that you were wrong. 'If you think that there can be no final truth to be arrived at, we might as well sit round this table discussing fashion tips.'

'What do scientists think of these theories? Do they know about them?' Mila asked.

'Of those who do, most scientists accept some or all of the weak programme,' replied Dalina. 'After all, they can see these kinds of things at work around them. But they are reluctant, to say the least, to take on board the consequences of the strong programme.'

'That makes sense though. They would have to stop work and go home if they agreed with it,' Sam said. 'It comes back to institutional interests – they won't accept the strong programme because it is not in their interest to.'

'But maybe they *should* give up and go home,' Jinsong said. 'If you're saying that scientific thought develops according to the impersonal working out of social forces, then they could all just go home, wait for the social forces to work, and hey presto! You say that science has no more truth content than mysticism, then why not become a mystic? All you need is some incense and a crystal, rather than a laboratory and a library. Or you could even become a sociologist of science: save on the incense.'

Mila was beginning to get slightly annoyed with the way Jinsong put his views into words so often and so easily (and always without seeming to look at his notes). She said, 'Well, clearly scientific advancement has to involve somebody actually doing something.'

Jinsong waved a finger at her. 'If that's the case, then you have to admit that mind comes into it somewhere. The interest group theory argument works both ways. It applies to sociologists, too.' Jinsong said you could see why sociologists might find this perspective attractive. It was hard to refute, especially if the refutation was contained in the original argument that nobody could make claims to authority and truth. But the root cause of all this criticism of science was sociologists' insecurity about the limitations of sociology. They thought – whatever they might say about it in their books and articles – that science *did* have greater claims to truth and objectivity than social science. This was why they tried to pull the carpet out from under the primary assumptions of science, even when they were benefiting from its methods and products. 'There's a bit of a mismatch here, though. Do social constructionists really not rely on electric light, or watch TV?'

Dalina said this was very clever. 'If one of them is tapping on his computer working on his latest tome and it crashes, does he phone an IT expert, or a psychic? Raymond Tallis makes the point that these thinkers never act as if their theories were true,' she said.

And Mila had to admit that Jinsong's point about the insecurities of sociologists really hit home. It summed up exactly how she always felt in any conversation she had with Jasmine about science. For some reason this made her a bit more annoyed, and a little reckless. She said: 'Sociologists are right to have an inferiority complex in one way: they don't know any science, or not much, anyway. And perhaps scientific knowledge is a more important *kind* of knowledge. I think that's the truth of what Jinsong said: that's the source of their inferiority.'

Then Mila went on to say, a little hesitantly, that this had big implications for the way sociologists studied science and they might even be the opposite of what you would think they would be. If sociologists didn't know much about science they could never be qualified to make any sort of judgement about the truth of science. If sociology was going to say anything about how scientific knowledge got made, it was going to have to avoid saying that a scientific theory got accepted because it turned out to be true.

Mila said she thought it would be OK for sociologists who wanted to write about how science got put together, and which bits got discarded, to pretend simply that nature, the thing against which all the truth claims are tested, did not exist. If they didn't do this, they were pretending to know more than the scientists – not more sociology, but more science. So, sociologists had to behave as if there was no real world to measure truth against and so they could not help but be relativists. They should look at – were only really qualified to look at – the way scientists agreed or disagreed according to the rules they played by.

Mila could not believe what she had said. She had given a short lecture on a subject she knew nothing about. She was worse than Jinsong, and what she had said seemed logical as she said it but now she was sure it must be nonsense. Dalina, however seemed pleased.

'Well, there is something to be said for taking an argument to its conclusion. The idea of proceeding as if the natural world was not part of the equation is put forward in the work of Harry Collins, who applies methodological relativism in researching science.'

Jinsong was unimpressed. 'But it's misleading. The natural world is part of the equation in some way. However much it is interpreted or seen through a paradigm, nature is independent of human actions. For instance, theories in physics suggested that it was possible to build a bomb using a fission reaction. It was built and tested, and then used. But if those theories had been wrong, the bomb would not have worked, no matter how much the local culture of physics said it should work. And if that had happened, the history of the Second World War would have been different.'

Mila thought that this would not alter the way sociologists approached the study of the science that led to the bomb. You would look at the way science was made relative to whatever criteria the scientists had for deciding that their experiments, or whatever, were good, you could not do it by saying such and such a theory was rejected because it was not true. But Mila did not say any of this. One long speech was quite enough and she was no longer feeling reckless, but Dalina was looking at her, smiling.

'Time's nearly up,' the tutor said. 'Last word, anyone? What did you read about knowledge and power?'

Assumpta read out something she had highlighted in her notes:

'Knowledge in our society is structured by power. Science is both the outcome and instrument of that power,' but, predictably, Jinsong was not going to let anyone else have the last word.

He told the group that arguing from power meant that you excluded the place of thought. The strong-programme people seemed to believe that nobody else – except for them – arrived at their conclusions through thinking. Ideas and mental events were 'just fireworks set off by the discourse monkeys sent out by the agents of power. To say that thought does not play some sort of a role in scientific ideas – even if power does too – is mad.'

To Mila's surprise, Coni stepped in. 'I don't know about the monkeys, but scientific discourse leaves a material residue that alters our way of living for better or worse – when you settle on a form of life, you can abandon it if you choose. You can quit the city's rat race and live on an island with some sheep for company and no cars for a hundred miles. But you can't uninvent the internal combustion engine or the pollution caused by it.'

As they packed up their books and notepads, Mila rehearsed what she might have said, if she had not been frightened of making another long speech. She thought that the strong-programme people were partly right. Scientific knowledge was a cultural construct, but not like any other, and this was not simply because of the authority given to science. It was the way that knowledge became independent of us, not just because it became imprinted on the social structure, like other forms of knowledge, but because it imprinted itself on the physical world, not always with an effect we would predict or even want.

The difference between sociological knowledge and scientific knowledge was that some scientific knowledge could have an effect across time, maybe for hundreds or thousands of years. It could become part of nature and its persistence would have nothing to do with whether human beings were aware of this knowledge. This was one good reason for thinking scientific knowledge was of a different order to sociological knowledge but maybe it was also a good reason for being glad you were a sociologist.

Later on, talking to Coni, Mila discovered they had learned something else from the seminar. People were reluctant to talk in Bertrand's seminar because he was so discouraging. Dalina was the opposite, but there were still problems with the dynamics of the group. Because Dalina made it so easy for people to contribute, this could create a situation in which one or two students dominated the exchanges. Coni and Mila had seen how Dalina had tried to head off this danger but it did not always work. There was clearly more to being a tutor than just being nice. Coni said she might tell Jinsong how interesting and stimulating Bertrand was: maybe he might decide to give Bertrand's seminar group a try? Mila sneezed.

'I think all that talk about alternative medicine has given me a cold.'

Visit the companion website at **www.palgrave.com/companion/ Bancroft-And-Fevre-Dead-White-Men-2e/** to access additional learning resources, including seminar questions based on the chapter's coverage, a jargon buster that defines key terms used in the text and a timeline which provides an overview of the development of sociological thought.

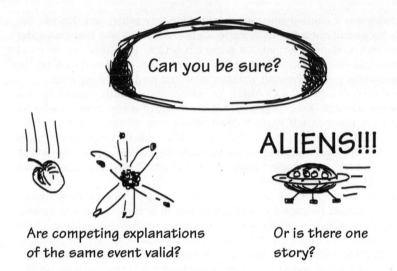

Can you be sure?

ALIENS!!!

Are competing explanations of the same event valid?

Or is there one story?

1. When it is said that we live in an information society or a knowledge economy it is implied that knowledge is easily recognised, and we can all agree on how to sift good knowledge from unreliable statements. There are many puzzles and disagreements on how to do that, or even if it is possible.

2. The placebo effect shows that a large part of the effect of a medicine can be attributed to what we expect it will do to us. So the effect exists, but is it 'real' or 'imaginary'? Related to that is whether knowledge about society can have the same status as knowledge about nature. Can it be as reliable and robust? Should it look like scientific knowledge and try to do what the natural sciences do – develop theories that can predict findings? Should science itself be treated like a social construct?

3. These are issues of epistemology – how you find and evaluate knowledge, and whether you should end up with one single account of whatever experience or event you are describing. For example, Chomsky proposed that every human being shared deep linguistic structures that made up the natural rules of language acquisition. One was the 'taxonomic assumption', by which we natively identify nouns with classes of objects. This is one example of a shared epistemology. Relativists on the other hand take the view that there are always multiple explanations and accounts and that any choice between them imposes a false sense of certainty.

4. Sociologists examine the natural sciences as being shaped by social forces to varying degrees, in the 'weak' and 'strong' approaches to the sociology of scientific knowledge. That perspective can be useful as it accounts for how some areas of research are far more developed than others – they are more politically convenient or socially beneficial. But it is a leap from saying 'nothing can ever be finally known' to 'nothing can ever be known at all'.

11
In Sickness and in Health

Mila wrapped herself in her dressing gown, and walked slowly and unsteadily from her bedroom to sit in the kitchen with Circe, Tuni and Jasmine. Every muscle in her body ached, her head throbbed, and her eyes were puffy and irritated, and yet she was feeling better than she had for days.

'Hello to the living dead. Don't look in a mirror darling,' Tuni said. 'It'll kill your self-esteem.'

'Would anything help, Mila?' asked Circe. 'I've got painkillers, strong painkillers, decongestant and three natural remedies including coneflower.' Tuni was outraged, or pretended to be. 'How unfair, you never offer any of that to me when I'm feeling ill!'

'That's because you've usually brought it on yourself,' Circe said primly, 'and you're a hypochondriac – last week you thought you had a brain tumour.'

Tuni was laughing. 'It's true, I had all the symptoms.'

'Why have you got so much of this stuff, Circe? Are you stockpiling supplies for assisted suicides or opening an alternative medicine store?' Jasmine asked.

Mila had been ill for nearly a week now and the women had settled into a comfortable routine of alternately fussing over and mocking her.

'You know what's the worst thing about being ill,' Tuni asked, 'you look weird.'

'No, it stops you working,' said Jasmine, 'and it makes everyone feel sorry for you.'

'We can't have that, sergeant-major Jasmine,' Mila smiled. 'I've missed one tutorial already and I've got to do a presentation at the next one. I've got nothing to present on, because I missed the lectures. I'll have to use Frank 'n' Stein. I think I'm about to feel very, very sorry for myself.'

'I think you need tough love,' Jasmine said. 'The place to start is to get you to a doctor. Who knows, maybe they'll even treat you?'

'I don't want to go out until I'm better,' said Mila.

'Good idea, go to the doctor when you're *not* ill.'

'I don't even know what's wrong with me.'

'Yes, you see, that's why there are these people called doctors …' Mila knew when it was better to give in.

An hour later, Mila's eyes had stopped being puffy, with the help of Circe's medicines, though they retained their redness. She sat in her room reviewing her tutorial assignment while she waited for Jasmine. The question she had to answer was 'Does Society Let People Do What They Are Best At?' To Mila, the recommended reading in Frank 'n' Stein did not appear very relevant to the question. It was about Talcott Parsons, a prolific writer from the 1930s to the 1970s, who had developed a theory called functionalism. Her lecturers' work was full of references to other writers, depending on their taste, or what they were writing about, but she could not recall them making a single reference to this man. The only reference to him she had come across in Frank 'n' Stein so far was the bit about him thinking that different roles for men and women 'complemented each other' to produce a stable social system.

Despite her lecturers' neglect of Parsons, her textbook told her that he was once the most influential sociologist in North America. Frank 'n' Stein's potted summary suggested he certainly had a high opinion of himself and that he was very ambitious for sociology. Parsons wanted sociologists to be like a set of doctors ministering to society:

> For Parsons, sociology was the science of a non-ideological age. Economics had emerged in the early days of industrial capitalism to help governments and society understand the new economic relationships that were emerging. Sociology could help us understand the new social relationships that characterised developed, capitalist societies. Parsons was trying to establish a model of how society worked, to synthesise the work of previous writers such as Marshall, Pareto, Durkheim, Weber, and others and explain features of modern societies like the nuclear family. He was also trying to solve a problem in sociology called the 'structure–action' problem.

Mila knew a little about the structure–action debate from several interminable discussions in tutorials which she had not seen much point in. You had one set of sociologists who thought sociology was all about the structures of society, those features of it that constrained people from doing one thing, or forced them to do another thing. Then there were other sociologists who thought sociology was all about the meanings people attached to what they did and the things they encountered. If she had paid much attention, it was simply to wonder why sociology could not simply do both of these things. She could not understand why you were forced to choose between action and structure. Maybe she simply didn't understand the problem. She turned a page and read.

> 'Action' means employing effort to use means for ends. A concept of action as financially self-interested behaviour had dominated classical economics. This had tended to divide human activity into rational and irrational action. Rational action was that which was of financial value to the individual concerned, irrational action was anything that did not have this goal as its end, and particularly, behaviour that appeared not to be in the person's own economic interests. Economic rationality is only one
>
> *Continued...*

kind of rational behaviour, however. All actions are rational, according to Parsons: they are oriented towards establishing and affirming commonly shared values.

For Parsons, action is never an isolated event. The economic rationality perspective, and many others, treats each act as an individual event and evaluates it in terms of its immediate consequences. Yet Parsons was sure people did not think in this way. They think about the future, the past, where they are and how their actions will affect others. Parsons called this the 'action chain'. Each act forms part of a sequence that connects it to a system of norms and values recognised by the participant.

Mila thought about the sympathy she had received from her friends just now – Circe's fussing intervention, Tuni's slightly self-centred humour, Jasmine's 'buck up and get on with it' attitude. What values were they 'establishing and affirming?' She knew they were all trying to show they cared about her, but Mila suspected that wasn't what Frank 'n' Stein were getting at. Mila wondered if the values they were demonstrating were how they expected her to deal with the situation, and how they would hope to behave themselves in a similar situation. This seemed more plausible. The values her friends were establishing and affirming were the values of a way of life.

Jasmine, she decided, had some of the Protestant work ethic she had heard about. Jasmine thought it was best for Mila to show her moral worth by not taking a little bit of illness as an excuse for shirking work and by making it clear she did not want to be ill. If she simply got on with things she would begin to feel better anyway: perhaps this would be God rewarding her upright behaviour by relieving her of her symptoms. Circe was like a Catholic Auguste Comte, the thinker who had influenced Durkheim. She thought Mila should trust in people who knew better than her and who could relieve her symptoms by applying their balms and potions, if only she would confess her illness to them. She also withheld her treatments from the sinful Tuni. Tuni was perhaps an interactionist, making Mila aware of the rule of sympathy for the afflicted by breaking it. That, or she was just a self-centred airhead.

This thought led to another. If Tuni sometimes seemed not to think before, or even after, she acted, she was not alone. Mila thought action was not always as considered or explicable as Parsons seemed to think. We often acted through habit or desire, sometimes from crazy impulse and mad intoxication. She felt herself start to drift into a doze – perhaps a side effect of the medication – when she was startled by Jasmine's sharp knock on the door. Circe was peering over Jasmine's shoulder.

'I'll walk with you to the doctor's, Mila,' Jasmine said. 'Better go before Circe tries to read your aura.'

***

Mila was called into the doctor's surgery and the doctor motioned her to sit. She quickly looked Mila up and down as she did so. Mila's patient history was also on view.

'What seems to be the problem?'

'I haven't been feeling too great.' The doctor left a pause. Mila felt her reply had been judged inadequate. 'Emm, I mean I've been unable to work ... I've been in bed all day, I'm tired all the time, my appetite has gone.' The doctor looked at her stubbornly red eyes.

'Are you upset or anxious about something: your studies, your family, problems with a boyfriend perhaps?'

Mila suppressed her annoyance. She expected the doctor saw hundreds of young women like herself every year: basically healthy but feeling vaguely, but persistently, unwell. 'I haven't been crying, it's not that. It's ... well, I don't know. I'm actually feeling better, a friend of mine gave me some medicine.' The doctor arched her eyebrows to express her surprise and disapproval. 'I just need a note for the course organiser to explain my absence,' Mila heard herself wheedle. This seemed to irritate the doctor more.

'I can't just hand out notes to every student who walks in here. And I'm very busy. If you have a cold there's nothing I can do, so you don't need a letter from me. Is there anything else?'

Mila shook her head, and mumbling a 'thanks for your time', left the surgery. She tramped back to her room with Jasmine, torturing herself with what she might have said to the doctor to justify herself. Back in her room, Mila was still consumed with embarrassment while she read Frank 'n' Stein's discussion of Parsons on 'the sick role'.

> Social phenomena should be studied because of their significance for society. This is the most enduring aspect of Parsons' work, and one which shows the power of his analytical approach. He firmly placed the experience of illness, and the role of the patient and the medical professional, as social experiences and roles. Sickness and health are part of the fabric of modern society. They are not biological phenomena independent of it. Being sick is a social experience and medicine is a moral, value-laden concern. It is oriented to requirements of individuals that are moral in expression, meaning they are about the fundamentals of society's continued existence. Parsons did not take sickness at face value, but sought to find out what social purpose was being fulfilled by allowing one set of people to define another set as ill or healthy. In this, medicine is like the function of the Protestant ethic in capitalism, which has nothing to do with its role in theology. Medicine tells Parsons about modern society much of what totemic religion told Durkheim about primitive society.

Mila was pleased and surprised to see that her guess about there being a connection between medicine and the Protestant ethic had turned out to be right. Then she dismissed it from her mind – it was just a lucky guess after all – and reflected on the rest of this passage. A doctor's letter had the power to excuse her from university work, in a way that a letter from her brother or Circe, would not. The document itself took on the power of the person writing it – or not really *their* power, but that of the social role they have. She thought about the role she and the doctor had played. The doctor had the right to ask questions about her, and she had to reply, even when no question was asked.

The sick role was performed, thought Mila. At first, this was a matter of her being unable to work, then it was being in the wrong place at the wrong time (in bed all day). Being unable to work, or unable to interact normally with others, and being in bed during daytime, were a violation of the normal social role. (Mila thought about what Jasmine would say about sociology students' role being to spend most of the day in bed.) To fit into the role, she had to show that she knew she was ill, knew why she was ill, and that she wanted to get better. Mila had tried a different tack – presenting herself to the doctor with physical ailments – but these meant nothing, apparently. They were reports on internal states which, unless accepted and validated by the doctor, had no worth in themselves.

Mila understood that Parsons intended something more here than that patients and doctors were trying to achieve a desired outcome. There was conflict and uncertainty between her and the doctor. The sick role allowed some people to be ill, and to take time out from work, while it maintained society's core values including the work ethic. There was an element of social control at play in the sick role. Circe refused to help Tuni when she was seen to have brought ailments on herself or exaggerated or imagined symptoms. To be acceptably ill meant being innocent, not responsible for the way you were. Tuni would have been a deviant patient.

Mila looked a little harder at her own behaviour and decided her action had deviated from the sick role in another way. She had gone to the doctor for purely instrumental reasons. She had not expected to get better because of it. She had medicated herself, a function that Parsons reserved for doctors alone. She had not been passive, and had challenged the doctor's interpretation of her symptoms. The doctor's disapproval of this may have been because she felt her role was being usurped, or because she preferred patients who would take their medicine. Perhaps the sick role had changed since Parsons wrote his article, or maybe it had only been like that for a short period of time, for middle-class Americans in the 1950s, or perhaps this had never been the case. She read on.

There is some evidence to suggest that Parsons was right about how the patient role would change. He predicted that the patient role would become more independent – and that the doctor would become more of a team member, an illness manager, than the bedside professional that he had been. This was exactly what did happen in affluent Western countries in the second half of the twentieth century. Patients began to behave like consumers, demanding information, specific treatments, and recognition for new illness conditions.

Mila read this over twice before she took it in. She had been right again! Maybe this time it was no fluke. Perhaps she was even getting used to applying theoretical ideas. Then she remembered the tutorial assignment question about people doing what they did best and she still could not make out what all of this discussion of doctors and patients had to do with it. But there was more to read:

Functional Differentiation and the Professions

This is a key feature of modern societies, according to Parsons. Industrial societies evolve towards ever finer structural differentiation. This means that systems are created which take on specialised functions. In medieval society, for instance, the family would have been an economic unit. It would have produced goods, it would have looked after its members, cared for the sick and the old. In modern societies most of these functions are taken over by the economy, the welfare state, the medical profession, professional carers, and the like. Doctors are one group in a set of people – the professionals – whose ethics are supposed to work for society rather than for themselves.

This was more than just an observation of how society developed a complex division of labour. Parsons thought that some of these systems became the places where ethics and values were played out. For instance, professions developed their own ethics. The medical profession required egalitarianism – every patient was treated equally. Doctors were not meant to act out of self-interest, but in the interests of their patients. Professional ethics operated in the general public interest. This was a way in which society adapted to resolve the ideological conflict between individualism and collectivism. However, this theory rapidly came under fire from all directions. Only some issues were defined as social problems for professionals to address, and the way in which they were defined reflected the power and interests of various sectors in society.

Mila began to write some notes for her presentation: 'a theory of functional differentiation doesn't see how medical systems reproduce social inequality. It tends to be interested in societal effects rather than content.' So presumably, thought Mila, the doctor could be performing voodoo rituals and this would suffice. That would be her doing 'what she did best'. Frank 'n' Stein said functional differentiation was like organic differentiation in the body and then she was back to structure–action again.

Parsons attempted to combine structure and action in a general theory. Sociology needed a general theory. It needed to be able to explain why social order (in other words, society) was possible. He developed insights from anthropologists, such as Alfred Radcliffe-Brown and Bronisław Malinowski, who had developed functional explanations for all sorts of human behaviour in the cultures they studied. They analysed actions and relationships as aspects of organised systems. All sorts of activity – religious rituals, kinship systems, sexual taboos, even joking and swearing, could be explained in terms of their contribution to the integration of the social system. They could see how particular practices, such as magic, fulfilled certain needs. Each contributed to one of four sub-systems or institutions: kinship, religion, economics, and politics. Talcott Parsons developed this in terms of modern societies. He argued that societies had four basic 'imperatives' or needs. These were adaptation, goal attainment, integration, and latency. Adaptation referred to the practical, biological needs of society's members that have to be serviced. Everyone needs food and shelter. Society has to adapt to the environment, or adapt the environment to it, in such a way that these needs can be met. Goal attainment meant society's declared fundamental values, such as prosperity, liberty, the pursuit of happiness. Integration was the process of ensuring society's members shared these goals. Systems such as religion and the education system exist to socialise individuals into shared values. Latency meant the requirement on all societies and institutions that they reproduce themselves over time. Economics ensures adaptation, politics goal attainment, religion and other belief systems, and cultural institutions service integration, and kinship ensures latency. There are many institutions which serve several functions, so the family is both a reproductive and socialising unit, and sometimes is also economic.

Functionalism is more than that, however. It tries to show how the system selects and evolves functions. Society evolves like organisms do. Conflict can be functional because it emerges from society adapting to changes in one or more systems or in the environment.

Mila considered whether student life could be seen in that way. There were plenty of socialisation and transitional rituals which were meant to transmit what being a student meant. The formal part, studying, writing essays and so on, was only a small part of that. She continued to write notes:

The university is also a system that assigns people to roles and gives them status. Like the medical system, the university is meant to instil values and abilities in students. But they may be interested in very different things. Students may see university as mainly about socialising, or finding a partner, or making connections – getting up the ladder.

So the university could be involved in recreating inequality. What had Parsons called it – latency? The university system was partly involved in reproducing society, socialising the next generation, but it also propped up divisions that already existed. She picked up Frank 'n' Stein again.

Criticisms of Functionalism

There have been many criticisms of functionalism. It has been said that functionalists focused too much on order and consensus, and only allowed for evolutionary conflict, whereas some conflicts are fundamental, for example there are conflicts about the type of society that we want to live in. In fact, functionalism was concerned more with equilibrium. Society has to change and adapt a balance of forces but also keep itself together as a going concern, just as walking involves constantly losing your balance and recovering. Stability and being static are not the same, and static unchanging societies, which are suddenly faced with fundamental challenges to their way of life, tend to be the ones which lose their equilibrium.

The French and Russian revolutions are good examples of systems which could not adapt quickly enough, or at all, and were swept aside, in each case with great loss of life and property and leading not to freedom but to terror and, in the case of the Russian revolution, enslavement. However, it is easier to declare oneself to be opposed to functionalism than to actually not be functionalist. Many critics of functionalism are themselves functionalist – indeed, most sociological explanations rely on a common-sense or elaborated functionalism. Any reference to the social order, or the usefulness of some behaviour or other, implies a functionalist explanation.

Mila could see how Parsons' version of functionalism fell out of favour, because it upset anyone who thought of themselves as progressive. It distinguished between primitive and complex societies. It justified the existence of professional power over lay people, and justified privilege and status inequality. It had a clear sense of progression in history, and worst of all, claimed that it would be better if we stuck to doing what we were expected to do.

Mila finally had some material for her talk. Parsons thought society consisted of social systems that performed one of the four functions, adaptation, goal attainment, integration, and latency. These systems ensured people did what was best in terms of each function, whether it was best for *them* or not. So, according to him, society was not ensuring that people did what they were best at, or what they wanted or would have liked to do, but that they did what was best to keep society running. So what happened when people's 'best' didn't work? She thought of her father: he had been 'doing his best' when he ruined the lives of many people, including his family. He had been adhering to the system requirements of making money. There were some situations where systems could undermine themselves, where people followed the values too closely, she thought, or where one element of the system came to dominate the others. In those circumstances, we could become slaves to economics, or to politics, or to religion.

Mila felt the basic structure of her presentation was becoming clear and thought it was now time for her to go back over what she had read, filling in the gaps. But, before she did so, she leafed through to the end of Frank 'n' Stein's discussion of Parsons and, as she did this, her eye was caught by a quotation from the man himself:

> 'the valuation and its expression in recognition and status, of ability and achievement by such universalistic standards as technical competence has, particularly in the occupational field, a far wider scope in modern Western society than in most others. No other large-scale society has come so near universalising "equality of opportunity". An important consequence of the universalistic pattern in these two fields is the very high degree of social mobility, of potentiality for each individual to "find his own level" on the basis of his own abilities and achievements, or, within certain limits, of his own personal wishes rather than a compulsory traditional status.'

Then Mila noticed the date of the first publication of the piece that this extract had been taken from. It had been published in 1947, a generation *before* the civil rights movement began to bring about fundamental changes in American society. How could Parsons have been so smug about a society that still had racial segregation and where racist intimidation, violence, and murder routinely went unpunished? The American civil rights movement grew up in a time and a place where people's best meant refusing what the system required of them. Mila thought of the way people had broken laws and customs that separated black and white people. In doing so they risked their own lives. At the time, many people, not just prejudiced white people, had thought that they were troublemakers. They had not been contributing to the system's functioning, but had thrown a spanner in the works of the system that was there.

It is rare that people actually watch themselves learning and see their interests and opinions changing as they come to understand the world in a different way. Most of the time this process is so slow that we only become aware that it has happened a long time afterwards. We are almost always unconscious of our self-transformation but there are special moments of heightened awareness when we can get a brief glimpse in the mirror at the moment when we learn. At these times, it is possible to understand both how we are changing and why this is happening. This was one such rare moment for Mila.

She thought of the civil rights movement and she saw in her mind's eye a picture of nine school pupils walking to school alongside soldiers carrying rifles on their shoulders. Mila was suddenly aware of how much she had changed from the girl who first heard of the American civil rights movement when she was at school, not so long ago. She had been interested, but indifferent, and now she cared about those people, now she wanted to be on the right side. She was not sure she would always know how to recognise the right side yet, but she did not want to be a bystander. She would not want to have been one of those who stayed on the sidelines in the civil rights era. She wanted to grow up and take her part in the great project of making her world.

Another remembered image came into Mila's mind: the image of the woman putting a flower in the muzzle of a gun. Some big ideas could be better expressed in pictures than words, she decided, and then Mila thought 'I want to judge what the big ideas are myself. I have had enough of checking them out with other people. That was a silly idea. I guess I knew it was because I always sought out people like my aunties who would give me a sympathetic hearing. If I didn't get the right reaction – from Arun's silly friend or his father or from Doni – I would put it down to narrowmindedness or prejudice. After that I took to making up my mind whether something was a big idea or not after I had talked about it and when people seemed impressed or, at least, didn't ridicule it.'

Mila laughed out loud at this point. She thought she had been like the person who pretends to trust a decision to the toss of a coin and then keeps tossing it until the right answer comes up. She had known what she thought anyway, she was making all the decisions all along and she was deciding in favour of sociology – why? She believed sociology was worthwhile because it had something to do with civil rights, and justice and equality. That's what she thought it was invented for: to find out how to improve things, how to change society, so that it worked better for everyone. Of course lots of people didn't like it, understand it, or think we needed it. Lots of people would even be hostile to it because they had much to lose. But even if she were in a marginalised minority, and sometimes thought abnormal or even a threat, she wanted to try to be on the right side of the line.

But that notion of testing the big ideas, finding out if they worked by explaining them to others, now seemed ridiculously childish to Mila and, more than this, it seemed irrelevant. Reading about Parsons had convinced her that the book was never going to be closed on any of these ideas because the object they sought to explain was a moving target, for example society's problems were changing all the time. What was more, sociology itself would make mistakes, big ones, and follow paths which led to dead ends.

But even if she had to go up and down those wrong paths and start again every time, Mila knew this was the only way to go. She thought she should have realised that when she was at the exhibition with Arun. As he said, being at university is about becoming a person who can learn, developing yourself, not being given the keys to the secrets of the kingdom. Later on, Mila had found that the ideas that worked produced their own problems. It had happened a couple of times but it was awful with Ana. Even though Ana was obviously in distress,

Mila had kept on single-mindedly explaining sociology in order to justify her own presence at university. The big idea had got in the way of being a decent person and a reliable friend. If sociology was going to be important to her, she had to remember it was the quest that was important and she should never think she knew all the answers and never stop listening.

Mila took off her glasses and blew her nose but she still had a moment more of reflection on her transformation. She had been foolish to think she would need to know what the big ideas were in order to make up her mind to stay or go. The big-ideas test was over but that didn't mean she had found out what all the big ideas were – far from it. Social life was just too complex, too interesting, too fast-changing. Parsons seemed to think he had been given the final word but it was still far too early to say. Parsons and any others like him who thought they had discovered the keys to the kingdom were doomed to fail. We needed hundreds of theories, and we needed to mix them up and synthesise them, and discard what was no good, revise and try again. She was smiling ruefully to herself. What a stupid idea it was to give people who knew much less than me about my own development the right to decide whether I go or stay – that was so childish, she thought. She should just be grateful she never really took it seriously but, as of now, she was going to be fully conscious that she was responsible for her own destiny.

The mirror was dimming now, but there was still time for Mila to realise that the painful but invaluable process of learning that afternoon she spent with Ana in the hospital also showed her that her search for validation had been in some way related to her father. She decided now it had been a way of diverting attention from something she had to face up to. If you want to be responsible for your destiny, she told herself, then here's your first task. Face up to the flood of public judgement that came after the trial. And then she cried a little, not because she thought this would be too much for her but because she actually felt relieved. Before she returned to her notes for the presentation, she composed her own doctor's note for her tutor:

> *I would like to explain my absence from the previous class.*
> *I have attempted to obtain a doctor's*
> *letter as requested. However, my diagnosis, unlike Parsons',*
> *remains uncertain.*

● ● ● ● ●

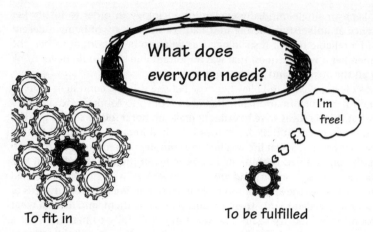

To fit in   **To be fulfilled**

1. Western societies emphasise personal fulfilment as a goal, so it is hard for their citizens to understand that there might be other goals motivating societies – such as service, duty, obligation. Yet these served and still serve many societies. Thinking of yourself in terms of function, how you fit in, is as typical if unglamorous. Functionalism is the kind of sociology that examines how all the different activities and roles people engage in serve a purpose. Talcott Parsons divided these functions into adaptation, goal attainment, integration and latency. By that he meant that society must serve its members' basic needs, have fundamental goals, ensure they are shared, and reproduce itself.

2. He took his idea in surprising directions. For example, he showed how being sick and healthy are social roles. They served social functions. Doctors are given the power to define someone as sick, and so free from their normal social obligations. Medicine is a great study for sociology because medical science has to work with the most bewildering spread of human behaviour and human problems. Often, medical science has to grapple with forms of behaviour that appear to be consistent, 'naturally occurring' diseases, only to discover that they are nothing of the kind. Psychiatric conditions are especially prone to that.

3. Parsons thought societies evolved as much as organisms do. In modern societies there was an ethical direction to this evolution. Functional differentiation involves a complex division of labour that produces new classes, such as the professions, which are supposed to embody an ethic of generalised social responsibility.

4. There is a strong divide in sociology between functionalists, who look at systems and how behaviour contributes to them, and others, such as symbolic interactionists, who examine meaning and the creation of social order in individual interaction. Functionalism has been criticised for a limitation of defining people as passive 'actors' playing out scripts, reproducing patterns and enacting norms, and for an overemphasis on stability and an inability to account for conflict.

12
In Two Acts

asmine narrowed her eyes at Mila. 'Your friends will desert you, your achievements will become dust, you will die alone and betrayed,' she said fiercely.

Mila met her gaze. 'Who cares for the ravings of a madwoman like you?' she replied in an equally emphatic voice. 'Go back to your weaving, you good-for-nothing hussy.'

The two women were sitting in the kitchen as usual. Mila was taking a drama class and Jasmine was helping her read lines from a play. Jasmine was playing the character of Cassandra, a figure from Greek mythology who had been cursed to know the tragic future but to never have her warnings believed. She was fated with foresight but powerless to stop what she saw from coming to pass. 'This play is a bit silly,' said Jasmine, calling a time-out.

'This woman keeps telling her menfolk that they're all doomed, but nobody takes her seriously because they think she's a lunatic. Why doesn't she just stop telling them what's going to happen?'

'I suppose the irony is that if she does stop telling them the truth, they will be more likely to believe her,' Mila wrinkled her mouth wryly. 'She was the classic tragic heroine, knowing everything but able to do nothing.'

'Rather like being a sociologist – you think you know everything about people but that knowledge doesn't seem to help you make them better people, or help you act better.'

Mila said this might be because nobody paid any attention to sociologists.

'It's true, though,' Jasmine held to her point like a hyena attaching itself to a wildebeest, 'if you learn about sociology, does that make you a better person?'

Mila had begun to learn to parry Jasmine's thrusts. 'That would be like saying that as an engineer you should be able to design artificial limbs for yourself; or if you were a doctor that you should be able to give yourself a heart transplant. It's more like if you're an engineer, you can look at a spider's web and understand what the spider is doing to create it, what makes the web so strong, even if the spider itself does not understand what it is doing in engineering terms. The spider is able to create the web without having taken an engineering degree.'

'The spider doesn't sit down and draw a set of plans. Humans can do that – it's what makes us human. But a lot of the time, what we do doesn't involve making plans,' said Jasmine.

'That's true,' Mila said, 'the actions we take make and remake society, or the group we belong to, without us consciously intending to do so, or thinking too much about their consequences. Sociologists have to think like that, though, and study our actions and see how they contribute to making a bigger whole.'

As usual, Jasmine wasn't satisfied. 'That seems very unconscious – as if we were ruled by the hand of fate, like Cassandra, but without the foresight. I believe we are in charge of our destinies.'

'Sociology can sound like that,' Mila agreed, 'you know, as if we are fated to live certain lives, take decisions that only appear to be free but aren't. That would be a tragedy if it were the case, but that's because we get things backwards. Most films, plays, and so on, do the same thing – they start out with an idea of where they want the characters to end up – the characters in the play don't know that, but you do. In romantic films the writers want the two attractive leads to end up together, the girl next door and the human rights lawyer, rather than her and the businessman who poisons the environment. Every action leads up to that. The actors have to act like they don't know it's going to happen.'

Mila thought that, when Frank 'n' Stein explained in the book why people did what they did, it seemed to be written as if every action people took was done with the aim of making things turn out as they did. As if everyone was following preordained scripts. Indeed, Frank 'n' Stein sometimes called people 'social actors', as if unwittingly admitting this view of things. She sensed this was not completely wrong – people did appear to follow scripts sometimes, but perhaps it could just appear as if that was what they were doing. She wondered what she would think if she had been researched by a sociologist and then written about like that, or what she would feel if she were a character in a play reading about her character. How would Cassandra explain what she was doing, if you could ask her?

'What's the assessment for your drama class?' asked Jasmine, ever practical, interrupting her thoughts.

'We all have to write and produce a short play, which will be performed in front of the class,' Mila replied. 'Some of the students are being highly experimental; one has put together a stage version of a cartoon sitcom. He painted his actors' skin yellow and made them act in only two dimensions.' Not a bad imitation of what many academics do when they are writing about people's behaviour, she thought.

Mila mulled over their conversation later on when she was trying to think of a theme for her play. She wanted to introduce this problem into it, this sociological problem – about people's conscious awareness of what their actions mean, what purpose they have. Often sociologists seemed to have written a script for people to follow, or allowed the hand of 'society' to do it. The problem was: could we have actions without a script? Did the actions write the script? Or were they just set responses to conditions? This was the same problem that Parsons had tried to deal with: reconciling structure and action, or structure and agency as it was sometimes called.

Some sociologists thought that human actions were best understood as outcomes of, or responses to, structural conditions. Others thought you had to start with what people did, the work that they did, to put their world together, to give specific meaning to specific actions. Mila still felt that sociology should be able to come up with a way of having both but she was not convinced that Parsons' theory did solve the problem. She felt like she was still bouncing between each one. The example she had used earlier was nagging at her. Were people like the spider, their actions making a web without ever knowing it was a web they were making? Or were they like a fly caught in a web other people had made? She was feeling a bit like a fly caught in a web herself, struggling but not finding any escape. She confessed this to Jasmine, who was enigmatic.

'Why don't you make your play about that, then?' and left it at that. Mila realised the significance of this remark later. A script can be like a web that traps our actions, or, in a way, like a maze that is designed to bring us back to a certain point, no matter what route we take. In the idea Mila was forming, the web would be created with the character's own actions – the true meaning of 'tragedy', which is not just something unfortunate happening to a character, but when their bad luck is the result of them trying to do right. She explained her idea to Jasmine. 'The play is going to be in two acts. The idea is that the central character moves from one act to a second act and the same actions are all rein-terpreted in a different context to have an entirely different meaning or different consequences. The first, that he is a hero; the second, that he is a coward and a traitor. But in each, he can't change his actions; they seem to him to be the only ones possible. The tragedy of the play is that his awareness of what is happening does not mean that events will unfold differently. So it's like Cassandra except with this character, he spins his own web for himself.'

In spite of Mila's confidence, she still needed to understand why this would have happened – could her character have agency or not? How could she explain why a character might be driven to take self-destructive actions? At the moment, though, she was more consumed with finding a convincing theme and setting for the play.

The following evening the two friends attended a screening of a classic gang-ster film. It was set among a Mafia family in the USA during the 1960s. The main character, the Mafia boss, had somewhat reluctantly inherited his Mafia empire from his father. He had to deal with the obligations on him to keep the family together and its members in line. He dishes out violence to others. Although gruesome, this violence was never random. Betrayal of the family was the worst crime in his eyes and would mean cold-blooded execution of the guilty party.

Despite the fact that he was a criminal and ordered terrible things to happen to others, the boss was a character that those who saw the film liked, or at least, respected. Indeed, respect was a big theme of the film – it made a big deal out of who offered the boss respect, who received respect and who didn't. The main character himself, despite the power he wielded over his empire, seemed at times pathetically keen to be accepted as a legitimate businessman and pillar of the com-munity, to be loved by his wife and children, to be accepted by American society.

The two women left the film chatting excitedly about what had happened in it. Jasmine found the behaviour of the family a bit outlandish, especially its 'code of honour', which everyone kept referring to, but which people also violated when it suited them. 'They're always going on about honour in these films but they aren't very honourable people. They rob and murder, beat people up,' she said.

'I think that honour doesn't mean behaving nicely,' said Mila. She told Jasmine it was more a particular kind of action and she tried to explain what she had read in Frank 'n' Stein about honour being the positive social estimation put on behaviour that exemplified the values of a particular group of people.

Jasmine thought it was more simple than this. 'Honour is where you can't back down because you've lost face. Like in cheap martial-arts films.' She adopted a kung-fu stance and shouted: 'You insult my honour.'

Mila remembered an author who had written a lot about honour, a sociologist that she had come across in her anthropology class. Pierre Bourdieu had studied the Kabyle people in Algeria and written about the ways in which honour was a big part of how they rated one another, as being high status, powerful, or influential. Not only that, honour governed a lot of their actions – although they were seldom explicit about it, and would think you very stupid or ignorant if you asked them why they did what they did. Economic exchanges, buying and selling, marriage and everyday interactions were about establishing and keeping one's honour. It was something that all group members subscribed to or at least acknowledged, even if they were at the bottom of the heap. Honour, according to Bourdieu, was group values in action; but also recreated in the moment of action, the moment of behaving honourably. Remembering this, Mila told Jasmine that: 'Honour isn't just about one individual being insulted and beating the hell out of someone in return – like you see in a lot of martial-arts films, or in action movies where the hero's best friend is killed and he goes on a revenge rampage. Honour in that film meant upholding the values of the family, and the Italian-American community that the family was a part of. That meant that even if you were from a rival family, you would hold someone in contempt if they betrayed an opposing family – as it was violating the code of honour that you all relied on.'

'What is the "code of honour"? Can anyone give me a copy of the code of honour? Is it like the government regulations for foreign students studying here, with rules for every conceivable situation?' said Jasmine, still not in a mood to take this seriously.

Mila said it meant that honour compelled a specific kind of action; but not in the sense of being rule-following behaviour. It was not like that because you couldn't have rules for every conceivable situation you might come across. Even in fairly simple and non-complex societies nobody could conceive of every possible situation, or would want to. She told Jasmine: 'Our spidery friend doesn't have that problem – there are only a few "moves" it can make to create a web, and they either work or they don't.'

Mila said a code of honour consisted of at most only a few explicit rules. If you were to ask the mafia boss in the film what he thought honour was, he would probably say it was having the right attitude: respect for the family, going to church, not butchering your rival on his daughter's wedding day. A 'disposition', she remembered, was what Bourdieu called it: 'A stance towards other people who are honourable or who should be honourable, a set of attitudes towards other people and one's world.'

Back at home, Mila mulled over her evening's entertainment. Honour was one way of compelling action, which made it a good subject matter for drama. But, she thought, in modern society most action was not compelled by honour – although respect was something people cared about, in the form of status. A lot of action was compelled by desire, necessity, following rules, the expectations of others, social forces, and so on. There were many frameworks of action, many structures. Did they all fit together, though, and, if so, how or, more importantly, where? Was there something that generated these frameworks of action? She continued reading about Bourdieu in Frank 'n' Stein and came upon the ideas that appear in most of his work – habitus, field, and capital. It seemed that the first of these, habitus, created the set of dispositions or attitudes Mila had mentioned in her conversation with Jasmine.

Bourdieu calls habitus the 'structuring structure'. It is the embodied sensibility that generates the set of practical logics and often unreflecting predispositions that govern day-to-day life. Habitus appears to us as 'second nature'. Habitus is what allows you to cope with the future. It brings the future into being without being oriented towards it. Habitus answers, or attempts to answer, a philosophical problem, that of the structure–agency divide. It is an attempt by Bourdieu to bridge this structure–agency divide by conceiving of how structures can work through agency.

Field is the context of action, the arena whose boundaries are set and landscape is shaped by power relations, by objective circumstances. There are many fields or domains of action. As a metaphor we might consider the field of play in soccer – it has agreed (if apparently arbitrary) rules, like the offside rule, and borders – the penalty box, the lines at the edge of the pitch. Now imagine if the field was not flat but one team played permanently up a slope; or another team had the right to redraw the lines as play went on (and choose the referee, call time, and so on). This is where structure comes in. For Bourdieu, it is not all in the mind, but in the end even the most powerful player is constrained. They cannot abandon the game; they cannot step outside the stadium.

Fields contain objective limitations on action. In the scientific field, it is the case that only certain people are allowed to 'do' science in particular locations and conditions. They can only be people who are qualified as scientists, in places called laboratories. Simply putting on a white coat and looking through a microscope would not mean you were 'doing science'. Field makes for the social and economic conditions of production and realisation of habitus; fractures, conflicts, and all. A field is a network of relations between positions, like hierarchies, or distinctions between types of people, or types of action. Field is what distributes capital in all its forms: resources, cultural, political, status, economic. Fields give value to capital (such as educational qualifications) but rely on others recognising their value, so there is an intersubjective element in field.

Mila thought she could understand this. For a Mafia family, capital might consist of their status, reputation, contacts within the police and the local government, various small corruptions that allowed their business empire to run. Field would be the underground economy, the state, the laws. Field gave value to capital. So, Mila reflected, her education – a form of capital – was only of value in a field in which it was accepted as such by other people. Her knowledge of social theory would not be of value in a criminal underworld where connections, the ability to do deals, display front, and convincingly threaten the use of violence were respected qualities. She couldn't be a gangster, because she couldn't go around threatening people.

In Bourdieu's theory, habitus existed between capital and field. It existed where there were individuals. Action (or practice, as Bourdieu called it) was generated in a spiral between field, capital, and habitus. Habitus was the location of action and practice, so it was always the point of force, but it was not (unlike symbolic interaction) explicable in itself. Practice was logical without having logic as its principle. Habitus was formed through 'experience' (this process of spiralling between capital and field). The process of selecting from past experience – of learned forgetting and re-narrating – was one element of practice. Appropriating multiple experiences as the singular 'experience' that constituted the self's orientation to practice was another form of practice, a practical reflexivity operating within a person's own life, their biography. Habitus was practical, in that we learned by doing, not just observing or being told what to do. This meant that we learned our place in the world – we learned what we could and could not say and what was appropriate, or not, for us.

This reminded Mila of her old story of playing football with the boys; girls in many societies learned early on not to play boisterously; they absorbed that physical disposition towards their own bodies. But she also felt she now had some sense of the world in which a gangster might live, or a way to make sense of it.

Mila started to write a short drama in which the main character was one of a mobster's 'family', although not literally a relative. Betrayal and honour would be her theme. She had a setting for the play: an organisation riddled by betrayal, which was run on the basis of honour and power. What would be the objective structures that would make the field? The head of the family, Boss No. 1, would set his henchman on the trail of finding out who had been selling them out to a rival organisation. In the first act of her play, the man tracked down the culprit, found him, and interrogated him before killing him – just as the boss wanted. In the second he did the same, but this time the traitor was the boss's son. The man would go through with the execution anyway, obeying the boss's orders, knowing that he would in turn be killed for having done away with the boss's son. In doing so, he was doing honour to the values of their 'family' that demanded that traitors were executed, knowing that he would suffer as a result. That was his honourable code and he would affirm it with the ultimate sacrifice.

'I still don't get how he can just do something that would destroy himself,' Jasmine commented when Mila explained the idea to her. 'It seems a bit too noble for a murderer.'

'I think his actions don't have to be meant as noble to appear as noble. Jasmine, have you ever done something where immediately after you thought, "Why on earth did I do that?" The kind of thing you may forget on the spot, or regret for ever afterwards. You put these actions down to a moment of madness, or stupidity, but your brain did not shut down when you were doing it. We like to pretend that these actions, these impulses, are not us, don't represent us. A sociologist called Pierre Bourdieu would say that they do, more than anything else. They are what we do when the mind isn't looking. You know that feeling when you read or see something someone has done and you know that it's wrong, and your first thought is: "Aaargh – how could they have been so stupid?" Bourdieu says we should rephrase that – the question becomes: "How could that person have thought that that was the only way of doing things?" – and take that seriously. When you have that thought about someone or something, you should always stop and think because there might be people in the future thinking the same thing about you.' That's what I'm trying to do, Mila thought: I want to explain that moment of apparent madness that leads to tragedy.

'I think that now and then, but it's always something I intend,' Jasmine interjected. Mila felt herself treading out over the ice.

'When sociologists observe people doing things, and write down what they do, we create a drama, a drama of life, in which it appears that the people we're studying are actors in a script written for them by someone else. It appears as if they're doing what they are doing just for our benefit, as if all action takes place in order to be observed. But who's writing that script? Not you, not me, not anyone but themselves. If so, how do they know what to do? How do two different people reach an end point without either of them knowing what that end point is, or consciously deciding to aim for it?'

Mila said that if you took a scene from a play, or film, or television drama, and tried to interpret it, you could only get so far if you thought that the meaning of it was contained entirely within the interaction of the characters, which was what many social scientists tried to do when they observed people or when they wrote theories of interaction. 'Habitus' was what each character brought with them to the scene: they had a history and they had a set of objective characteristics that had an existence outside the scene.

'What characteristics are objective and who decides?' Jasmine asked.

'For instance, you're watching a soap opera in which one woman has had a daughter by her husband's brother. Only she knows this. Her daughter doesn't, her husband doesn't, and the brother doesn't know she is his child. Only you – and the mother – know this objective truth of the situation, and given that you then understand a lot more about it. You can see why the mother tries to keep her daughter and her brother-in-law apart. She does not want them to get too close and start to suspect the truth.

If you tried to work everything out from the interaction itself, you might assume that she thought the brother-in-law was a bad influence, or had designs on her daughter, for instance.'

'Which would all be equally plausible in a soap opera, I suppose, which is why I don't watch them, ever.'

'It goes much deeper than that. It might include someone's relative power. So, the wife doesn't confess because if she does her husband can divorce her and claim her daughter on the grounds of her unfaithfulness – perhaps this is a society in which women have very little power in these matters, and which values fidelity among women very highly. These features of the situation are most likely to be hidden.'

'The wretched soap opera just put me off, Mila. Think of another example.' Mila tried to think of an example Jasmine would be familiar with, but could not get her mind off the drama class. 'We did a session of improvised theatre. Anything can be said or done; there's no script, just actors playing characters. The characters, or the director, give you the motivation and your "cognitive structure"; for instance; you are a vengeful woman out to right a wrong done to her by another character in the play. Very quickly your actions prompted other actions that produced a storyline; there was no single person writing the story. The responses of the others were contained in the actions of each performer – they anticipated the others' actions while they were still being formed and began to formulate their own responses when they were being performed. Every interaction was full of these anticipations. It was like a collection of potential being made real – one footballer running towards another and trying to anticipate which direction they will move.'

Mila told Jasmine that you had to anticipate what other people would do when you acted on the basis of your habitus. That meant we could not reduce the meanings of actions to the individuals' conscious intentions. Interaction was not free, but took place within the objective structures of the habitus. In Mila's play, the lead character terminated Boss No. 1's son knowing that there was a very good chance he would have his brains blown out. This meant that you could not look objectively at a character in a play and say that she should have done this or done that, because in doing so you were, as Bourdieu put it, 'substituting the observer's relation to practice for the practical relation to practice.' You were assuming that each character had every option open to him or her, to choose from a limitless field of possibilities. The henchman's code of honour was a habitus that had become second nature. Mila realised she had the title for her play: 'Second Nature', but Jasmine was still was not fully sold on what habitus actually was. Could you find it anywhere? Mila did her best to explain what she had read in Frank 'n' Stein.

Bourdieu said habitus consisted of what every human has – the ability to relate with other humans through symbols (linguistic, pictorial, aural, pointing at objects). In truth, habitus is very hard to show (but not hard to find) because it appears to us as what is natural. What is seen as natural is unquestioned, as nobody thinks that there is anything to question. Habitus is congealed history, but history forgotten. Bourdieu was trying to explain the way that our actions appeared to be well organised, but were not, not in the sense of having been organised that way by someone. As Bourdieu has it: 'objectively organised as strategies without being the product of a genuine strategic intention.'

Mila said that, according to Bourdieu, every reaction was contained within every action. There were two major errors in understanding action. The first was to see a mechanical action–reaction at work. Every action was produced mechanically by the environment and the stimulus the individual received, like that wretched spider. The second was too see what Bourdieu called 'teleology' – assuming that everything took place because people wanted to arrive at the end point they did arrive at. The spider's web was an end point, sure enough, but the outcomes people produced rarely got made in this simple way. The spider responded to a very limited set of factors in its environment but in the actions we took, the actions of others and our anticipation of them fed back into what we did.

'Isn't that just your sociological idea about there being rules that we follow,' said Jasmine, 'stating the completely obvious?'

'No. According to Bourdieu, social life is underdetermined by "the rules". For example, the rules of being a gangster are not enough to tell you how to go about being a gangster in practice. Look, would you help me to get started writing the play? It'll be much better if you're there to try out ideas on, and you can help me act them out. Maybe I can explain Bourdieu a bit better too?'

Mila was not surprised that Jasmine agreed to help her with the play – she was always generous with her time – but she was surprised at the enthusiasm Jasmine showed for acting. When they got together the next day to have their own little drama workshop, Mila began by passing on some of the directions from her drama teacher (with a little bit of added Bourdieu).

'Habitus, Frank 'n' Stein said, "is embodied principle. It is embodied experience and practical sense. It is pre-reflective, non-symbolic and visceral". The characters need to embody power, weakness, humility, respect, masculinity, femininity. First of all, each character is embodied. Embodiment means the sense that you are your body, not a pilot in it. How do the powerful speak and act? How to get an impression of power for the boss in the play?'

Jasmine did not appear to need this guidance. She was leaning back in the chair and made her body take on the demeanour of one who never made a move or said a word that wasn't effectual – that did not lead to something. She fixed Mila with a cool, unimpressed look.

'How's that?' she asked Mila.

'All too good. Now, Bourdieu said that language is an instrument of power. The boss commands in a commanding voice. Bourdieu said there were "no innocent words". There are words of betrayal and loyalty, words that are actions in themselves. Alice in Wonderland's Queen of Hearts said, "Off with her head!" – those words had a real effect – if they were felicitous. For instance, if I said: "Off with Jasmine's head!", I would just be laughed at, but the boss says: "Take care of him", and soon a character is swimming with the fishes. So the boss commands his henchman with his embodied power and his powerful words but he is going to find his words have consequences he had no control over.'

The two friends thrashed out the scenario further. The boss would be told by his son that someone in the organisation was on the take, creaming off the profits from an illegal gambling operation, and covering his back by selling out other members of the family to the police or to rival gangs. He would set his henchman, his 'best man', on the trail. Writing the character of the henchman was harder than that of the boss, because the audience had to like him a little in order to put up with seeing him on stage as the centre of attention for the whole play. Mila thought it was necessary when writing a play or any other work to have some sympathy with the characters. There had to be some empathy, too: some appreciation of both the ties that bind and the opportunities that presented themselves. 'We have to establish how the henchman works.' Mila said. 'Let's call him …'

'Don't call him anything,' Jasmine said. 'They don't need names, just characters.' She went on. 'Everyone has their SOP – standard operating procedure. You see cop shows in which they catch serial killers by following their pattern and predicting where they will strike next. I always think, why don't the serial killers just change their SOP – kill someone else just to put the cops off the scent. They must have televisions too. But serial killers can't and won't change their SOP, just as the cops will not change theirs. Because they do not consciously master their SOP.'

Jasmine wanted Mila to make the henchman more sympathetic and less of a cold-blooded killer. She said mafia men must spend their time taking the rubbish out, going to the shops, worrying about their kids' performance at school – all the things you never see in gangster movies because those activites are not 'gangstery' enough. But this behaviour also has a quality that could make the characters more sympathetic. Mila thought about what was involved in habitus. 'Routine,' she said. 'Routine evokes sympathy. We can see the henchman doing ordinary stuff. Most of our behaviour is not reflected on. Routine is one type of behaviour that is clearly predictable – but that aspect of it doesn't make it fated.'

Mila explained that, for sociologists, routine was as meaningful as those outbursts of interest. It was as if you had taken all the best bits from your favourite book and made a shorter, more exciting read – you realised rapidly that you need all those other bits, even the tedious parts. For example, looking at interminable edited sports highlights was often very boring, like eating only ice cream. You needed the routine, the humdrum, as counterpart to the highlights. 'It's the kind of stuff that never appears in a film or a play because it's unsaid – we all know that the characters annoy themselves with their own quirks, forget their computer passwords, and lose the TV remote control. How do we know that? Because we live in the same world he does, with the same stupid things that bother us. But we don't like thinking about it.'

'Because that would make him too much like us,' Jasmine said. 'What routines should we have, then?'

'Let's say… he listens to his favourite radio programme. He always has a coffee and a cigarette while he writes his diary. Routine makes the henchman more understandable – we can see how he has the same habits ordinary people do. His work is routine to him, and that's how he copes with it – the horrendous things he does are just work. He doesn't kill because he particularly likes it. This also allows us to see how he might pursue a lead without thinking much about the consequences – it's what he does.'

They continued to work on the scenario. The henchman was going to track down a minor functionary in the organisation, who the Boss's son has led him to. He would tie the man to a chair and interrogate him. Unlike the Boss, the henchman needed a reason to kill someone; he wouldn't just do it on suspicion, he had to hear it from the traitor. What happened next presented further difficulties: how could they make it believable without simply having the henchman slap his prisoner around? Every gesture of an actor had meaning, Mila thought. So we should think that gestures are meaningful – embodiment again, they embody power.

Mila and Jasmine broke up their workshop for the day, but Mila found she was still wondering how to present the interrogation scene when, later on, she was reading about Bourdieu's book *Language and Symbolic Power*. She struck on something Bourdieu had written about this kind of power.

> 'The ways of looking, sitting, standing, keeping silent or even of speaking ... are full of injunctions that are hard to resist precisely because they are silent and insidious, insistent and insinuating.'

According to Frank 'n' Stein, this embodiment of power was part of the habitus. A sense of social worth was embodied in posture and comportment. That gave Mila an idea of how the henchman should act, how he stood with and over other people. Dispatching the suspect was easy enough. The henchman would point his gun, the lights would go down, and the play would break for the second act.

When their informal workshop reconvened the next day, Jasmine asked:

'What changes in the second act? Is this the same sequence again? We can't just write the same thing again. That would be *boring* routine!'

'No, it should follow from the first. Let's say, he finds he was wrong. All his heavy mob technique did was to get the poor soul he was torturing to tell him what he wanted to hear. His actions produced that outcome, not, as Bourdieu would agree, by intention, but by being oriented towards the future, towards producing an outcome of some kind.'

Jasmine suggested: 'First of all, the social worth of the henchman changes. Why don't you have him interrogating a superior, or someone who might be his superior? Then he finds that it's the Boss's son who set up the guy in the first act!' Jasmine was thoroughly pleased with her clever twist to the plot, but Mila did not give her the credit she was due, because she was so absorbed in her thoughts about Bourdieu.

'That outcome, that outcome learned through practice – is absorbed into his habitus. It does not make him into an angel – because habitus doesn't just change overnight, but the experience does subtly shift his orientation to those around him. Let's say, he trusted the Boss's son, who set him up to finger this guy. Well, now he feels wronged and, remember, he is the kind of man who is "naturally suspicious". His habitus means that suspicion is a quality you have to develop quickly – he doesn't think that this was an innocent mistake. In his world there are no innocent gestures – which is pretty much like any world – and any action that has meaning comes loaded with the conditions of its production that give it meaning. That's the difference between routine and action. Actions have to be responded to.'

'Why doesn't the henchman just run away?' Jasmine asked.

'I think it's because it would not be what Bourdieu calls a valid move in the game. He could try and escape, but would probably be found and killed. Just like a chess player can't make his queen move like a knight. The other gangsters would not accept him deciding to opt out.'

'Why not? They could probably have easier and longer lives working as door-men. Or middle management. Or blogging as anonymous wiseguys'.

'They won't let one person opt out, because that would mean the game is meaningless.' She told Jasmine it would make all their investment turn to nothing – all the horrible things they had done, all the violent acts – would be for nothing. And his capital was of no use outside the field in which he existed, like drug dealers who ruled the roost in a few blocks of a New York barrio, but were lost outside it. She said: 'Think about the henchman: what was practical was what could be done, what was done, and what had to be done. This didn't mean being cynical – it could even be idealistic.'

'Let's say,' Mila carried on, 'that most other gangsters would just be glad they'd got someone, received their boss's praise, and not care if it turned out to be the wrong guy. But his adherence to the code of honour means that he can't take it that way – to do so would be impossible; it would turn his whole habitus inside out; it would mean that the only thing justifying his monstrous behaviour throughout most of his life, was meaningless. Therefore his action in following his code of honour and doing in this innocent guy is the author of what happens next because he has to follow it through – not because he is trying to be noble. Again, it can't be as if we are watching and judging what he's doing and he is doing it for our benefit.'

For Mila, the crime family – with its hierarchy, status, age, gendered, biologi-cal, legal, and other relationships – was a field. These objective criteria were not as hard and fast as you might imagine. The family might include some cousins but not others, some non-relatives who were 'close'. Jasmine wanted to know more about the final scene. 'The final scene, in every sense. He kills the Boss's son. He goes back to his routine, writing his diary, listening to the radio, waiting for vengeance to come. The radio programme is burbling in the background. He pours his coffee, lights his cigarette, there is a knock at the door and ...'

'Lights out,' whispered Jasmine.

Visit the companion website at **www.palgrave.com/companion/ Bancroft-And-Fevre-Dead-White-Men-2e/** to access additional learning resources, including seminar questions based on the chapter's coverage, a jargon buster that defines key terms used in the text and a timeline which provides an overview of the development of sociological thought.

●　●　●　●　●

Why habits are hard to shake

coffee

**Habits help
us function**

Generic
Coffee
shop

**And remind us
who we are**

1. You often see people involved in activities that to an outsider might seem short-sighted or self-destructive. They become unquestioned parts of people's nature or personality. Bourdieu wrote that these were one aspect of the 'habitus' that becomes second nature for people. The habitus is the set of dispositions towards life that everyone has. It is developed through routine — unspoken learning by doing. It is very powerful as it appears to be human nature. We forget we have even learned it.

2. For that reason, trying to explain people's behaviour through the conscious choices they make often gets it wrong. I never chose to go to university, it was 'just what people like us did'. My aunt never chose NOT to go. Bourdieu used the idea to cut through the divide between structure and agency in social writing. That is the tendency to rely on explanations that say people have a script which they act out, or that they freely choose everything they do. Neither is really true. Habitus is the structure within us, the embodied, personalised sense that this or that is the right and proper way of acting.

3. Social capital is a resource held by individuals. Field is the arena in which capital is given value. Field was Bourdieu's term for the structure in which habitus made sense. Field meant the limits of action. Practice is the way each individual brings social capital into play. Much like players in a game, when you are outside the field, your talents have no function. That is why most people like to stay close to 'home'.

13
In Essence

A long, curving corridor was closed off at the end by a dark wooden door. It was the kind of place where you expect to find a single fluorescent strip light buzzing on and off, and possibly a stunted race of minions serving some dark plan. The stencil on the door announced 'A Museum of Humanity'.

Mila pushed open the door, hoping for an ominous 'creak'. Inside, rows of wooden glass cabinets displayed skulls, facemasks, ethnic costumes, and various trinkets. Each was neatly annotated with a small typed note. It was the kind of place run by a man who is one step from sewing together a few corpses and breaking out the lightning conductors.

Mila had begun writing for the student newspaper. Her assignment was to cover an until-recently forgotten museum at the back of the university's old public health department (now the VIP hospitality suite with complementary homeopathic bar). It was a slightly sad building with blackened walls and forbidding, shadowy doorways. It was of the kind that sparked legends among the students of ghosts, hidden tunnels, and forbidden science. Long ignored, the museum had become the focus of protests. It had been said that the museum represented the racist foundations the university had been built on. It had been scheduled for destruction.

She slung a camera. She intended to record it while it still stood.

Mila wanted to understand why the museum had been created. She had dug around in the university's records of bequests, and she had searched out a book in the library on the history of 'museums of humanity'. She had snapped a section called, 'White Dreads' by Cassie Sun, on her phone and read as she went:

> These museums were part of an intellectual enterprise, called scientific racism. 'Colonialism' in social theory was normally used to refer to one specific instance of this, the colonisation of large swathes of Africa, Asia, and to a lesser extent Central and South America by Western European countries in the nineteenth century. It also meant the intellectual climate that grew up to justify these actions, which declared the colonised to be of different, inferior, races and nations. The coloniser would lead the colonised out of the darkness, with the white light of Enlightenment science, reason, and the rule of law. Edward Said called this 'Orientalism'.

Mila looked up at a chart which reached from floor to ceiling. It was called 'Types of Mankind'. At the top were male heads drawn in profile, emphasising their presumed racial distinctiveness. The 'Negro' was charcoal grey, the (native) 'American' actually red, the European had a huge, cartoonish Greek nose. Below each was a drawing of a skull and then of animals native to the region where each race was supposed to have originated.

According to Sun,

Humanity was classified into superior and inferior races, each of which had its own special qualities. Black people were suited to working in the fields because they lacked intellect and grace, and were relatively impervious to pain and physical effort. 'Orientals' were naturally devious and untrustworthy – obsessed with byzantine intrigue and feminine disputes. Hearing the term race science now, it is often assumed it was inherently bad, because racism is bad. The people who were involved, for the most, were not especially prejudiced, or only so far as they shared the general sense that England, or the USA, or white people in general had a destiny. They viewed themselves as dispassionate scientists, trying to bring light to a topic marred by bigotry and naivety. They were challenged and satirised at the time as fruitless skull measurers, starting from the blindingly obvious and working backwards. Although much mocked, these divisions were not trivial. US sociology was effectively split into black and white traditions until the 1960s. Intellectual traditions are not immune from society, just the reverse.

Following the end of the colonial period many Western and non-Western minds turned to development. The question was asked, how can we, or they, become wealthier, more modern like the West? Post-colonial theory asks a different question: how and why has the West made these countries poor and how does it continue to do so? It makes the claim that a big part of that 'how' is presenting the West as both better and the only way to be. The post-colonialists argue that we still think and act in terms of essential, solid categories of humanity and the historical uniqueness of European industrial and political development. In acting and speaking as a black person, you confirm the category of white; as a woman, the category of male. As long as you do that you confirm rather than overturn the system of thought that led you to that point originally. Post-colonial critique aims to do what they call destabilisation.

That means taking issue with these binaries. For example, if you were keen on liberation you would question how the white Europeans defined black people as inferior. If you wanted to destabilise the binary, you would question the other part, the way whiteness was defined as a superior identity.

Mila took a photo of the chart. She moved on to a map of the world divided into empires coded by colour. British, French, German, Portuguese, and Spanish divided the world. This was the high energy particle physics laboratory of its day – a triumph of science, in an institution which trained and sent out young men to conquer the world.

She read further, about Frantz Fanon, who was a psychiatrist born in Martinique, who was involved in the Algerian revolution against French colonial rule. His patients included both Algerians tortured by the French forces, and torturers themselves. He resigned his position to join the Algerian independence struggle, arguing that colonialism damaged the psyche of both white masters and black underdogs, and so it was impossible to practise psychiatry ethically under colonial rule. Fanon wanted black people to achieve independence of mind, as well as the literal independence of colonised states. He was often dismayed by the black elites of newly independent states whom he thought mimicked the departed overlords, with their contempt for and fear of the masses.

Sun wrote,

> For Fanon, European Enlightenment thinkers talked endlessly of the rights of man, but happily destroyed real men and women. Critics like Said and Fanon examined colonialism as something that affected the coloniser and the colonised – psychologically, culturally, and socially, as well as politically and economically. They pointed to the way in which good intentions could be as harmful as bad ones, when those on the receiving end were thought of as less than full human beings capable of governing themselves. The ruler needed the ruled to define themselves as superior to.
>
> In sociology many people came round to the conclusion that the ways of thinking which developed from the Enlightenment allowed some people, people in power, to treat other human beings in pretty despicable ways. Although they might have long since departed from the ideas of the thinkers who made the Enlightenment, these ways of seeing the world had allowed some of us to treat other men and women as if they were not human. So, although they talked and spoke and had voices that could be listened to, they were treated as just things, as objects, to be used and then destroyed – slavery, genocide, the examples were far too many and too sad to go into. Many sociologists have made a big effort to counteract this.

One of the glass cabinets contained a row of skulls, each labelled neatly as one example of 'behavioural deformities of nature'. 'Criminal'; 'Skulker'; 'Wastrel'; 'Moocher'.

She wondered where they had come from – dug up from what pauper's grave. The label explained how each one represented a degenerate type of humanity.

'The consequences for the white race of the poor breeding will be further exam-ples,' it said. At the time, as Sun wrote, social problems were being attributed to inherent differences between social classes. The tools of race science were applied to social class. The poor were poor because they were so very bad at being rich. This was essentialism.

"Essentialism is one of the deadly sins of post-colonialism. It means implying a fundamental quality to one group or culture that it does not possess. Race science was involved with codifying this, attributing differences in intelligence, physical aptitude to the human races and also to the genders. It takes passing appearances to be permanent attributes. It is more than a mistake; it is taking a temporary aspect that a group acquires by virtue of its history, social status, power, and resources and making it their fundamental essence. We cannot really live and talk without drawing on some essentialist categories or acting as if they are real.

"Essentialism is in many processes that have in common a claim to an authen-tic insight into human nature and which use it to categorise humanity. That is what makes it dangerous. The history of racial segregation is a good example of where the category people were in made a vast difference to everything else about them. If you were 'coloured' or 'white' in the USA of the segregation period in the Deep South you ate in different restaurants, went to different schools and churches, used a different entrance for the cinema, and everywhere were remind-ers of this difference. That division was imposed by the state. Even if you wanted to live side by side in perfect harmony, you were unable to. As a result of this, being defined one way or another became so important, more important than class or sex. Many in the South had mixed racial ancestry. Those who were in a position to do so were 'whitened', redefined as white, and those who were too poor, or badly connected, to resist were 'blackened'. When new ethnic minori-ties arrived in the USA the same process was applied. The Irish were for a long time poor and discriminated against. They were 'blackened'. When they gained political and economic power in the cities of the Midwest and Eastern Seaboard they were 'whitened'. The most effective part of this process is that it is forgot-ten. Each group appears to have always been white or black, making race appear as if it was an essence beyond history."

A nasty process, Mila reflected, but how does this affect sociological theory? Is this a problem of thought, or of memory?

She looked at the portraits of humanity in the museum. The whites were in full garb from different eras, Renaissance Italy, Industrial Revolution England. The 'natives' were half naked, standing in forests and plains, with no evidence of human handiwork in sight.

Why it matters, she read, is identified in the work of Gurminder Bhambra who writes that claiming modernity is a fundamentally new stage in human develop-ment assumes there is rupture and difference. Rupture means there has been a historical upheaval separating pre-modern, pastoral life from that which came after. Difference means that European, Western ideas, ways of life, organisation, states, and really everything about the place is different from elsewhere.

Every culture tells myths about itself. One of the blinding successes of European cultures has been to exclude their own imagination from the category of myth. Bhambra summarises these myths of singular splendid uniqueness –

the Renaissance, the Enlightenment, the French Revolution, and the Industrial Revolution – which are powerful and which every white European and American implicitly lays claim to solely by being white.

They are myths because they are presented as singular moments of self-invention, as if for example China and India had not developed many technical and organisational techniques which would play a part in the Industrial Revolution. They do two things: they present Europe as having sprung fully formed from its own fundamentals, and they hide the role of European empires in shaping the world system to support them. One example would be the British Industrial Revolution, which was supported by a skewed trade with India, in which India produced raw cotton and the more profitable textile manufacturing was restricted to Britain. Not surprisingly every nation on Earth would prefer if their achievements could be directly attributed to their own genius.

'Bad ideas are never unique to bad times,' Mila noted.

Mila took her photographs and notes to her editor, and gave her pitch.

'Let's see it,' her editor replied.

Mila began her article, which she wanted to call *Around the world in several wrong ideas*.

'Misunderstanding people is normal. Knowing why you misunderstand them is the first step to enlightenment, the Buddha never said. Controversies about history rarely give light to the past. They usually signal who would like to feel good about themselves in the present. It is possible to feel good about getting rid of the Museum of Humanity because we think it shows how superior we are to those who put it together. We can then tell ourselves that we would never make the same error. But what student does not learn through errors? Knowing why those in past eras thought the way they did about humanity tells us more than we might like to know about how we think of humanity now. They arranged humanity by its racial essence. They thought themselves to be the centre of the world thanks to their innate worth. Now we arrange humanity by its similarity to what we would like to be and think our innate worth means we can erase its history. Destroying this museum erases a history. It should be updated as a museum of misconceptions of humanity, retaining the original exhibits.'

She pinged the article to her editor and walked home.

***

When she got home she found that a parcel had arrived for Tuni. Tuni was in the process of tearing the wrapping off. She beamed as she saw the shoebox inside – it was a pricey thing, designed to impart an air of quality. She pulled the pair of pumps out. These were not shoes for walking. She caught Mila's eye. 'They'll get me from the limo to the nightclub door.'

A piece of paper had fallen out when Tuni had opened the box. Mila picked it up. 'I've heard of these. Factory workers leave notes as protests, or to let you know what they got paid to make them.'

'It'd better not be a photo of someone else wearing these. I pay for ex-clu-sivity. Don't tut.'

'I didn't tut.'

'You were thinking about it – I can tell when you're about to disapprove.'

Mila looked at the note. She thought of the history she had read before, of the Industrial Revolution, and the way the European countries had arranged trade so that they kept hold of the valuable manufacturing work. Now they arranged it so that mass manufacturing was far away.

She expected a statement about the maker being enslaved and chained to their factory machine. It was just a series of numbers: −0.180653 ; −78.467838. She showed it to Jasmine. 'GPS coordinates. They must make i-thingies there as well. Other shiny lifestyle objects are available. Let's take a look at where it is.'

Entering the coordinates into the map programme on her phone showed a satellite view of a dense set of tower blocks. Nearby was a flat-roofed building. Workers' housing and a factory, Mila thought.

'Here's a little trick' Jasmine said. She entered a code into the browser and date. 'It rewinds through past satellite imagery.' The tower blocks quickly vanished, showing a complex network of alleyways and dense streets. 'These were cleared out by the local government to build houses for factory workers. Your shoes changed the landscape,' she said to Tuni.

Mila stuck the note in her purse and forgot about it until the following day, at a seminar with Dalina entitled, 'The World System and the Global Value Chain.'

Dalina was setting the class up, 'The global value chain is the total sum of all the activities that go into a product or service – marketing it, designing it, making it, transporting it to you, or transporting you to it. These chains stretch around the globe, running through homes, factories, streets, and markets, across borders and time zones. They tie us together when we are working, shopping, eating, watching TV, and everything else.

Families are affected by it. The global care chain is the name for the way that some domestic labour and caring duties are farmed out to poorer women, often immigrants from the developing world. Cleaning the home, looking after children, is the work of women from the Philippines, the Caribbean, Africa, and elsewhere. Even the womb is globalised. Women in India and Thailand are paid to be surrogate mothers for wealthy couples.

We often hear that we live in a globalised world, and this is what it means. Globalisation is the integration of economic, political, and state activity across the globe into a system that works independently of the actions of nation states. It involves many different activities. Companies are detached from any one country and move their activities from place to place in a heartbeat. The ability of national governments to tax and regulate is diminished. Instead they have to make themselves as attractive as possible.'

Mila thought of the VIP building that the Museum of Humanity was attached to.

'So when the university tries to attract the donations of the wealthy, is that what it is doing also? Making itself look good so it reflects well on them?'

Dalina grinned. 'Hmm, awkward!' She decided to redirect Mila's challenge. 'It is a fact that academia has to respond to, and not always willingly. The fact of globalisation is at the heart of world systems analysis, which challenged the in-country sociology that fixes on national societies and the disciplinary boxes of anthropology, sociology, economics, and politics.

Sociology and those other disciplines developed as single country or single culture disciplines in Europe and North America. That means they studied each society or culture as a singular entity. They sought universal theories of social and economic development. Developing countries would be able to use them as a model for their own growth towards modernity. In the case of Britain, France, and to some extent Germany, these disciplines justified the existence of those empires. The countries in their purview would soon come to benefit from the white man's laws and education system.'

Mila remembered a poem she had read, by a British poet, Rudyard Kipling. She found herself saying,

> *'Take up the White Man's burden, Send forth the best ye breed*
> *Go bind your sons to exile, to serve your captives' need;*
> *To wait in heavy harness, On fluttered folk and wild –*
> *Your new-caught, sullen peoples, Half-devil and half-child.'*

Dalina caught her meaning. 'Kipling believed that the British Empire was beneficial to the people they ruled – but he also was not an idiot and saw through some of the pomposity and arrogance of this viewpoint.

He wrote that at the end of the nineteenth century. Even at that time there were plenty of people who thought that the burden of imperialism was being borne by the people who were colonised, and not the white man.

Empires disintegrated in the second half of the twentieth century. If empire was the cause of underdevelopment, the end of it would free peoples to pursue economic and social development.

As inequality persisted in any case it became apparent that there was not a universal path of development by imitation.

Interventions by critics such as the United Nations Economic Commission for Latin America suggested that the fundamental issue was not underdevelopment, but unequal exchange. A 'core' of Western countries had created a system for sucking the surplus from the Third World. The centre-periphery relationship required a switch in perspective. Traditional analysis saw international relations and trade as a set of relationships between equals, where each country is a unit able to act largely as suits it. World systems analysis takes the relationships between them as key to understanding what is going on within and between. To take one example: Brunei exists as a country because it suited Britain to have oil wealth concentrated in a number of small states who could not be in any position to use that wealth independently.'

Pallo, who was ever ready to challenge the tutor, said 'Are we not mired in the past? There are many countries – Singapore, Japan, South Korea, China – which are far better at benefiting from global capitalism. Most of them are becoming richer than the old European colonial countries. A wholly exploitative, imperialist world system describes the Spanish Empire quite well, British India from 1857–1930 fairly well, and the currently eroding predominance of the USA less well. China is building a resource network in Africa and Russia, a centre-periphery resource extraction model that does not make it into the post-colonial critiques.'

Dalina replied, 'One argument is that those countries that developed fast, like South Korea, were those that partly separated themselves from the world system. They protected their industrial development with trade barriers and state sponsored corporations. Japan had its own empire, so the theory should not be only a way of explaining persistent white guilt.'

Mila interjected, 'Is it a world system, or several systems? A country that is large and resource rich like Russia is able to act on its own against Western interests.

Dalina agreed, 'You could say that it sits at its own centre and has its own periphery of states that look to it. Then again, any system is composed of subsystems. It does not have to be harmonic, but they do respond to each other.

The implication is that we have to drop either the model of Western-centric progress towards modernity, and say that there are many different modernities, or drop the model of progress altogether. We do know that there has been a lot of change, but that change turns out not always to be progress. The idea of linear progress – so that capitalism must come after feudalism and is inherently better because it leads to socialism – is something specific to Europe and not a fundamental law of human development.'

'What we do have are economic systems that reach across states and encompass distant activities, some of which may not even be recognised as economic, like caring and reproduction.'

Pallo said, 'But it is better to be working in a capitalist factory, than in a field all day. If you are a human being and not a horse.' He smirked at his own cleverness.

Mila thought it was time for the big reveal. She took the note out of her purse. 'Can we talk about someone real? I found this in a parcel of … er … well it doesn't matter, let's say it was a high value, low utility product, this morning.'

She showed the numbers to the others. 'It is a location, a factory.'

Dalina said, 'Let us imagine who that person is.'

'Maybe it was the shoes (oops) but I had an idea that she was a woman.'

'Why not? Plenty of factory workers are,' Dalina replied.

'Say the person who made these shoes is a migrant worker. She travels from one part of the country to another, leaves her children behind. Her mother supports her by looking after her children.

The upshot is that the capitalist economy reaches back deep into peasant society and peasant homes. Paid labour is just one kind of work that is drawn into supporting the worldwide capitalist system. The world system appears to benefit from a traditional, patriarchal default that old women look after their grandchildren. But that is to get it the wrong way round – the need to send daughters to the cities to work makes this the default by necessity.'

'It's a good thing' said Pallo. 'This woman would have ten kids and be dead by 30. Thanks to your shoes –'

'They're not my shoes,' Mila insisted, 'she can spend her time at the local Corporate Exploitation Bar and Nightclub.'

'Maybe nothing works without helping those it exploits. Commodity production can and does benefit them. Does she choose that though?' Mila asked, thinking, 'I wish we could hear from this person.'

'Choice is the challenge to any theory that relies on saying one bunch of people is exploiting another,' Dalina said. 'It is what we call agency – the sense that people take advantage of the choices available to them, however limited they might be. The whole arrangement could just as easily be seen in reverse – and this is one of the criticisms of theories about "the other". Western theorists have been obsessed about what "we" do to "them" and how they are affected, disciplined, labelled, and reproduced by the powers acting in their name.'

Mila said 'Don't people resist that?'

'That set of theories does acknowledge that people who are exploited resist it. They form labour unions and they migrate away from these places. However, talking of what they do as resistance defines what they are doing as reacting against Western exploitation. If we think of them as having some agency in it we could see them as taking advantage of the money economy knowing that at some point in the future things will be better than they ever could hope to achieve living as rural agricultural workers.'

'In either case, there is a political economy that means that your shoes, his cigarettes, her car, are not just produced by a system of free exchange. The ideal free market where labour is allocated by cost and buyers and sellers enter into free contracts might exist in a computer model whirring away on the Trade Ministry's server. In reality economic exchanges are also relationships and obligations – of family, state, neighbourhood, nation, moral debt, and credit.

An effect of privilege is thinking that you are without these obligations, that you live in a 'light' world of free movement and free exchange. Institutions like the state weigh heavily though. For example, if you want to make people sell goods or their labour for cash, because you need the cash to fund a war, you make it a requirement that they pay their taxes in cash. And this was the origin of the money economy. European states created credit markets to fund wars.'

Pallo said 'Is all economic development then tainted by exploitation and imperialism?'

Mila interjected, 'We cannot make a value judgement about that person who works in that factory without getting in her head. We can only judge the ideas that explain that system.'

She thought back to Bhambra and the way European writing tended to think of everything else in reference to it.

'What perspective are we arguing from?' she asked everyone. 'Are we assuming that all people have the same choices, and the same wants?'

Dalina said, 'What you are criticising is universalism – the application of humanity-wide characteristics and experiences which derive from a small, usually privileged, segment. It has been asked how can feminism exist when there is a global division of labour and value chain? On what basis does it make sense to imply a universal character to womanhood, and a universal oppression, between a female CEO in Shanghai and a female illegal migrant working on the sly in Rio.'

Mila thought again about the museum and what it said about having a universal perspective on humanity. 'When we say that ideas have had their day, or we say that anyone who held them was so wrong headed, I like to think 'what is being thrown away?' What was wrong, and what mistakes are we still making – even when we condemn others for doing that same thing. Humanity still has a unique set of properties, which change the world around ourselves to make sense of what we as humans are doing. The production of my friend's shoes made the life of that factory worker completely different from what it could have been. My friend thinks the shoes will make her life different, and they won't. They won't make her more glam than every other person in the nightclub – or not for long. But they have changed that worker's life for ever.'

Visit the companion website at **www.palgrave.com/companion/ Bancroft-And-Fevre-Dead-White-Men-2e/** to access additional learning resources, including seminar questions based on the chapter's coverage, a jargon buster that defines key terms used in the text and a timeline which provides an overview of the development of sociological thought.

● ● ● ● ●

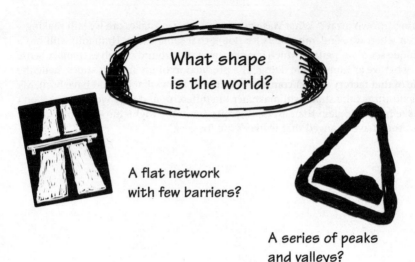

What shape
is the world?

A flat network
with few barriers?

A series of peaks
and valleys?

1. Post-colonialism is the study of global relations in the light of the rise and fall of the great global empires. It implies that humanity is still living with the political, economic, psychological and cultural legacy of those times, if they are indeed past. Frantz Fanon was one who argued that the new world of liberated nations mimicked the old.

2. Myths were vital to the modern empires of Britain, France and others and some persist. They are that the development of modernity in Europe involved unique qualities not found elsewhere, and that could be attributed to unique qualities of its society and people.

3. World systems theory looks at how global development recreates dependence through a network of core and peripheral states. The core states can arrange global trade in a way that benefits them. That perspective emphasises the power of nation states. Other views emphasise the diminishing power of nations and the growing power of transnational trade and network technology which 'flattens' the world.

4. Whichever perspective is better it is true that activities that take place in one corner of the globe affect many other places far distant from it in deep and lasting ways.

5. The question of whether sociology can come up with universal claims is a bone of contention. Some critics, such as feminists and post-colonialists, have argued that sociological thought is flawed in that it claims to be universal when it is in fact particular. The dominance of European countries in the globe shaped social thought, and in particular, the idea of that progress involved societies moving towards a West European or USA model. Post-colonialists, among others, have challenged this.

14
In and Against

The holidays were approaching and Mila needed to know what her brother might be intending to do about visiting their mother. From the start of her phone call to Doni, she guessed that her brother was far too wrapped up in his business affairs to spare the time. Mila told him there were other things in life than money, but he didn't seem to think so.

'Money matters, Mila. You can't have any of the other things without money. Even sociologists know that, don't they?'

Mila knew that arguing with Doni would make him more determined not to come home and, in any case, she was secretly relieved. When she said that sociology was all about the other important stuff in life, Doni's reply was sarcastic.

'Oh, really? You've heard of Karl Marx, haven't you?'

In spite of herself, Mila was amused. 'I've heard of Marxism. I know that back in 1989 all those people in Russia and Poland and the rest of Eastern Europe showed they preferred freedom. Surely you are not becoming a communist, big brother?' Her brother chuckled to himself before he answered.

'Of course not, but I understand Marxism's ideas about how things ought to work are not the same as Marx's ideas about how things do work, about the importance of money. Actually, it's not so much money, as the economy, the importance of the economy in all our lives. You don't have to be a communist to work that out, and you should work it out little sister.'

Mila was sure her brother was trying to provoke her but she steered him back to the holidays. She had guessed right: there was a business deal in the offing and he could not come home. She wasted little effort on trying to persuade him and, with a clear conscience, she heaved a sigh of relief when they said their goodbyes.

Mila went off to find Frank 'n' Stein. She didn't know a thing about Marx's theories and nobody had mentioned any plans to study him as part of her course. Was Marx even a part of sociology? She found it irritating that her brother should know something about sociology she did not know. If Marx was in Frank 'n' Stein, then Mila was going to read about him, even if it did break her rule of only reading something when she was going to be assessed. She told herself it wasn't sibling rivalry but a sensible precaution. If Doni had heard of Marx, then other people might expect a sociology student like her to know all about him.

Frank 'n' Stein had a chapter on Marx, and his collaborator Friedrich Engels, and Mila took the book with her when she went home for the holidays. The journey was so long and tedious that she began to read the chapter as she travelled. She quickly discovered, to her annoyance, that her brother was right, in at least one respect. Marx, who had written all his important works in the second half of the nineteenth century, when industrial capitalism was starting to take off, seemed to have learned how important money was early on, because he was always asking Engels for it.

Marx earned little money of his own, and Engels, who ran his family's textile factory, made the money that fed Marx and his growing family. Without this money, there would have been no writing (in fact it seemed Engels did a lot of the writing as well). As she read on, Mila found that Marx and Engels did say that the economy was the key to everything, the key to society – and to history – and even to how different groups of people (they called them 'social classes') thought. But the foundation of their theory seemed to be something called 'surplus value' which Mila was having a hard time understanding.

In common with the economists of their day, Marx and Engels thought the value of any good that was made, or service that was provided, was the amount of labour that went into it. Marx and Engels parted company with most of the economists when they said that capitalism was only able to grow in the phenomenal way it was doing because some of the value the labour produced was creamed off. The workers only got paid enough to keep body and soul together and make sure they turned up at work the next day. But they created more value than this when they worked and the capitalists cashed in this value when they sold the product the workers made.

Some of the money the capitalists got from selling the product went on workers' wages, raw materials, machinery, the cost of buildings, and so on, but there was still an extra bit that came from the labour of the workers. This 'surplus value' did not get created by the capitalist but the capitalist used it anyway. In fact this was really what capitalism was all about: exploiting the workers by getting them to create value and then creaming off the surplus beyond what was needed to pay the workers to make sure they turned up in the morning. If capitalism wasn't able to exploit the workers in this way, there would be no profits to reinvest and capitalist enterprises would not grow.

Once she had grasped this, Mila decided there was really not much to it. It was not a surprise after all: of course capitalism was a kind of uneven exchange. Everyone knew the workers never got rich, and capitalists did, but there was rough justice in this because the workers got jobs out of the exchange and without those jobs they would starve. What's more, these days, workers in many countries did pretty well out of capitalism. As her aunties had said, the workers were not exactly rich but they were more prosperous than they had been, and there was always the possibility that they might be even better off in the future.

What was there to set against this? How would people get jobs? How would they get any money at all, if it weren't for capitalists? The state might give jobs to some of them (as teachers or bureaucrats) but the money for those people's wages had to come from the taxes of the capitalists and their employees. It might be a very unequal system, but there was no way out of it, not that Mila could see. Yet Marx and Engels apparently wanted to persuade us that there *was* a way out. While they readily admitted that exploitation was inevitable within capitalism, this did not mean we were stuck with it. They thought that we could have another kind of economy which would be even more productive than capitalism but would not involve exploitation.

If you looked back through history, you could see that capitalist exploitation had not been going for very long, and Marx and Engels did not think it would go on for much longer. In other words, you were meant to conclude that exploitation was central to only one sort of economy and there would be others. Capitalism was only one *phase* in the development of economy and it was a phase that Marx and Engels believed was nearly over. But they were writing this stuff in the mid-nineteenth century and, with hindsight, you could see capitalism was not nearly over at all, in fact, it was just getting going when they were writing.

So what had made Marx and Engels so sure they would live to see the end of it? They thought you could tell how near we were to the next phase because the capitalist economy was failing. Mila knew about recessions, booms and slumps – the business cycles that meant some people lost their jobs every five to seven years or so. Marx and Engels thought that these slumps were proof of another defining feature of capitalism: its inevitable failure.

This was another point that Mila found hard to understand. Exploitation was how capitalism worked, and surplus value was reinvested in order to increase the size of the enterprise and make for more exploitation. In other words, exploitation was what made capitalism worthwhile and it was how capitalist enterprises grew. But Marx and Engels also said that the exploitation at the heart of capitalism was like a design fault which meant it was bound to fail. Mila thought this was wishful thinking: how was it meant to work?

Capitalism was also about the competition of one enterprise with another and so each capitalist was continually driven to cut costs in order to keep profits up while prices were driven down. This pressure caused constant changes in work organisation and technology. Mechanisation and the increasing division of labour were amazing achievements which were unique to capitalism, but they also created problems. For instance, mechanisation meant replacing workers by machines and it was from workers that surplus value came. More machines meant that there were fewer and fewer workers to provide that necessary surplus value. Marx and Engels thought this would put pressure on capitalists' profits and contribute to the business crises in which, every few years, many firms went bust and thousands of workers were thrown out of work.

Capitalism also needed workers to make sure that the surplus value that was put into the things workers made could be turned into profits. This was because capitalists had to be able to *sell* the things workers made if they were ever going to see their profits. Some of these goods had to be sold to workers and, if lots of people were out of work because capitalists were trying to cut costs, there would not be enough people to buy the goods and so capitalists would never get their profits. This meant that recession would deepen into depression and an increasing portion of the population would sink into poverty. In fact, through the money they paid to keep the poor from starvation, the capitalists would end up paying to keep the poor people alive rather than exploiting them. Marx and Engels thought this showed how an economic system which depended on exploitation could not last very long.

Gradually, Mila understood that Marx and Engels had some positive things to say about capitalism. They argued that, because it was based on exploitation, capitalism could not help but make possible the development of industry in ways never even dreamed of before. With all that new machinery, and with everybody being brought into production, capitalism was very efficient and highly productive. But, at the same time, because it was based on exploitation, it was certain that people could never benefit from the full potential of this development. In fact, more and more people would actually get poorer and poorer.

Capitalism was a necessary part of progress, but it was a phase that would not last very long. Apparently, many of the philosophers of the time thought of history in terms of phases, but usually the phases were marked by different kinds of ideas. It was as ideas changed that history moved along: there was an age when religion dominated, then the Enlightenment, then maybe an age when science dominated. Over hundreds of years, people came up with better and better ideas and this was how progress was made.

With a bit of time, and not too much effort, Mila had got to what she understood to be the heart of the theory. Marx and Engels's big idea was that it was not changes in ideas that moved history along but changes in 'material' things. There was just one problem with this (for Mila): what did 'material' mean? Obviously it was meant to include new technology and new forms of work organisation, but there was more to it than this. When they mentioned 'material' objects, Marx and Engels did mean mechanisation, steam power, and new forms of transport but it turned out that they also meant laws and structures like patterns of who owned what (they called the last of these 'social relations'). It was all of these material characteristics that were the real defining characteristics of each phase of history, according to Marx and Engels. The change that mattered most was that hundreds of years ago there was slavery, whereas in a later phase there was paid labour, the railroad and the electric telegraph. You would not expect people to think the same way in these two phases but ideas were the result, not the cause, of the changes.

Their materialist view of change meant Marx and Engels were confident that capitalism would not last. It had brought some progress, but the changes it had brought in material circumstances meant it was bound to run into trouble and, in fact, we would end up seeing it was just the foundation for the next stage. Marx and Engels made a lot out of these 'social relations': what was most important to the theory was how we dealt with nature and the relationships we set up with each other in order to do this. Masters and slaves had one sort of relationship, capitalists and workers had another. Buyers and sellers on a free market did not have the same kind of relationship as the feudal lords and the subjects who, by law, had to give up their money and goods to the lords.

These differences in relationships, backed up by differences in the legal framework, were some of the key differences between phases and, when the relationships began to change, then so did everything else, including the ideas. Marx and Engels thought you could see this going on in capitalism. What they called the 'material forces' – both the technological changes and the changes in 'social relations' – were driving historical change. The most important changes in social relations were the ways in which more and more people were forced to work for a wage to get by, and capitalist enterprises were getting bigger and bigger while smaller capitalists were taken over or went bust. These changes were so important that lots more changes, including changes in how people thought about their families and nations, followed.

As Mila read on, she gathered that it was meant to be through further changes in the social relations between people that the eventual change from capitalism to communism would come about. The 'contradictions' which were built into capitalism would finally come to a head and cause a massive breakdown of the system in which the way forward to a new kind of economy would become obvious. This would also be a new kind of society because everything else, like our ideas about how to live, for instance, followed the change in material things.

The most important contradiction in capitalism was between the 'forces' and 'relations' of production. The forces of production were all that stuff that actually made capitalism so productive: the labour of the workers, the mechanised technology and the steam power. The relations of production were the relationships between people which capitalism built up and relied upon. Marx and Engels meant by this that most people were selling their labour to the capitalists in order to survive and the capitalists depended on this reliance to create their labour force. This was the exchange that everyone understood, the one Mila had thought produced a kind of rough justice.

Because this mutual dependency was obvious to Mila, the contradiction between the forces and relations of production became a bit easier to understand. It meant the tremendous potential of the forces to produce benefits for all humankind would never be realised; in fact it would look to be further away than ever, because the relations of production meant the majority of the population had to be kept in poverty and were actually getting poorer. Mila decided this must be another way of looking at what she had read earlier about capitalism breaking down, there not being enough people in work to buy the goods capitalism produced, and so on. Recessions and people being thrown out of work must be proof of the contradiction at the heart of capitalism.

Mila was already convinced that history had proved Marx and Engels wrong. If capitalism had contradictions, it had proved capable of living with them quite happily – but it was an intriguing view of progress all the same. Marx and Engels apparently had their own idea of what the various phases of human history might be, and they saw the key differences between these phases as being the differences in the social relations of production and associated differences in technologies.

At the start Marx, and particularly Engels, imagined there was a stage of 'Primitive Communism' in which there was no private property and people related to each other pretty much as equals. Then there was 'Ancient Society' where production depended on slaves, and the key social relations were between the slaves and the slave-owners. In 'Feudal Society' production depended on the 'serfs' who could not move away from the land on which they were born. They weren't slaves but they were bound to labour for the feudal landowners all the same and so their relationship with the landowners was the key social relation.

Of course the key *capitalist* social relations were those between the capitalists and the workers who had to work for a wage in order to live. Mila supposed that, in the transition from each of these stages to the next one, there would always have been a growing contradiction between the forces and the relations of production.

After capitalism would come communism, where the means of production – the factories and machines – were in common ownership and everyone would benefit from the development of the forces of production. Marx and Engels said it would mark the beginning of the real story of humanity. Up to that point, people had had very little real choice in what happened. Marx said, 'they made history but not in circumstances of their own choosing.' After capitalism had been overthrown, people would have real freedom to determine how things turned out. Marx and Engels thought that, when the human story really began, it would do so with us returned to our real selves and with real human relations between each other.

The journey home had taken Mila much longer than normal. She had been reading this stuff for hours and hours. She now understood that Marx and Engels were saying that the *economic* stuff had *social* effects. This was what their big idea, the materialist theory, was all about. The new capitalist arrangements in which workers sold their labour power, and worked in factories, affected every part of their lives. But Marx and Engels weren't saying that the economy would always matter.

They were saying that the economy mattered in a particular way in capitalism but it had not always been this way and it need not be this way in the future. What was more, they were saying that after capitalism the economy would not matter at all. People would become so productive that they would be able to concentrate on other things instead.

Marx and Engels believed we could have an economy which made it possible to achieve all of our human potential. There would not be a spectacular, and growing, chasm between a shrinking number of ever richer people and the increasingly poor majority. Everyone would work, but nobody would have to work for very long, and that work would be fulfilling. This was what Marx and Engels thought the world would be like if the means of production, the factories, and the machines, were owned in common. This utopian world would be the product of this kind of common ownership: the social and political consequences of this kind of mode of production would be uniformly happy ones.

Mila looked up from her book, quite exhausted and incapable of reading any more. So, what did that mean? That her brother was wrong, surely? Marx and Engels had said the economy only dominated everything *for now* and we could look forward to a time when it didn't, when it could be put more in its place. Mila could feel her brain was now well and truly overloaded. She closed her eyes and fell to thinking about her visit home several months ago. Mila vaguely remembered having some kind of revelation that things did not have to stay the same as you saw them now. Hadn't she come to the conclusion that modernity could be just a phase too, and wasn't this what Marx had been saying?

***

Mila later told her mother that Marx and Engels had tried to find out how things had actually changed in the past and how they might change in the future: everybody's work would be valued and worthwhile, enjoyable, everyone would be comfortable and prosperous. Her mother said that was probably what people meant when they said Marx's ideas were hopelessly idealistic.

Now Mila was thoroughly confused. 'But I don't think Marx and Engels meant that change would not happen without people fighting for it, at least ... Oh, I don't know what to think now. I think I need to read some more.'

Mila did more reading. She worked out that what she needed to know was how people fitted into the big idea of materialism. It turned out to be much more complex than she had expected. Mila was getting used to this but she needed time to get to grips with the ideas so it was as well her mother seemed to be quite self-contained, and even preoccupied, in the days that followed. Mila certainly saw less of her than she had done when she was living at home. She had no idea what was taking up so much of her mother's time and it made her curious, but not curious enough to ask. She thought it would be too much like role reversal for the grown-up daughter to be caught out nagging her mother to spend more time with her. So she read Marx and Engels instead and, without Mila noticing, it was soon almost time for her to go back to university.

Mila told her mother that she had sorted out the tangle she had got herself into on the first night of her visit. 'I may be slow to grasp ideas but this was not my fault. Marx and Engels want to have it both ways. They say that we do make our own history but we don't get to choose the circumstances that we do it in. We have to play with the cards that the past has put in our hands.'

'Ah, I see, it's like when someone stops to ask directions in the countryside, and the person says that if they wanted to go there, they wouldn't start from here.'

'Very funny, but, yes, I suppose so. You have to set out for your destination from wherever you find yourself and that means some people will be in a better position to influence history than others. I think it also means that there needs to be people *doing something* in order to make the history happen. You see, Marx and Engels do have it both ways. They stick to their materialism but they also make it more like real life, real history, where people have to struggle for ideas. It's complicated but I think it makes sense. It explains the arrival of capitalism itself, for instance. Some people argue for new ideas of liberty, and so on, but the time has to be right for these ideas to move people and that means material conditions have to be right. Feudalism needs to be on its last legs.'

Marx and Engels were sure capitalism would break down but Mila had found out that they also thought there would need to be more than an economic breakdown to bring about all the changes that were needed. You could not simply have people saying, 'OK capitalism was a bad idea, let's have a new one.' The materialist theory also had to explain how the transition to the next kind of society, the next phase in history, was going to happen. This was where classes came into it: they were the *agents* of the materialist juggernaut that was driving history and it was different classes that brought in new forms of society. Mila told her mother: 'Marx and Engels said capitalism depended on some people selling, and others buying, their labour. These were two different *classes* of people and classes are defined by their economic position and that means what property they own and how they get by.'

Mila said that Marx and Engels thought capitalism was all about classes but they also thought that this was true about the other stages in history too. In previous economic systems, or 'modes of production', there were not only different kinds of laws and different sorts of property – slaves could be property in ancient society, for example – but there were different classes. In fact each of the previous stages had been defined by relations between classes: in ancient society it was master–slave; in feudal society it was landowner– serf; and in capitalism it was the 'bourgeoisie' – the capitalists – and the 'proletariat' – the workers. Mila said Marx and Engels made classes the agents of history. At times they even talked of classes thinking in this way or that as if they were people. In any case, Marx and Engels saw classes as the agents of change from one mode of production to another: 'Look at the way the bourgeoisie grew up in the cities in late feudalism and became more and more powerful. Eventually they rose up, usually violently, to grab more power from the landowners and monarchies. They often set up a sort of democracy but what they really wanted was to get power over what happened in the economy and in the legal system. The most important freedom they needed was the freedom to exploit and one of their key aims was to get the workers released from the land, with nothing to sell but their labour power. The landowners did not necessarily want this and so it was a further source of conflict.'

As she spoke, Mila was thinking this materialist theory was quite some achievement – it had so many interconnections and ramifications. The bourgeoisie, for instance, grew and got more powerful as part of material change and the inevitable conflict with the landowners was a material conflict over power and resources. OK, ideas like liberty figured in the conflict, but Marx and Engels did not want us to mistake them for the cause. The bourgeoisie wanted liberty but it was their material circumstances that led them to fight for it. Mila carried on.

'Yes, there was class conflict between the bourgeoisie and the feudal landowners, and the bourgeoisie had been the revolutionaries, the ones who brought in the new phase in history. But Marx and Engels went on to say that, in the future, it would be the proletariat that would be the agent of change from capitalism to communism. The main reason for this was that capitalism was turning everyone into workers. All the peasants and all the shopkeepers, and even the small employers, became workers.'

As capitalism turned everyone into proletarians, the proletariat began to behave as if capitalism had already ended, working communally in huge enterprises, living together in the new towns. The proletariat glimpsed the future and, moreover, they lost all their ties with the past. They had no interest in bourgeois society, they did not believe in any of it. The workers did not have any property, or any reason to respect property laws. Again there were the material influences hard at work on history, driving it forwards and, in this case, condemning outmoded ideas to the garbage heap.

Hard work and poverty made sure that, for the workers, family life was nothing like bourgeois family life. Nationality meant nothing to the proletariat because they knew capitalist exploitation was the same everywhere. They had more in common with the workers of other countries than they did with the capitalists of their own. All the values the bourgeoisie said mattered most – patriotism, respect for the law, morality, and family values, even religious beliefs – would then be seen not only as alien, but as a kind of smokescreen behind which the bourgeoisie would go on grabbing what they wanted. Increasingly, the proletariat would no longer allow themselves to be fooled and they would revolt.

Mila said that Marx and Engels thought they knew that the proletariat would be the agent of social change but that they would not be doing it unopposed. There would be class struggle and class conflict, as there always was in revolutions. And, as was always the case, there would be a revolution in everything, not just economics. You had to have a revolution for the forms of property to change in the way that was needed. For example, there would need to be a new law making it illegal for individuals to own factories and other means of production and making them the common property of everyone. This meant that law, politics, everything had to be changed, and this would mean there was going to be a fight, but this was not a surprise. The bourgeoisie themselves had to struggle to overthrow the feudal system and put capitalism in place. In fact, they were in a minority when they did this, whereas the proletariat were very much in the majority, and in time they would be irresistible.

Marx and Engels said that the whole of history – not just the revolutionary bits – was a tale of class struggle. What went on year to year while capitalism continued was explicable in terms of class struggle. And there was more to class struggle than you might imagine. For example, the bourgeoisie appeared at the end of feudalism but, in reality, feudalism already had lots more classes than landowners and serfs. There were also free town-dwellers including independent artisans and merchants. And in capitalism there were classes in intermediate positions between the proletariat and the bourgeoisie – artisans, shopkeepers, small employers – not forgetting other classes like the *Lumpenproletariat*, the intellectuals, the different sorts of bourgeoisie. Mila's mother wanted to know why there were so many classes. Mila was amazed she could remember the answer. 'Because there were this many different ways of making a living and this many different relationships to property!'

Mila explained that Marx and Engels believed that in time all the members of these other classes would be reduced to the level of the proletariat who had no property but their labour, which they must sell to survive, but in the meantime there was scope for numerous diverging class interests and complicated patterns of class alliances and class struggles. When Marx wrote about the political struggles in France in 1848, he described all sorts of different classes. There were several different factions of bourgeoisie: those who owned factories, those who owned property in the city, those who owned property in the countryside, the bankers, and financiers. There was also the petty bourgeoisie, the proletarians (who got massacred in 1848), the *lumpenproletariat* (who did some of the killing) and smallholding peasants. The peasants were the eventual powerbase for Louis

Bonaparte. Louis was Napoleon's nephew, Mila said. He became President of the Republic in 1848 and made himself Emperor in 1852. According to Marx, it was the peasants' nostalgia for the days of Napoleon that made them support him. Napoleon had given them land of their own and there was nothing that peasants liked better than land. They also liked the idea of a return to the good old days when the French Army used to take on the might of the European monarchies. Marx thought any resemblance between Louis and his uncle was something the peasants imagined. They were being persuaded by an 'ideology' which was not in their real best interests.

Mila was sure she must have said enough now, and ought to give her mother a break from sociology, but her mother was interested in this notion of ideology and asked Mila to tell her more. So Mila told her that, in the materialist theory, ideas always arose from the economic system and this was obviously also the case with the ideas that made up class ideology. Mila said that Marx taught that ideology arises from an economic position: classes think the way that they do because of their economic position; and in their ideology they are thinking about their position (and their interests), although this may not always be obvious. So the peasants in France in 1848 were fervent supporters of armed nationalism, and therefore of Louis, but their economic position depended on the land they had been given by Louis's uncle.

Marx said this was not unusual. Classes frequently came up with ideas which happened to be very convenient for them and which also helped to whitewash what they were up to. The landed aristocracy made a big deal out of 'honour', because they were the ones who were supposed to have all the honour and it justified them keeping hold of all the power and wealth. Similarly the bourgeoisie were very keen on 'liberty' because they were in the best position to take advantage of it.

'So are you saying it's always a conspiracy, Mila? Is class ideology a conscious attempt to fool people?'

'I don't know for sure, but I don't think that each class realised that it had to come up with ideas which would justify its hold over resources. Perhaps the people in the class, or some of the people, completely believed in the ideas, but their thinking was flawed. They could not understand that the ideas that were so good for them might not be good for everyone. So the bourgeoisie were keen on liberty but the workers, who had to scrabble for a living each day, were not actually in a position to get much benefit out of liberty.'

Mila explained that Marx thought that not all ideologies were equally effective in protecting or advancing class interests. Their effectiveness depended on the material circumstances of the class. The peasants were different to the proletarians living and working side by side in the towns and new factories. They were insulated from each other on their smallholdings spread across France, and so the ideology that they believed in, particularly armed nationalism, did them very little good. Mila thought she could now see very clearly how all this class–ideology stuff linked into the big idea of historical materialism. Just as classes were the agents of history, so it was through classes that ideas (and laws, and forms of politics, and family types and artistic forms and everything else) arose from the material factors.

The higher classes could come up with ideas that are much more useful to them, Mila said. Indeed the top classes always had the material circumstances which allowed them to actually impose their *ideas* on others. Marx said: 'the ideas of the ruling class are in every epoch the ruling ideas.' He said that the people who owned everything – the factories, the warehouses, the mines and the docks – would most likely own the things that they needed to make sure their ideas were dominant too. He called these things 'the means of mental production', meaning something like factories for making people think in a particular way. The most obvious example in Marx's day was a newspaper, but you might also think of a radio or TV station doing the same thing.

'And what about universities, Mila? Do they teach the ideas of the ruling class too?'

'I don't know,' said Mila uneasily, pressing on. 'Marx said the people who did not own anything would not be able to get their ideas across at all. They just wouldn't be able to compete with the bourgeoisie and so, in time, even people who were outside the bourgeoisie started to see the world in the same way as the bourgeoisie. They ended up thinking capitalism was good for them too and they could not see that they were being exploited.'

Then Mila and her mother realised there was someone at the open door leading into the garden. For a moment, the light from the garden made it difficult to see who it was, but then Mila recognised Lin, an old friend of the family. Mila wondered how long he had been there, as he sat down between her and her mother.

'Who's learning about Marx? Surely not little Mila who I thought was not interested in books?'

Mila had not seen him in eight or nine years, but Lin hardly appeared to have aged at all. She was sure he was some years older than her mother, but now they could easily be taken for the same age. To look at them they might even be brother and sister and, as they chatted, it was clear that they were very much at ease in each other's company. With a sudden jolt in her stomach, Mila thought she understood why her mother had had so little need to spend time with her since she had come home. Mila suddenly felt very jealous and not at all grown up.

Lin seemed to be very interested in Mila's experience of her university course, but her mother seemed determined to steer them away from any kind of serious conversation. She told Lin that Mila was going back to university tomorrow and Lin said he envied Mila this period of time on the sidelines of life, when you could seriously think about what kind of person you wanted to be, and what impact you would make. To Mila this all sounded a bit forced and she wondered if it was just politeness that made Lin and her mother carry on engaging her in conversation. She decided they probably had things to talk about and, a little awkwardly, she took her leave, saying she must go and check all her clothes were clean and ready to pack. When Mila went to find her mother later in the day, Lin had left and there had been a subtle change. It was not of Mila's making, but there seemed to have been another shift in her relationship with her mother. The ties that had only just now been re-established were straining a little. Mila had felt for a short while like a little girl again but perhaps a bond between a grown-up daughter and her mother could never feel like that? But did that mean they could not share everything with each other, all their secrets? Then Mila remembered Arun.

That night, Mila could not sleep because she was trying to find, in her mother's words and behaviour, clues as to what her relationship with Lin might be. Her mind was restless and she thought over what she had said today about Marxism, and the concept of ideology that had so interested her mother before Lin arrived. Mila had told her mother that the poor people, or, at least, people who weren't capitalists, ended up thinking capitalism was good for them and that was why they could not see that they were being exploited. Then Mila had said that the capitalists could not get it into their heads that the ideas which made capitalism sound so good might be good news for them, but not for anyone else. Was this what had happened to her father, and were the poor people he duped being fooled by an ideology?

Mila was wide awake now. Her mother had said she no longer thought about the trial and its aftermath but thought about why Mila's father had done what he did to those people and why he hadn't seen it was wrong. Mila knew that her father had said all along that everyone knew the rules; they knew what could happen if they invested, nobody forced them. But maybe he did not need to force them, maybe he gave them a view of the world that was good for him and not for them and told them it was the right view, the only view.

But did he genuinely believe it or did he set out to deceive? Even if you concluded that he fooled the poor people into believing his ideology, you still wouldn't understand why he did it unless you enquired into the content of his beliefs. Maybe they would justify, at least to her father, going ahead and fooling people? Perhaps he genuinely believed he knew better than them what was in their best interests. Mila had to know what her father really believed. If she didn't, these questions would worm away at her just as they had done to her mother. And, if she could find answers to them, Mila would, she was sure, be able to reassure her mother by showing her that there was nothing that she could have done to persuade her father that his beliefs were wrong.

Visit the companion website at **www.palgrave.com/companion/ Bancroft-And-Fevre-Dead-White-Men-2e/** to access additional learning resources, including seminar questions based on the chapter's coverage, a jargon buster that defines key terms used in the text and a timeline which provides an overview of the development of sociological thought.

● ● ● ● ●

Do you earn
what you own?

Do you create
economic value
for others?

Do they create it
for you?

1. Capitalism means judging activities on the basis of their market value, the process of accumulation of capital, and money becoming a value in itself. Karl Marx put flesh on the bare bones of capitalism. He cut beneath the story it told of itself to see what the real relationships were. In his view these were economic relationships that appeared to be free and equal but in reality were founded in exploitation.

2. People who worked, the proleteriat, created the economic value for people who owned, the capitalists. That was called surplus value, the wealth capital earns solely because it is capital – not because of any innate genius of the owner. Workers produce value but do not receive all of its worth. The 'surplus value' is added to the wealth of the capitalist employer, which strengthens their hold over the worker, so workers create what enslaves them. That is the 'labour theory of value'.

3. He developed a theory of social change. Society changed through class conflict. Each economic system, each relationship of production, created the class that would bring the new society into being. Feudalism created the capitalist class who soon found that they had no need of the aristocracy. Capitalism created the working class who he thought would find they had no need of capitalists.

4. Marx has been described as an economic determinist, someone who reduces social relationships to economic ones. There was a lot more to him than that, for example, he thought that social classes have their foundation in the economy but that class struggle involves much more than economic relationships. Marx tied together intellectual and economic life. Capitalism might stay in power through ownership, but it rules through appearing not to have power at all. Ruling relations of power produce ruling ideas which are the most powerful when they appear to be the only way of being.

15
In Between

The following morning Mila's mother mentioned that Lin would be visiting again before Mila left at midday. 'Yesterday, after you left us, Lin was telling me he read some sociology as a young man. He is a civil servant, as you know (Mila did not know), a bureaucrat.' Apparently, when he began his career someone told him that a sociologist called Weber (she pronounced it 'Veber' in the German fashion) was the person you had to read if you really wanted to understand what you were getting into when you went to work for the state and for politicians.

Mila remembered nothing about him and she felt there was something odd about her mother's little speech. She felt an underlying uneasiness about the relationship between Lin and her mother and had the impression that her mother was forcing a connection between her and Lin. To add to her sense of unease, she dreaded the thought of a conversation with him about sociology. She thought this theorist would be some oddball Lin had latched onto – that would explain why she had never heard of him – and that Lin would lecture her about him like Arun's father did about philosophers.

Lin arrived just as Mila was carrying her bags downstairs. The three of them went to sit in the garden which was now pleasantly warm. Mila was sitting between Lin and her mother and felt that the full force of their joint attention was concentrated on her. There was very little small talk before her mother referred to their conversation, the day before, about Marx.

'You were saying people are happy with capitalism because they are being persuaded by an ideology but your Aunt Ima would say that, although not everyone is rich, capitalism has given millions of people quite comfortable lives. Capitalism may be competitive but that doesn't mean one person wins and everyone else gets nothing.'

There was nothing in her mother's words to feed Mila's sense of unease but her mother's seriousness made her apprehensive all the same. Was this what it felt like if you were the child who could play the violin being asked to show off her repertoire? She said: 'Marx would say that, yes, capitalism has made a huge difference to people's lives but it can't make good on its promises. I guess if he was alive now, he'd still say the same thing: we do have much more prosperity, and it's more widely spread, but this is still a flawed system and we can make a better one.'

It now crossed Mila's mind that her mother was behaving in the way that parents behaved when they had important advice to impart, or some upsetting news to break, to their children. Lin seemed much calmer when he spoke.

'But what if you were to ask other theorists, Mila, people who thought about all of these questions after Marx did, a little nearer to our own time? There was another German who was writing three decades after Max died – he was very aware of Marx's theory but wanted to go beyond it. As you say, Marx was saying capitalism might be good in some ways, and bad in others. Because we could see that it was bad, then we should not settle for it, but struggle to change it for something better. This other theorist showed you don't have to be a communist to want to criticise capitalism but, all the same, it was pretty obvious to him that there was no alternative to it. The question that he thought we should be asking was ...'

Mila's mother pitched in, smiling now. 'You're talking about Max Weber aren't you, Lin?'

Mila thought her mother sounded as if she was reading a script but what Lin was saying seemed interesting, even if it was like a lecture. She asked him to go on.

'Your mother's right of course – Weber is my special subject, really my only subject. I am like an amateur conductor who only knows one symphony. Weber said that there was no alternative to capitalism because capitalism was the thing that made most sense. The more reasonable societies became, the more that capitalism came to seem like the system that would work.'

Mila was not sure what Lin meant, but she gathered she was now expected to say something. 'You mean like the Enlightenment when everyone starts to question everything and begins to apply reason everywhere. They no longer say "God made poverty and illness so that's OK; we can live with that", instead they look for reasons and then try to do something about it.'

Lin smiled in a way that Mila liked – there was not a trace of the condescension Arun's father could convey – and continued. 'Yes, the Enlightenment kicked off the move to more and more reason and that eventually led to wider acceptance of capitalism.'

Mila had to force herself to respond with the obvious question. 'Marx didn't think there was any alternative to capitalism either – it was a necessary stage – but why *did* the Enlightenment mean capitalism was the only way to do it? Weren't there any alternatives?'

Lin said this was the key question, but to answer it would take a little time. He started off by saying that a lot of Weber's ideas came about as he debated with 'the ghost of Marx.' There was, apparently, plenty of implicit criticism of Marx in Weber's writings, nevertheless, much of what Marx wrote was simply accepted by him. Weber had no problem using the idea of workers being separated from ownership of the means of production for instance, and, along with much else in Marx, this was simply taken as read. Weber knew about the dispossession of the workers, and the concentration of ownership of the means of production in the hands of the bourgeoisie, but he knew this explanation could only be a partial one. He wanted to get a fuller explanation of the origins of capitalism, and get it historically right, so the question of *exactly* why people latched on to capitalism was the most important one.

'Elements of capitalism had been around for hundreds of years but Weber wanted to know how some of us had got to the position where our everyday wants were provided for by capitalist enterprise. Yes, you had to have land, machinery, and so on, controlled as private property by those enterprises, and you had to have free labour, but you also needed *rational* organisation of the machinery and the labour.'

There we go, thought Mila. It's because capitalism is the rational way to think that it goes arm in arm with the age of rationality. You did not get capitalism when you are still prone to think in an irrational or superstitious way. Mila was racking her brains to think of what she might say when it was her turn to speak, but she soon realised that Lin was nowhere near to stopping. Lin went on to explain that 'rational organisation' meant thinking about the best way to do things in the abstract manner of 'what means do I need to achieve this end?' The capitalist enterprise was then run solely as a profit-making enterprise and other things like tradition could not get in the way. Lin paused and Mila spoke.

'He didn't believe in simple answers, did he?'

'That's right. He was always looking for more complexity in his theories to match the complexity he saw in the real world.' To demonstrate this, Lin went on to describe how Weber said that the free market was essential to rational organisation, especially the free market in labour. Only where it was supposedly voluntary – but actually compelled by 'the whip of hunger' – could the costs of labour be worked out in advance. But Lin said that there were other motivations you needed as well as 'the whip of hunger.' Rational organisation depended on being able to *calculate* the effect of each decision on your income. The enterprise had to be able to work out whether it was making money so it had to have accounting, in other words, it had to be able to keep the books and work out a balance. The enterprise had to be able to rely on other things being calculable as well, the law, for instance. The enterprise had to be able to rely on the consistency of the law.

'Lin trained as an accountant,' Mila's mother put in, casually. Lin laughed and said he had always liked Weber for pointing out how important the boring jobs were – bureaucrats, bookkeepers, accountants – but he had not worked in this capacity for the government. 'But you did use your qualifications in your charity work, didn't you, Lin?'

'Oh,' said Mila interested, 'you do charity work?'

'Yes,' said her mother in a matter-of-fact way. 'Lin was the treasurer for the main charity that your father was involved in.' Mila did not really have time to take this in before Lin was off again.

Lin explained how businesses could never have functioned without bookkeeping and a legal framework to govern relationships with suppliers and customers. For instance, Lin said, all of this helped businesses to forecast costs and profits in future periods with some reliability. And Weber said calculability also meant having a rational technology – where calculation had gone into the design of every bit of it – and this implied mechanisation. By the mid-nineteenth century, all of this was apparently so well developed in the West that you could say capitalism was general; not universal, but so important that economies would collapse without it.

'Now, to get back to your point about Weber not believing in keeping things simple, Mila. He could not keep things simple because he knew reality was not simple.' Lin said that whenever he moved from discussing things at the abstract level to concrete historical cases Weber always made things more complex. For example, he knew the West got to capitalism by way of the creation of mass markets some time before. These came about through falling prices putting manufactured goods within the grasp of many more people. If prices fell, then manufacturers had to be able to do something to reduce their costs and this increased the need for rational organisation of labour and rational technology. Weber pointed out how this innovation depended on proper patent laws – it seemed he had a thing about bringing the law into his explanations – because without this people would not bother with technological innovations. Mila's mother interrupted with a laugh Mila found forced (what was she so nervous about?).

'This time it's boring patent lawyers that turn out to be really important. Did Weber have more to say about the law, Lin?'

'Oh yes, Weber thought we might find out more about the origins of capitalism by comparing Western Europe with the East, and especially East Asia. The West had developed the key features you needed to have capitalism: rational law; a rational state; the concept of citizen; science; and what he called a "rational ethic for the conduct of life". For instance you might call Eastern settlements "cities" but they weren't like the Western cities in which citizens were supposed to treat each other as equals when they exchanged things.'

After that surprise about Lin's charity work, Mila was wondering exactly what the relationship between her father and Lin had been. How involved had Lin been with her father and might this explain her mother's odd behaviour? Did this have anything to do with the way she kept prompting Lin? Now she was asking Lin to tell them more about the law as if there was something specific she was reminding Lin he had promised to tell Mila.

Lin explained that, according to Weber, irrational law and magic obstructed capitalism in the East but these obstructions were swept away in the West. For example, Christianity (following Judaism) was hostile to magic. Christianity also played a role in the rationalisation of law because old law (trial by ordeal or combat for example) was thought to be heathenish. Lin said this related to Weber's point about citizens being free to exchange goods and services with each other without fear of being cheated. 'Part of the obstacle in magic is that it sets up differences between people so that you can't work with these people, or sell to these other people, or buy from those, or can't give this person their real due because you must give it to someone else because the magic tells you to. These differences were overcome in cities where *everyone* was a citizen and of course they were overcome where everyone had a rational attitude.'

Lin said Weber thought that in the East there was always a special sort of difference made between your group (the tribe, the brotherhood, the community, the religious community) and the rest. You could steal from the rest but had to be very generous with your own group. This distinction was abolished in the West and this made it possible for there to be commercial dealings between all sorts of people.

It crossed Mila's mind that this would amuse Doni. He seemed to think that businesspeople were like a tribe who had their own code and knew what to expect of each other, but deceived and cheated everyone else. If Doni was typical, then Weber wasn't really right about capitalism, Mila decided, but she wasn't going to say this directly. Instead she said: 'But what about everyone having a rational attitude? And didn't you even say something a while back about people having to have a rational ethic for the conduct of life before they thought capitalism was the way to go?'

'Yes, you'd think that's to do with the Enlightenment and the way that people wanted to understand things in a rational way without bringing God into it all the time. But Weber didn't think it was that simple.'

'I'm beginning to think he complicated things on purpose, just to make it harder to understand,' said Mila.

Lin laughed. 'Weber certainly can be difficult. I was just saying that he thought Christianity helped to push magic aside and make the law more rational. This was just one example of the way Weber thought the Christian religion offered a route to more rationality. You could see this clearly with the *ascetic* religion of monks who deprived themselves of any worldly pleasures, and sometimes any contact with the outside world, because they thought this was the best way to be religious and, ultimately, save their souls. They set about rationally organising a way to make sure they served God in the best way and so they ordered and organised every detail of their lives. They even used clocks to mark off each phase of the day when hardly anyone was using clocks.'

That was it, thought Mila. That was what Lin looked like: he didn't look like an accountant, he looked like a monk. She was trying hard to avoid smiling at this revelation while Lin told her how the Protestant Reformation in the sixteenth century, in which many Christians broke away from the Catholic Church, brought the monkish sort of religion out of the monasteries. Ordinary Protestant believers were now supposed to organise things as a means to an end – their salvation. Among other things, this would mean that people no longer stopped work and started having fun as soon as they had made sure they had enough to eat.

There was a particular Protestant group called the Calvinists. Lin went on to say that in *The Protestant Ethic and the Spirit of Capitalism*, Weber's first important publication, he had described the 'salvation anxiety' resulting from the Calvinist doctrine of predestination. Calvinists believed that, when they were born, some people were already marked out for salvation but you couldn't really know which people they were. You didn't know whether you were going to heaven or hell, and this made people very anxious. To help them cope, people looked for signs which might give them some sort of hint about the future.

Regarding her carefully, as if to gauge her reaction, Lin continued.

'In charities, like the one I was involved in, there are always lots of businessmen who get involved. You know, they make money but they also want to give something back. Some of the most wealthy have been enormously generous.' Mila was thinking: not my father, he took rather than give back, and she realised that Lin would know she was thinking this. Mila was now very suspicious about where this talk was leading them.

Lin simply carried on: Calvinists began to think that someone who performed 'good works,' by giving money to set up hospitals or almshouses, for instance, must be a good person and therefore one of those predestined to be saved. But in order to perform good works, you first had to amass some wealth. They thought the only godly way to do this was through hard work and enterprise, because stealing, or inheriting, a fortune could not be a sign of someone being predestined for heaven. So, because good works were a sign of being saved, they began to think of work as a duty to God. Mila thought she knew there was something wrong with this.

'So being wealthy was a sign of being saved? But didn't I hear that the Christian Bible says the wealthy man cannot get into heaven?'

'Calvinists felt they had to work together with others in a rational and disciplined way. They were like the ascetic monks except that, unlike the monks, they rejected the idea of flight from the world being the quickest route to salvation. They thought God did not want them to reject worldly things. They believed they might be wealthy but saw themselves as only administering, and not enjoying, this wealth. As I said, they saw this as their duty, or *calling*. This is a word that only occurs in Protestant Bibles and it means you are called to do something by God: accumulating wealth becomes a *religious task* demanded by God.'

Mila was struggling with her memory. 'Is the "Protestant ethic" the same as the "work ethic"?'

'Well, that's part of Weber's theory, too: the workers worked hard because they thought it was their duty to God and the only way to be saved. This was why they no longer took time off when they had earned enough to cover their subsistence. But Weber said the *Protestant* ethic was just as valuable to capitalism for what it made the capitalists think. Weber said the idea of a calling gave them "an utterly clear conscience". The capitalist could be shameless about exploiting the workers because it was through their labour for him that the workers got the chance to save their souls.'

Lin wanted to make sure Mila understood the wider significance of this. Capitalism did not get a boost because religion was declining as a result of the Enlightenment but because religion still mattered to people very much. The crucial historical event was not the Enlightenment, but the Reformation which changed the nature of Christian beliefs for millions of people. In the Protestant ascetic communities, people were only going to be saved from damnation if they were fit and worthy, and success in business was a sign of that suitability. All the same, it turned out that once it had got going, capitalism no longer needed religion and Weber thought the old Protestant ethic was a dead letter by the early nineteenth century.

Mila recalled how her father and his cronies had used religion for their own ends: a shared religion helped to explain why the people they took advantage of had trusted them. That was more like Durkheim than Weber but, once again, she wondered whether there was an ulterior motive to this conversation. It was almost as if Lin were telling her some tortuous fable which she was meant to realise was a deep and meaningful parable about her father. 'Oh, stop it,' she told herself, 'not everything is about you, remember!' Lin was saying you could see the traces of the old belief in a calling to be a successful entrepreneur but now what Weber called 'the Spirit of Capitalism' took on its own life. It led to the same sort of behaviour in the end but it was no longer religious and relied instead on the notion of individual greed being good for society. Of course the Protestant ethic eventually died out among the working class too. They were no longer content to wait for their rewards in heaven either, and started to organise themselves and take on the bosses. All of this meant that capitalism could cope quite happily with the decline of the power of religious belief which followed on from the Enlightenment. Mila now felt as if she was getting back on firmer ground. 'OK, so now we get back to the idea about people thinking capitalism was the only way to do things because they were used to applying reason everywhere.'

'I guess so. We know Weber thought the spread of reason was necessary to remove a lot of the obstacles to capitalism and also to make the conditions right for capitalism to grow. Weber called this *rationalisation*, the process in which more and more of life was conducted on the basis of abstract calculation of the means needed to achieve defined ends.' Then Lin explained that rationalisation was not only vital to Weber's explanation of capitalism but also to his understanding of the modern state. It was also the underlying theme of Weber's interest in the growth of bureaucracy.

'This was how I got interested in Weber,' he said. Weber could see bureaucracy increasing all around him – it was how you would have to organise things in a rationalised society. So the capitalist enterprise had its bureaucracy, as did all the other organisations, including the state. Not that bureaucracy was always such a good thing – just because it came with rationalisation, didn't mean it didn't have disadvantages.

'Early in my career, the government of the day had wanted to find ways to eliminate wasteful bureaucracy and bring wayward local government back under central control. We used Weber to analyse the problem. From Weber we learned that, just as capitalism had disadvantages (like exploitation), so did bureaucracy. In particular, once you set up a bureaucracy, the rules you made tended to become an end in themselves. Even if the end result of applying the rules was the opposite of what had first been intended when the rules were thought up, bureaucrats kept on applying those rules. In fact the whole process of rationalisation in modern societies risked increasing the use of formally rational procedures while actually undermining people's capacity to get the results they really wanted.'

Mila had a flash of inspiration. 'Like the spirit of capitalism: you don't set out to spend all your time working. You set out to make money, so that you can do all these great things with your life, but then you get stuck into working to make the money and you never have any time. People are always saying they want more time, and making plans to work less, but they never do anything about it. So are we meant to think that rationalisation is not always good?'

'There were certainly some things that worried Weber about rationalisation. He felt that it all seemed like a really good idea until, after we had jettisoned everything else in favour of reason, we found we had closed down all our options. Weber felt a rationalised world was a dull one, almost a kind of prison, and he thought that we were bound to miss the things we had thrown out, and all the mysteries that had now been explained. Maybe there was more fun in not knowing everything because it kept things magical. Weber thought increasing rationalisation couldn't help but spread "disenchantment", meaning we could not feel that magic anymore.'

In Mila's mind some ideas were starting to come together. 'So, all the time Weber was explaining why societies seem to find no better way to do things than capitalism (or bureaucracy or the state) he wasn't saying that these were the only possibilities and he wasn't saying they were beyond criticism.'

Lin sounded pleased. 'Yes. We don't need to pretend things are different to how they are – like pretending capitalism is going to collapse tomorrow – in order to criticise them and suggest how things could be changed for the better. You can see this most clearly in what Weber thought about inequality in capitalist society. Weber wanted to know how all the good things that capitalism was producing got shared out.'

Lin started to talk about class. For Weber, class was based in economic relationships, just as it was for Marx, and Weber saw the bourgeoisie as a class and the proletariat as a class. Weber recognised lots of other classes as well but, unlike Marx, he didn't restrict his discussion of the economic basis of classes to what went on in production. Marx defined all their classes in terms of their relationship to production but Weber said that what mattered was the relationship of classes to *markets*. Weber thought other classes were trying to do what the bourgeoisie did. The bourgeoisie monopolised ownership of the means of production and they profited from this, but what else could people monopolise? They could try to corner the market in a good or a service: the market in credit, or land for residential building, or diamonds or uranium, or a particular type of labour like engineering or window cleaning.

Mila thought about her father and his cronies: what had they cornered the market in – information about investments? No, they didn't really have any expert knowledge, they simply pretended to have it. The pretence to be experts persuaded the poor investors to trust her father and his friends with their money. Her father then used that money to double his own gains but ruin the investors. Since her father only pretended to have expert investment information the crucial factor in his enterprise was getting people to believe in his non-existent expertise and this, Mila assumed, was where his charity work came in. 'Did Weber think it mattered whether people really had monopolised something that other people wanted?' she asked.

Lin looked confused. 'Weber pointed out that some people were more successful, and some people were less successful, when it came to building or defending such monopolies. For example, among professionals, some groups like lawyers are good at it and they usually get the highest pay. Is that what you mean?' Lin explained that it really made a difference how good you were at monopolising a market because it affected the distribution of resources. Because it mattered so much, people would be prepared to fight each other, sometimes literally fight each other, in order to break or defend a monopoly. OK, thought Mila, if there was fighting there could be lying and cheating. Meanwhile, Lin was saying this meant Weber thought there were lots more different sorts of resources to *fight over* than Marx had thought of but, like Marx, Weber said we did not just fight about them as individuals, but as classes.

Weber thought social classes were made up of the people who gained control of some market or other – the market for a type of work, or product, or raw material, or anything else that was bought and sold. Most of the time, gaining control meant keeping other people out – this was what class struggle was really about – and it was often the case that the classes which controlled the more valuable markets were the most successful at keeping other people out, and the numbers of people in these classes were small. This was why there were often much smaller numbers of rich people than poor people. Social stratification – the way society was divided up into a hierarchy of different classes – was a reflection of the different relationships people could have to the various markets. The top classes had a monopoly on a market that gave them lots of resources and the less dominant classes got only partial monopolies or monopolies on markets which give them fewer resources.

'So, is this where it makes a difference what kind of market you can monopolise?' asked Mila.

'Yes, there is a huge difference between monopolising the local cab rank and monopolising the investment banking business. But you have to remember you still get conflict over access to cab ranks.'

'Why?'

'Because it matters: members of classes who monopolise nothing have no alternative but to compete with each other without protection and they get the fewest resources in consequence. This is what happens to unskilled manual workers for instance – the poorest of the poor. But Weber didn't just use the idea of class to explain inequality and stratification. He also used *status* and *party*.'

Mila thought she knew what status meant. 'Status is all about ranking people in terms of what they can afford to spend their money on, like the clothes and cars they buy.'

Lin shook his head. 'Status is certainly concerned with culture but there is a lot more to this than ranking people in terms of what they can afford to spend their money on. For Weber, status was not simply a matter of having a more expensive car than anyone else you work with. You really miss the point if you only think about individuals or families ranking themselves against other individuals or families.'

Lin said that status was more to do with identifying with people than competing with them. It was about identifying with people you thought were like you (or maybe 'the you' that you would like to become). So, status *groups* were communities of people who thought of each other as being on the same level. They had the same lifestyles and this meant they thought the same things, did the same things, including spending their leisure time in the same way.

'And were they meant to spend their money on the same sort of things?'

'Yes, and people from the same status group would value some kinds of goods and not others. Status was not about buying a car that was better than your neighbour's because it was more expensive. It was about buying the kind of car that the members of the status group that you identified with would think desirable.'

Mila found herself thinking of the way Doni talked about 'people like us,' as he gestured to the people sprawled on the leather sofas at his club. She had thought that they all looked a bit alike: all those older men and young women. Mila spoke. 'So, you might think your new car was great, but if the neighbours were from a different status group, they might think it was horrible?'

'That's it! Different status groups have cultural differences which are reflected in their members' likes and dislikes.'

Lin went on to explain that Weber was trying to improve on what Marx had said about classes being actors and the agents of history. Weber didn't think that it was right to think of classes as if they were people who could think. He wanted to make it clear that it was individuals who actually did things like making history, but you could see how the individuals in a status group would all come to think the same sort of thing. Since these individuals would then behave in the same sort of way, it might look like the status group was behaving like one person.

Status groups behaved like actors because they were groups of people who identified with each other. Classes, with their purely economic base, were not like this and so it did not make sense to pretend classes could be the actors of history as Marx believed. Weber said there were two aspects of status groups that made them different to classes. They had cultures and they were communities. Saying status groups were communities did not mean that all the members of these communities had face-to-face contact with each other like in a small settlement. But it did mean you recognised a degree of likeness in a stranger once you could place him or her in the same status group as you.

'Think about how we scrutinise a stranger looking for subtle, and less-than-subtle, clues which tell you about their status. We do it all the time. We don't always treat people differently if we think they are from a different status group, but status can determine our behaviour. For example, we might well behave differently with a stranger depending on what we think we know about their tastes and opinions from the assumptions we make about their status group membership.'

Lin said that, for Weber, class difference and status difference could often coincide, in fact they *had to* coincide for some of the time, because Weber said the success of classes in monopolising resources depended on them becoming status groups. This was a key point in Weber's theory. It was almost as important as the idea that there was no alternative to capitalism because capitalism was the thing that made most sense. Different status groups thought different things made sense, and different things mattered, and what they thought affected their chances of monopolising the market. For example, if doctors said they should monopolise surgical operations because only they had the necessary scientific knowledge, they were more likely to win a monopoly and earn more as a result.

'I think I get it. It would be hard for a group of skilled manual workers to make the same kind of convincing case for their monopoly of a particular kind of work. But what about monopolies in other kinds of markets?'

'The same thing applies. The elites which have figured in the history of so many countries have always been status groups and cultural communities. This meant they had cultural values which made them powerful in particular markets – usually land and other forms of investment.'

Mila was still thinking of Doni and the people at his club making their own rules and their own morals. This certainly helped her to understand what Lin meant. 'So the cultural peculiarities of status groups really matter? They are not just an amusing sideshow to the business of fighting over resources. Cultural differences bring an economic payoff.'

'Yes, and culture becomes much more important than Marx ever imagined. First of all, nobody is going to monopolise anything unless they become a group and Weber said it was the manufacture of cultural similarity that made the group. Second of all, what Marx called class ideology was, for Weber, all to do with the culture of the status group. The group had to believe it was right to monopolise resources. Status groups of all kinds believed it was justified that they should have what they had or get what they wanted to get in the future.'

Lin said the group might also have to persuade others its monopoly was legitimate and this too depended on the culture that the status group generated. You only had to think about groups of professional workers to see how they tried to do this. Lawyers and doctors were always saying that it was their knowledge and expertise, their values and their ethics, that meant they were the only ones who could handle the responsibility for some money-earning opportunity. So, 'class ideology' turned out to be necessary in creating the class and status turned out to be intimately tied up with class. Indeed, it could not be otherwise since no status group could be noneconomic, for example their cultural characteristics (including the money they had to buy cars and clothes) depended on economic resources.

Now Mila was thinking of the way her father and his friends had claimed they had a legitimate monopoly on their insider knowledge and she said she understood: status groups believed they were justified in grabbing what they wanted. Lin asked her, very quietly, if she was thinking of her father and then Mila knew that they were coming to the end of a slow, elaborate dance around the subject that they had always been intended to reach. There was, she was absolutely sure, going to be a hard lesson to come, or some news that was very painful to hear.

'In my charity work,' Lin was saying, 'I learned that your father and his friends played by their own rules. They needed someone like me, a boring professional who people thought was a stickler for the rules of bureaucracy, to keep up appearances.' Lin said he was foolish and felt deeply culpable for going along with them.

Mila was determined to get whatever was coming over with, now. 'Going along with what, stealing?'

'They would say it was more like public relations,' her mother put in, 'but you might think it was a kind of confidence trick. That's what I believe, and Lin, too.'

They seemed to be expecting Mila to say something – to argue with them perhaps – but Mila could think of nothing to say. The silence was too much for her, so she spoke. 'I think I have understood this now. In Weber's theory about class, status and party he says that some – or all? – of the success of a class in monopolising market position depends on its becoming a status group.'

Lin seemed almost relieved they had stepped back into the parable. 'Yes, that's right, and that's one way in which culture can become very important to economic relations. The culture of the status group gives it the justification for monopolising the bit of the market it has managed to corner.'

'And Weber's big idea was that there was no alternative to capitalism, because capitalism was the thing that made most sense?' asked Mila.

'Yes.'

'So it might just be possible that it's the culture of a status group, or groups, that says capitalism, or bureaucracy, is the reasonable solution, the best reasonable solution. In other words, it's not really the best solution for everyone – maybe we never know what the best solution for everyone is – but according to the culture of the people with most resources there is no contest. Their culture says it's capitalism, and particularly the aspects of capitalism that benefit them, that is the most reasonable way do to things.'

Mila's mother seemed a little perturbed that they had begun talking about sociology again. 'I think you are getting confused, Mila. Lin did not say Weber was writing about ideology.'

'But I think what Lin's been explaining has got a lot in common with the ideology of the ruling class, although the theory is a lot more complicated. In Weber's theory there are lots of competing ideologies but still, as with Marx, some are much more successful than others and that's part of the reason why, however hard people try, they seem to be able to do nothing to get rid of inequality in capitalist societies. That may even be why inequality gets worse: it gets worse because the causes of, and justifications for, inequality seem so reasonable!'

Lin sat back in his chair and looked at Mila with amazement. He turned to her mother to say something but, before he could open his mouth, Mila's mother spoke up.

'Mila, Lin and I have been a bit clumsy. I think you have guessed we wanted to tell you something and we, I, had the idea it might be possible to get to the subject gently by talking about your interests.' Her mother glanced pointedly at Lin. 'I'm sorry, but we're going to have to be a bit more direct.'

Her mother said that she hoped Mila didn't mind, but she had told Lin some of what Mila had said. They had talked it over and decided Mila ought to know more about what had really happened, now that she seemed ready to hear it. As Lin had said, her father and his friends played by different rules.

'We felt that we must have wilfully ignored all the clues that would have told us what was going on, if only we had recognised their significance. We decided separately that we needed to atone for this, but we've been trying to do something about it together.'

Her mother told Mila that she and Lin provided grants to people who had lost money because of her father's deception. 'We have to do it behind the scenes because nobody would trust us since we are associated with your father. The charity helps us. Its reputation is intact because anyone who was connected with your father and his friends resigned. Lin gave up being treasurer before the trial, so he has no official connection. We channel the money through his replacement as treasurer.'

Angrily, Mila said: 'My father has made us all into deceivers, hasn't he? Because of him, none of us can be ourselves, even if we are doing something really good, like this. Where does the money come from? Is it from other wealthy businesspeople who my father knew?'

'Some. But Lin has been very generous with his own money and I have given back all the money that I could find when your father went to prison. This is what I wanted to tell you. Lin has found me somewhere I can stay and I'm giving up this house. I'm really sorry, Mila.'

In spite of herself, Mila became even more angry. 'Why isn't the law compensating the investors? Why do you have to do it? It's more of the same: the inequality can never be tackled. If it gets better on its own, fine, but the state doesn't do anything to make it better, even where people have been tricked and cheated! The bureaucracy mustn't do anything to rock the boat that produces inequality even when it's produced such an unfair outcome.' As she had begun to speak, Mila had been aware her anger might suggest she was only thinking of herself and that this was the old Mila she hoped she had left behind. She reasoned that the anger that she felt must therefore come from somewhere else. As she spoke, she began to wonder whether, if Lin and her mother could be righters of wrongs, why couldn't she be?

Lin had begun to explain why the state couldn't do what Mila thought was obvious. Party was the last bit of Weber's theoretical toolkit for explaining inequality in capitalist society, the third way of competing for resources. Party did not just mean political parties, but any kind of association people got into to try to influence all of the different political levels from the local to the global. Nowadays, this would include special interest groups and all sorts of campaigning organisations.

Weber taught that political conflict helped to decide how resources, including the sometimes vast resources of the state itself, were shared out, and conflict went on all the time, not just when there were election campaigns. Conflict took place between parties, and sometimes between factions within parties, and Weber was sure that this conflict was not just a matter of conflict between status groups. Lin said you couldn't really understand what was going on in politics if you thought parties and factions were simply the representatives of classes or status groups. In fact they could be representing an *alliance* of classes or status groups, or only sections of some classes or status groups. What's more, parties also had interests of their own. For example, Weber said all parties and political factions had their own *economic* interests. They didn't just try to determine the distribution of resources for other people, but they were also concerned with the resources the party and individual party members might have.

Mila's mother interrupted. 'In lots of countries, individuals can get very wealthy as a direct or indirect result of being in parties.'

Lin exchanged a look with her mother that Mila could not interpret, then continued. 'More importantly, there is the whole power and wealth of the state itself to compete for and play with.'

Although, for Weber, the state was not just the object of party rivalry, it had something of an independent life of its own. For one thing, states ran the armed forces and this put them in constant need of cash. This might mean compromising the interests of the party and, indeed, the coalition of classes and status groups which made up the party. Similarly, states always needed to look after their own legitimacy in the eyes of the population or be prepared to exercise physical force to maintain state power. Lin said this confirmed that the state was not simply a neutral instrument wielded by the party that controlled it. States also had to compete, and sometimes cooperate, with each other and fight their own battles over power and resources. It was the conflict and competition between states that really interested Weber the most. Lin said Weber saw geopolitics as rather like a global version of status group competition with states struggling to control power and resources. For a moment Mila found herself thinking of that nightmare ride in the taxicab months before, then she regained her train of thought.

'Are you saying we should never expect the state to do anything about inequality and unfairness?'

'Not exactly, Mila. I am just saying it's not all that straightforward. If party is one of the ways that an alliance of classes or status groups can enshrine its cultural values, then a party – and also, I suppose, the state itself – can became a way of monopolising things and keeping the poorer people out. But I believe politics can offer a way to do something about inequalities. Those cultural values can be turned into laws and regulations which back up monopolies or weaken them. And what Weber shows us about all that parties and the state can do, shows us that we don't just have to throw our hands up when we see injustice.'

Mila was thinking that the first thing you needed to do was to show how the cultural justification for inequality was being presented as reasonable. This was what gave it such power in modern societies. But then you had to find a way of unpicking this, of going beyond reasonableness to find some other kind of thinking to appeal to. 'So, the state plays a big role in saying what is reasonable and, if another class-status group got control of the state, perhaps they could start to change what is seen as reasonable.'

'But other parties which might get hold of the state also have their complicated relations to classes and status groups, and all of them have some sort of stake in capitalism because they will all be cornering the market in something. If you got rid of one party's cause for thinking inequality was reasonable, you'd just end up by replacing it with another party's cause for thinking inequality was reasonable.'

Mila thought it really *was* like the ruling-class ideology from Marx all over again, but with the special twist that any viable, competing ideology would simply end up proving the same thing: that capitalism was reasonable. You had to find a way to step outside all of the cultures on offer, maybe even take the view of the excluded and the dispossessed, in order to show that it was not. 'But aren't there some people who would not believe inequality is reasonable? What about the people at the very bottom of the pile who have no monopoly on anything: the unskilled, the displaced workers, the peasants wandering into big cities from the countryside?'

Lin told her that Weber would say that the dispossessed and excluded people would need to become a status community before they could act together and start to play a role in defining what was reasonable. Mila was not sure but she was certain that there would need to be a new way of thinking that would challenge the ideas everyone seemed to have about inequality – and maybe even capitalism itself – being reasonable and, in fact, inevitable. For reasons that were not yet clear to her, this certainty, together with her new found idealism, were making her more determined than ever to ask her father exactly why he thought his behaviour (now revealed, she was sure, to be the opposite of idealism) was justified.

Visit the companion website at **www.palgrave.com/companion/ Bancroft-And-Fevre-Dead-White-Men-2e/** to access additional learning resources, including seminar questions based on the chapter's coverage, a jargon buster that defines key terms used in the text and a timeline which provides an overview of the development of sociological thought.

● ● ● ● ●

Society – what is it?

Is it a hierarchy like this?

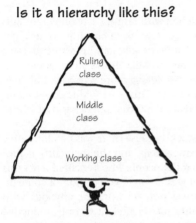

Ruling class

Middle class

Working class

Is it a plural set of competing groups?

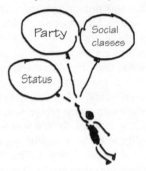

Party

Social classes

Status

1. Where does society start, where does it stop and what does it look like? Lots of sociologists like Max Weber thought society usually ended at the borders of the nation state. Commentators like Karl Marx emphasised society's nature as a hierarchy of social class power and wealth. To him, the state is the ruling class. Weber thought that nations had lots of institutions and relationships which did not involve social class and these were equally important. The state was one institution and it did not just represent the interests of the ruling class.

2. Weber theorised that the origins of capitalism lay in religion as well as economics. Calvinist Protestantism saw creating wealth as a sign of divine blessing. Keeping that wealth and using it to generate more in a rational and self-denying way made the economy more rational and disciplined. That 'Protestant Ethic' sparked the immense growth in capital and industry that reshaped the economy of Europe and then the world.

3. Marx viewed the problem of capitalism to be one of ever increasing exploitation of the many by the few. Weber identified a different problem, the iron cage of rationality. As society becomes ever more rational and carefully organised we lose the joy, the surprise, the messiness, that makes life bearable. Rationalisation comes to dominate every human need. Weber was concerned that the very things that developed society and the economy also hollowed out what made life worthwhile.

16
In Pieces

A week or two later Mila was in the kitchen with Jasmine late one night, just like that first night so many months ago. They were firm friends now, but it was not an easy friendship borne along by jokes and gossip and small talk. Jasmine did not do small talk, instead she and Mila always talked about serious questions and, as she had come to take her course more seriously, Mila had felt Jasmine's respect for her go up a few notches. This is why Mila could admit to Jasmine that she was struggling with a real intellectual puzzle, and of course Jasmine wanted to help.

Mila explained to Jasmine how she was stuck, because there was no alternative to the orthodox view which said the current system, and the inequality it produced, was rational. Even if you realised that the people who benefited from this inequality were the ones who argued that it was rational, you could not come up with an alternative view which showed it was not. For instance, anybody who said that the system that produces inequality was inefficient or not productive enough would be laughed at. You were only allowed to say that inequality was an unfortunate side effect; you could never come up with an argument that undermined the system that produced it. In reply, Jasmine relied on what she knew most about, science:

'In science there are lots of examples where a theory is not proved wrong but simply overtaken. Nobody has ever proved Newton's theories were really wrong, but if you just followed his theories there would be some parts of modern physics that made no sense to you. In science you don't always win an argument by proving someone else is wrong, you might agree they are right but you show they missed out important factors.'

Mila wanted to discuss this further with Dalina, her tutor. Dalina said that it had a lot to do with the way the politics and economics of the twentieth century turned out. History was always written by the winning side – whether in wars or any other kind of conflict – and what counted as sociology was determined in the same way. Marxism was one of the big losers of twentieth-century history; Weber's concern with conflict and competition over resources no longer fitted with a world in which global development was portrayed as a boon to everyone. But Dalina said there was something else wrong with Marx and Weber, a kind of inbuilt design fault. If you understood this fault, you would see it was not simply a big part of the causes of their declining popularity but the reason why Mila had ultimately found their theories unsatisfactory or, at the very least, seriously incomplete.

Dalina went on to tell her about Eleanor Marx and Marianne Weber. Eleanor, Karl Marx's youngest daughter, was brilliant and precocious, a natural intellectual heir to her father. But of course she was a woman, and she lived in the nineteenth century, so, instead of pursuing her own career, she became his secretary, helping him to put together the pieces that became the three massive volumes of her father's book, *Capital*. Then she nursed Marx and her mother at the end of their lives. She had two long-lasting relationships with men and the last of them required extreme examples of the same self-sacrifice that had characterised Eleanor's early life. She still managed, however, to become a well-known feminist, revolutionary, trade union agitator, journalist, and writer of several books in her own right. Then she committed suicide while still only 43. When he had been at that same age, her father was still six years away from publishing the first volume of *Capital* – who knew what Eleanor might have gone on to do?

Of course Mila wanted to know why Eleanor had committed suicide. Dalina said that nobody knew for sure, but that there were theories. The man she was with at the time, Aveling, was never faithful to her and may have humiliated her one time too many, perhaps by secretly marrying someone else. Or perhaps Aveling had defrauded some political or trade union funds. At this point it seemed that Mila might say something and Dalina stopped, but Mila shook her head and Dalina carried on. There was also another theory that Aveling black-mailed Eleanor by threatening to reveal that her friend, Freddie Demuth, was not the illegitimate son of Marx's collaborator Engels, but the illegitimate son of the father she worshipped and honoured. Perhaps Eleanor thought she could not have endured the way her fathers' enemies would have gloried in his disgrace.

'Maybe she preferred to die, we don't really know. Anyway I haven't told you about Marianne.'

Dalina said that Marianne Weber was a leading light in German social democracy and that country's early women's movement at the beginning of the twentieth century. Her childhood was blighted by the effects of the mental illness that plagued her family and which would eventually affect her as well. Max Weber was her cousin and with tragic inevitability, he fell prey to serious mental illness after their marriage. Marianne nursed Max through his illness for seven years only to see him fall in love, and begin an affair, with a mutual friend. It was ironic to think that Marianne's most famous work was called *Marriage, Motherhood and Law*!

Marianne kept the marriage going and, as Max's fame and importance grew, the Webers became the centre of an intellectual circle that included the sociologist George Simmel and Marie Baum, the feminist. Marianne herself continued to publish feminist works and became the first German woman representative elected to a state assembly and the president of the Federation of German Women's Organisations. Then Max's sister Lili committed suicide and Max himself died suddenly. Marianne suffered through four years of depression before becoming active again in public and eventually adopting Lili's four children. Although she continued to publish in the underground press, her public activity came to an end in the early 1930s with the rise of Hitler. She lived to a ripe old age, but her own mental health was badly affected by the experience of Nazism.

'What sad stories those are,' said Mila. 'Do you think they were heroines, Marianne and Eleanor – noble and self-sacrificing – or do you think they were mad to put up with such treatment? How much choice did they have?' said Mila but, as she said it, she was not thinking of Marianne Weber or Eleanor Marx, but of her own mother. She could see the parallels between her mother's life and theirs and she thought her mother was noble and self-sacrificing.

Since she had come to terms with the fact that Lin was an important person in her mother's life, Mila felt very close to her mother again. But now she knew that she felt close to her mother *as an adult* who admired her mother's strength of character rather than as a child who questioned nothing their parent did and made no judgements of her own. Mila felt she was no longer a little girl running home to her mummy, but a woman who was admiring, and strongly identifying with, another woman who happened to be her mother. If she admired her mother, then how could she not admire Marianne or Eleanor, how could she not think she would have been proud if she had acted as they did in their place? So she told Dalina that she could not believe they were foolish. 'No, they *were* noble and anyone who thinks otherwise is giving in and seeing the world the way men saw it.' And she had to stop herself from adding: 'men like my father.'

'Well, that's one way of looking at it, but you might think they rather overdid the self-sacrifice. Perhaps for their good and ours it might have been better if they had thought more of themselves and given their ideas the proper space and time to develop. But that was not what happened in the societies they lived in, or rather endured, and that's the point. Maybe I wouldn't make their mistakes, and you wouldn't either, but back then there was no alternative. Whatever they might have thought of their bohemian credentials, Karl Marx and Max Weber were still part of a world in which women's voices were silenced, not always because they were told to shut up, but because their precious time got used up doing other things. Now the world has moved on – at least it has in some places – and maybe this gives us the answer to your question as well. There is one big problem with Marx and Weber: they claimed to speak for everyone and that will no longer wash. They never had the right to speak for Eleanor and Marianne and neither do their successors.'

Dalina told Mila she thought the world had changed and the way sociology saw the world had changed too. There was no longer one perspective: Marx and Weber and all the rest came up with their answers which were meant to apply to the whole world but they were missing out big bits of the picture. Because of the way they received the ideas of the Enlightenment, they thought that progress for people like them, white European males, would be progress for the whole of humanity.

Mila experienced this as a revelation. She was looking for a way of finding the voice of those who suffered most from inequality and here was Dalina explaining exactly why she had been unable to find out up to now: the exclusion of such voices was apparently part of a basic design fault in the theories of Marx and Weber. Mila felt vindicated and rather proud, but she could not help but feel a little puzzled by what Dalina went on to say next.

'Do you remember the seminar on scientific knowledge, and the discussion about how we come to know things? In any social situation, be it sociological research or a conversation, the answers you get often, and maybe always, depend on the questions you ask, and this means not only what you ask but who you ask it of, and how you ask it. Sociologists have been aware of this for some time. It isn't that different from natural scientists who try to screen out observer bias and make sure that the observer has as little impact on the experiment as possible. The difference with sociology and the other social sciences is that you can never really get rid of the observer.'

Dalina then went on to explain that in sociology the observers, the sociologists, were also affected by what the people who were being observed were doing. 'Unlike the natural sciences, in sociology the observer and the observed are the same – we're all people. The knowledge sociologists produce influences how other people behave, how they talk and what they talk about, and – this is less often noticed – the knowledge other people produce influences how sociologists think and talk and behave. So, in the case of Marx and Weber, their theories were very much affected by the behaviour of other people at the time.'

'If the story about the illegitimate son was true, Marx covered it up because of how other people would react. After that, it's pretty clear what he says in his books was affected by other people as well,' Mila said.

'Yes, but don't be too hard on Marx, either. I am not saying simply that he left women out because he was worried about social convention. There was also a problem, will always be a problem, in finding out what the people who are being excluded want to say.'

'I don't get it. Why couldn't he just ask? Why couldn't he just ask Eleanor? And why couldn't Weber just ask Marianne, or at least read her books?'

'As sociologists, and as people, we speak languages that can be understood by each other, we can make ourselves heard, we can ask and listen to the answer. Things should be easy. In practice, nothing could be farther from the truth. Sociological categories are full of instances which miss people out, or define what some people do as less important than what other people do. For instance, women's domestic labour was for a long time ignored by studies of work, as if it didn't happen. The social sciences have had enormous trouble just working out who people are and what they want. Anthropology, sociology, economics, they've all had great difficulty defining what they were studying. Hardly a research paper goes by without someone arguing that the way we define ethnicity or class is wrong and, furthermore, that the questions that we have been asking are the wrong ones – and even when they have been the right ones we haven't bothered listening to the answers.'

Mila thought this was good. It made sense that the way you conceived of a problem, the way you chose the basic building blocks of your thought, could close off all sorts of opportunities to bring in the people whose voices were not heard from the very start. It was as if you were in an elevator, concentrating on pushing the button for the right floor, and unaware that by closing the doors now you were leaving lots of people who wanted to ride with you on the ground floor. 'Are you also saying that sociology tends to close the doors on – sorry, I mean, miss out – the people who are different to the sociologists in some way? Like the sociologists are men, and they exclude women, or they are Christians or Jews and they exclude Muslims?'

Mila could see Dalina's point, but it gave her no pleasure to be able to antici-pate the stages in her argument because Mila was still puzzled as to where all this was ultimately leading. She had believed that the basic ideas of Marx and Weber were on the right lines, that they had the potential for changing society for the better, but were seriously incomplete and so the potential stayed unrealised. Now Dalina seemed to be saying that Marx and Weber were not worth saving. Mila was beginning to feel dispirited.

Dalina was now saying there were two lines of objection to the old sociological project. The first was that the classical sociologists (including Durkheim as well as Marx and Weber) had a rather blinkered view which ignored a lot of people. They thought that they were stating timeless, universal truths. They thought of themselves as staring reality in the face but were only describing what they saw in the mirror – their truths and their realities. According to Dalina, people who raised this sort of objection were not rejecting the *possibility* of creating univer-sal truths, they only suggested that Marx and the rest of the crew failed in their objective. By including more voices and more experiences, particularly those from the bottom rungs of society, more accurate universal statements could be made and sociology could come to reflect a truer version of reality.

This was fine, Mila thought, it's the elevator theory: Marx and Weber forgot to open the doors wide enough but it is still possible to open the doors and we can get it right next time. Fine, but Dalina was saying the second type of objection was harsher.

'It says that not only did these dead white males fail to take account of, and listen to, certain people's voices, they never could have. They – and all of us – are incapable of ever listening to and understanding someone who is different.'

Mila was desperate to find a way of dismissing this version out of hand.

'So, some voices never get heard – but how do we know which ones are being ignored if our very method of asking questions prohibits some answers or some voices from answering. And is any of this really true, anyway? From when I first started studying sociology, I learned that sociologists pioneered work with people who have been shut away from the rest of society – psychi-atric patients, criminals, ethnic minorities. From this work, they developed insights not only about the situation of these groups of people but about our entire society.'

Dalina seemed to ignore Mila's first point and answered the second.

'I wouldn't quarrel with you, Mila. Sociology has been at its best when listen-ing to these hidden voices, but it has still been reluctant to admit when its own practices are excluding some voices in favour of others. There are many examples of people being ignored in this way: theories of class are a top-ranking offender. Class has been a major part of sociological research and theory. For a long time it was the only respectable way of looking at what went on in society. The prob-lem has been that attempts to actually apply theories of class to society have relied on ignoring a whole lot of people who didn't seem to fit into one class or another, or lumping different sorts of people together with others who were nothing like them. For instance, women were assigned to their husband's social class, and their domestic labour was brushed aside.'

'I agree that this is wrong. It's obvious it's wrong. Sociology has a special responsibility not to act like this. But it was the classical sociologists like Weber and Marx who designed it this way. They wanted sociology to point out to society aspects of its working that might not be what members of society would like to hear. Part of this has been to try and speak up for people who haven't been able to have their voices heard directly.'

'It's fine to take care not to ignore or silence people, but isn't it a bit arrogant to think you can speak *for them*? Can we really describe things for other people who are very different to us? Can we understand what it's like to be in their shoes? Can we really understand people who have had different lives to us?'

Dalina went on to say that the harsher critics of Marx and Weber said that it was wrong to suggest that we could speak for other people in this way. For a long time we had lived with the idea that progress – human beings getting on better with each other, developing socially, economically, morally – meant the same to everyone. Sociology's role was meant to be weighing up the merits of competing ideas of progress (Marxism, social democracy, and so on).

The first set of critics adhered to this premise, adding only that we needed to get more people, more voices, on board this project for it to work right. But, after the 'second wave' of the feminist movement in the 1960s, and separatist black nationalism in the USA, and the waves of migration in the twenty-first century, it turned out that there were a lot of people who thought the premise was utterly flawed. They pointed out that the achievements of liberalism – universal rights to vote, outlawing discrimination – had not done very much to eradicate inequality, to get rid of racism and sexism, to make the world a fairer place. Even worse, they said, these liberal rights had actually made things worse by masking all that racism and sexism and classism, because they gave the impression that everything was alright now. Sociology, they said, was a guilty partner because, like all the social sciences, it had operated with the assumption that what society had to do was get everyone on board and make sure that everyone was treated fairly. After that, everyone else's problems became their own fault.

'Yes, I know there are some feminists who don't think that universal rights, legal equality, anti-discrimination laws, and so on are enough. There are people who think the same thing about race and ethnicity then?' asked Mila.

Dalina said theorists of race were just as concerned as some feminists were with the inequality that liberal concepts of equality and justice cloaked. They pointed out that there seems to be an injustice in every justice, a wrong in every 'right'. Then she had a question for Mila.

'When you were reading Marx and Weber, didn't it always seem to you that the classical sociologists were talking about someone else?'

'I see what you mean. They wrote so long ago and I am a woman in a different kind of society, but I *could* identify with what they were saying, all the same. It made sense to me in a way. It made me feel as if I could do something.'

'Maybe, but is that a genuine feeling? It's because you buy into the Hegelian idea of a *universal subject* that you think this. The universal subject is both inside and outside of society, because they are partly representing the society that is about to come into existence. The universal subject represents the future state of society. It is the "motor of history", in Marx's rather odd term, as if history was a car that needed an engine, with him in the driver's seat.'

For Marx, the proletariat would be the universal subject of capitalist society because they and their leaders, which included of course Marx himself, were able to speak from the perspective of the socialist society which would replace capitalism. When the proletariat became politically mature (i.e. Marxist) enough, they would also revolutionise society and overthrow the capitalists. Dalina said lots of people just did not buy into the idea of the universal subject. It did not seem real to them: it was always too abstract, existing more in the heads of Marxists than in society.

Feminists criticised Marxism because the universal subject of the proletarian was implicitly assumed to be male, and black nationalists criticised Marxism because it was assumed to be white. Working-class women were in a very different position from working-class men and didn't always have the same interests and certainly didn't have the same views. The organised, Marxist proletariat represented only a small part of the working class. To deal with this problem, some feminists tried to set up women as the universal subject, while others abandoned the whole idea as inherently flawed. The whole structure of intellectual thought, social and historical, reflected a tradition that was quite narrow but thought itself broad and all encompassing.

'It's a matter of perspective, where you are looking from, as well as who you are,' Dalina said. 'That "where" and "who" need a closer look. Take the "where". When we think about intellectual traditions we often put ourselves within Europe, looking down on all the rest – without knowing that we are doing so – and even if we are not in Europe!'

Dalina said that because of colonialism, and the economic and political success of European countries and their inheritor, the USA, it is assumed that progress spreads outwards from Europe. Asians, South Americans, and Africans begin the race from well behind the starting line. Thinkers like Marx and J. S. Mill, who prided themselves on thinking of all humans as equal, thought that they had not yet reached the level of civilisation required for self-government.

'To think like that, we have to ignore – or be ignorant about – non-European intellectual traditions. For instance, we often say that sociology started in the Scottish Enlightenment, or with the work of August Comte. Ibn Khaldun, a fourteenth-century North African polymath, wrote what we would now call a sociological–historical analysis of world history. In the process he laid claim to a science, *ilm al-umran*, that would explain how societies came to be the way they were – a "science that has its own peculiar object – that is, human civilisation and social organisation". Sounds familiar? He developed what are distinctly sociological ideas on conflict, cohesion, urbanisation, power, historical change, and how things come to have value – all events and ideas we assume began in Europe, around the time of the French Revolution and the Industrial Revolution. Marxist analyses of history often gave the impression that history began then and there – and that countries like India or China had to get up to speed before they began to have a history as well.'

Dalina explained that we think that the 'who', the universal subject, is a universal standpoint, but it is not. It is specific – in ways we are not aware of because they are deeply hidden. Stuart Hall was one sociologist who began to explore this. He started work in Britain in the 1950s having come from Jamaica. He found himself out of place – middle class and well educated, so an insider, but black, so outside the boundaries of British identity. He found that what appeared to be an inclusive and colour-blind identity, that of 'British', was one that he could not be part of because of his colour.

Hall thought about the way our identities and ideas about everyday life are created and reflected in popular culture. He wanted to see how ideologies – meaning sets of hidden values – are created and reproduced in culture. By 'culture' he meant the array of objects and experiences that produce meaning. He included television, popular magazines, music, radio, magazines, films, books, adverts, newspapers. One of the great things Hall contributed was the idea that it was necessary and desirable for academics to study popular culture, what most people use in their lives.

Up to that point, only high art, literature and music had been OK to study – the culture that the elite liked. Hall and others thought that they should look at the cultural objects and experiences people used to make and make sense of their lives – the media that they lived their lives through, and which provided a window onto the lives of others. First that meant things like TV but after that it was websites, podcasts, and video games. 'He used the theory of Antonio Gramsci, that there was an all pervasive "common sense", the assumed meanings and biases in apparently neutral media, discourse, structures like the state, fundamental assumptions about what society is like, what relationships are like, people who are deviant and not to be imitated. The media persuades.'

Dalina said there were 'dominant meanings in the media and social media – the accepted story that everyone believes. Some subjects are for ever off the agenda or taken on in a way that tells you what all right-thinking people believe is true. So if you have an exam question asking "What policing methods are effective in reducing crime?", it presumes that there is agreement about what crime is, that it should be reduced, and that policing is the way to do it.'

'So how are we part of that? asked Mila.

'Hall thought that there was not just a right way of being – there had to be a wrong one implied too: what is called "the other". Identity is always created in terms of what it is not – so British at the time meant, among other things, not being black.'

'And being a man is not being a woman,' said Mila. 'But is that not just everybody's normal way of thinking? For me, being a woman means not being a man – obviously!'

'Hall's point is that it makes the second part of each of these pairings, white–black, man–woman, into a residual, what's left over – not something in itself. The "others" are marked, and ourselves are unmarked. Homi Bhaba wrote that a process of forgetting is done which hides the uncertainty at the heart of all claims to "we" and "I".

Dalina went on to talk about the way nations had a myth of singularity – of a single cultural history, that of the dominant social class and ethnic group, which usually hid mixing, mongrelisation and conflict. 'This also goes for members of minority groups that suddenly rediscover venerable and spotless cultural traditions that are claimed as a profound part of their identity, or expatriates who become obsessed with the mother country. This can be a response to alienation, or perceived racism; and it can be born of a sense of cultural superiority. But they make it up of the things they have to hand. Modernity has meant high levels of emigration and immigration around the world. There are many "diasporas", people who live in a place different from that they claim as theirs. Hall thought that being in a diaspora was a common feeling, having to negotiate where and who one is, was something more and more people have to do.'

Mila thought of herself and Jasmine – never quite able to be what they were, with slippery or questionable identities. They were in-betweeners.

'The USA, Canada, and Western European countries were becoming more multicultural from the 1950s on and into the twenty-first century. Other countries were going in the opposite direction – changing borders, moving populations, often violently, to make themselves more "pure". As Hall had predicted, this involved creating myths of past racial and linguistic purity. Croatia and Serbia rewrote their histories. The Taliban in Afghanistan erased evidence of Buddhism in their country.'

According to Dalina, Hall thought that Enlightenment liberalism could not explain these events without reference to 'barbarism' which itself just made the problem another example of 'the other'. Race and race relations problems were treated in a liberal sort of a way, requiring education among the ignorant majority, and ending discrimination. Hall thought this was not the case – problems of interethnic conflict and racial strife were projections of much larger issues of exploitation, post-colonial economics, and power politics. The universal subject obscured these processes and made people think that racism was an individual problem, or leftover from less enlightened times. In fact, racism was very modern.

More and more criticism was made of the universal subject until it collapsed under the weight of its own contradictions. The problem with it was perhaps not so much that the universal subject was flawed in conception, although that may very well have been the case. It was more that nothing could bear up under the weight of the expectations put upon it by Marxists and others. 'It's a tall order, being told that you are the motor of history and furthermore that you represent a uniquely moral point of view. Few of us would like to be informed that the future of society rests on our shoulders. Marxists worried about how the proletariat never behaved like their theories said it would or should. If they had looked in the mirror a little bit harder they might have realised that the problem rested with their theory of the universal subject, not the proletariat.'

Dalina had now got back to the place in her argument when she had asked Mila if it had seemed as though the classical sociologists were talking about someone else.

'Does the abandonment of the universal subject mean that the questions you ask and the answers you get – about life and yourself – are always different depending on who you are? Is there any common ground between different people?' Mila was beginning to feel quite miserable because, if the answer to this question was no, she felt she might as well give up.

Meanwhile, Dalina was saying that those sociologists who wanted the hidden voices to be heard still claimed that there was a universal truth which could be attained so long as we adhered to the correct, value-free methodologies. But objectors to the idea of the universal subject argued that the distinction between facts and values was fallacious. Value-free research had fallen out of favour, with a lot of people arguing that such a thing was impossible. They said that all research was biased one way or another:

'Feminist standpoint epistemologists go further and argue that the answers you get depend entirely on who you are. They say that women are the truly oppressed, and that only women working from a feminist perspective can really tell it like it is. They aren't the only ones. Postmodernists deride attempts made by classical sociology to speak for everyone, saying that this is both impossible and harmful.'

Mila remembered the 'feminist standpoint' people were the ones whose names she always forgot, and she also remembered why she distrusted their views.

'Aren't they just saying that since you are going to be biased anyway, you might as well choose which bias you adopt, and be honest about it?'

'Let's take this a bit more seriously,' Dalina said. 'The 'real' is changed by social status and power. Social psychologists have noted the conformity effect in their experiments. The judgements people make about such things as basic as the length of two lines changes depending on the judgements of others around them. And it changes much more towards those of a perceived higher status than them.'

'We all want to please teacher,' Mila commented.

'I should hope so,' Dalina raised her eyebrows. 'So then take that question and apply it to everything that we do to gather knowledge about the world. What if these unconscious biases are not simply errors, but systematic facts about the world created by the systems of privilege and inequality that surround us?'

She took a breath.

'If you find that people disagree on what is real, or they agree on what is real when they should be disagreeing, you are taking on the most basic question of knowledge. It is called ontology: what is, and what is its nature?'

'It is a difficult topic to tussle with so I like to think of it in terms of questions to ask. Do you think reality is the same in all places, and for all observers? Quantum physics shows that some very basic facts of reality only come into existence when they are observed. Take that to a level we can work with in sociology, you might look at some basic definitional errors. Defining two things as distinct when they are the same, or have an underlying sameness. Or vice versa.'

'So,' Mila said, 'saying that male and female brains are different when they are largely the same, and this difference represents a fundamental fact about human nature. Or in the reverse, asking only men's opinions on a topic or for only men's experiences and taking them to be representative of human experience as a whole.'

'This happens a lot,' Dalina said. 'Social class is defined in terms of male occupation. The ageing process was defined in terms of what was supposed to happen to men, so it was assumed that men would naturally move into retirement and be put out to pasture. But for many women, they take on caring responsibilities later in life, so work continues long after retirement age. The fact that care was often not recognised as work is another epistemological error.'

'That does not happen because everybody is confused, or prejudiced, or holds the wrong set of values. The scientific and social scientific practices bring things into being. How we create knowledge does this. Which makes this a relevant question for us.'

'You can see this happen every time when uncertainty becomes certainty – as in a lot of medical diagnosis. For instance, the longstanding sociological concept of sickness owed a lot to Parsons. He defined the sick role as being unable to fulfil one's social duties. Doctors had the special power to allow people to legitimately withdraw from their obligations by defining them as sick. This relies on an idea of illness and obligation that depends on a stereotypical ideal that most of our social obligations take place in public – basically, work and socialising in public places. If many of your obligations take place in the home, or involve caring for people close to you, as is the case for many women, you cannot just happily withdraw from them when you get ill. Your obligations do not stop at the front door of the home.'

Mila wondered if this also applied to the views of the marginalised, the ones whose voices had been suppressed. Were sociologists always comfortable with what those voices had to say when they were raised so that everyone could hear? Dalina thought this was a good point. Left-wing sociologists tended to ignore or explain away uncomfortable facts – about racism or homophobia among the downtrodden, or women's acceptance of traditional female roles.

'Well then,' said Mila, hardly bothering to hide her exasperation and disappointment, 'we've gone full circle; where do we go now?'

'You mean the situated, standpoint subject is as limited as the universal subject?'

'That's what you mean isn't it? "Bad things" said by those hidden voices are ignored or explained away. How does that help anyone? It seems that the standpoint theorists and the postmodernists are saying that the things one set of people say only make sense to people who are like them. If I want to be understood, I have to expect other people to adhere to some common set of standards. If I expect them to, then I should as well, otherwise it's all pointless, isn't it?'

'Sociology has tended to be stuck between the feeling that it should wear its heart on its sleeve, and the knowledge that it is only persuasive when it conducts work which is unbiased. If people think you have an agenda, they tend to either tell you what you want to hear or ignore you altogether.'

'So, if I have understood what you have been telling me, there are two strands to the "hidden voices" criticism of Marx and Weber and other classical sociologists.' Mila continued, a little wearily. 'The first is that they were blinkered in their approach. Because of their cultural background they couldn't see that what they thought were universal truths were only very specific truths about people. If we take off our blinkers, we can be better sociologists, and likewise better people, by including all the voices. There was nothing wrong with their perspective or their aims, they just fell down on the job. They did bad sociology, but their hearts were mainly in the right place. The second strand suggests that their hearts, basically, were not in the right place. It is not just a case of filling in the blanks, but only people with the right mindset can listen to those voices. Only people who've been on the downside of the Enlightenment can really see the truth, really understand what is going on. Only they can speak for themselves. If the second lot are right, then how can there be any universal truths? If people can only speak on behalf of people like them, then how does anyone end up listening to and understanding anyone else?'

'But the critics are asking good questions: who chooses what gets studied, who speaks for, and about, whom? Are we fundamentally defined by difference or sameness? Framing the argument in those terms means we lose it. It is only women who were ever required to reproduce for the nation; and men who had to die for it. Men's dying for it mean they could be full citizens. Women, who produced the men dying for it, were subordinate citizens. Both exist alongside each other. That theory of the citizen has been fragmented, as women in the USA can be soldiers, and can die alongside their husbands and brothers.

We often come back to motherhood as the fundamental difference. Only women can create new citizens, and this fact has been used to tie them to the home and the birthing bed. Yet that is also mistaking it for one thing. There are many different perspectives on motherhood and ways of experiencing it. If all women have in common is screaming pain at the end of nine months, that is not a great standpoint to start with. Especially when some can afford to rent other women's wombs, and purchase their eggs.'

Sociologists and philosophers – and other social scientists and humanities scholars – have a special responsibility. They all spend a lot of time talking about what other people do, rather than doing it themselves, or thinking about the terms on which they do it, which is where the feminist epistemologists and the post-colonial theorists come in. Those other people seldom get a chance to talk back and, when they do, what they say is often not taken at face value. There is a danger that sociology only sounds convincing because it tries to offer explanations in terms of a pre-set framework, explanations that are bound to seem persuasive because they can't be disproved except by moving outside that framework.'

'Where does this leave us? Does this just apply to sociology, or to everyone? Is it really impossible to understand the experiences of someone else? Can a black middle-class woman only understand other black middle-class women? You hear this from non-sociologists too. You know, "you would never understand – it's a black thing, a Catholic thing". I think this just means "keep your nose out of my business, you could never understand me". But sociologists used to think that they could help people understand each other, appreciate each other's varied experiences and in so doing help make things better. If people could understand that there were people worse off than them, they would do something about it. But you're saying that this may not be possible at all. I am sure it's an overreaction, but this makes me feel completely demoralised.'

'And I was trying to help! I'm sorry, Mila, but let's not give up too easily. A philosopher, Wittgenstein, asked how he could feel another person's pain. He wasn't too sure if this was possible. According to his philosophical system, it wasn't, yet the reality was something else. If you see someone else get hurt – even if they are someone you don't know – you often experience a gut reaction, a squirming feeling of pain. You *can* share their pain. Some men get birth pangs in sympathy with their pregnant wives, apparently. At least some experiences can be shared, and not always with those who are close to us.'

Dalina said she thought some sort of understanding, a literal fellow feeling, was possible between individuals. Indeed, it could be said that communication – and hence basic agreement about meaning and the form of communication – was both possible and necessary. Society could not exist without it, and as individuals we would be pretty much lost as well. The fact that society did exist, the fact that you could translate Chinese philosophical texts into English and retain most of the meaning, must imply that it was possible to talk to, and understand, and be changed by, people and ideas from very different cultures. 'We have at least got the potential to feel things across apparently intractable barriers. It might just mean that we can say things, make statements, that apply across those same barriers as well, statements that have meaning for a man in Delhi and a woman in New York.'

Dalina seemed pleased and was giving the impression she thought her impromptu lesson had reached a successful and satisfying conclusion, but Mila still felt depressed. She thanked Dalina profusely for her generosity with her time. To the embarrassment of both of them, Mila even said Dalina was as self-sacrificing as Eleanor Marx and told her she thought that their talk had helped her make progress. But in truth Mila really felt a great deal less positive than she sounded.

If she was persuaded by the arguments that Dalina had laid out, what on earth was she to do about it? She might understand why Marx and Weber's theories were not enough, but where were the missing pieces to come from? She was still looking for more inspiration and, in fact, she seemed worse off than before, because, if she believed all she had been told, she knew now that the search for inspiration would always be fruitless. Mila was feeling a kind of emptiness even, to her surprise, a kind of despair. Apparently people like her were not allowed to speak for the oppressed. The sketchiest outline of a possible plan for Mila's future that had been slowly taking shape in her head had fallen into pieces. The same could be said, as far as Mila could see, of the whole sociological enterprise. If that was in fragments too, then why bother carrying on learning about it?

Dalina could tell from Mila's expression that she was not being entirely honest and asked her what was wrong. Then Mila had to admit that, even though it was not really sensible, she felt disappointed and deflated. When Dalina asked her why, she began, hesitantly, to explain.

'Leaving it to the hidden voices is letting power and privilege off the hook, isn't it? What if the voices stay silent? And, even if they don't, won't they probably be ignored, or, at best, fobbed off? Doesn't there have to be some universalising insight into whatever it is that creates the inequality and oppression? I wanted a sociologist to *really* question the basis of the society that produces all of this, in fact to help us look at the whole way we live now, everything we take for granted, in a completely new way. I wanted somebody who threw it all up in the air and made it come down in a way that would help everyone to see that things could be made better.'

'You could always try reading Simmel – he was one of those bright sparks Marianne Weber used to entertain in her salon. It's a long time since I read him, but that was what he was all about, as far as I can remember. Not that everyone takes him seriously: he was a dilettante, a maverick who did not find work in a university but wrote lots of odd things, just as it pleased him. He wrote essays on how to say hello, love, the sociology of smell, secrecy, and the social significance of chairs.'

Mila was laughing in spite of herself. 'Yes he sounds just about mad enough for me.'

Visit the companion website at **www.palgrave.com/companion/ Bancroft-And-Fevre-Dead-White-Men-2e/** to access additional learning resources, including seminar questions based on the chapter's coverage, a jargon buster that defines key terms used in the text and a timeline which provides an overview of the development of sociological thought.

● ● ● ● ●

What do you hear when you speak?

Your voice?

The sound of others' voices?

1. A trick of the sociological imagination is to look at a specific experience or problem and link it to a system problem. That is the question that relates what is said to who is saying it — linking knowledge to power.

2. The Enlightenment was an eighteenth-century revolution in thought, which claimed to replace religion with reason. Many of the approaches common to sociology, other social sciences and the natural sciences are grounded in the Enlightenment. The Enlightenment sought to cut down the voices of those who spoke FROM authority — from tradition, or divine right — and replace it with those who speak WITH authority — the authority granted by scientific, objective knowledge.

3. Standpoint epistemology is critical of this position, and points to how that 'objective voice' speaks by silencing others. A truer objective standard is necessary, one that comes from recognising how the most cool and level headed perspective might in fact be partial after all. Feminist epistemologists have pointed to how supposedly universal ideas of the human subject — rights, wants and needs — are in fact based on male rights, wants and needs. Black feminists, among others, have criticised the way in which feminist ideas that claimed to speak for all women in fact only spoke for a few.

4. Yet some ability to represent others — to speak on their behalf and with their voice — seems to be necessary for public debate and democracy. Otherwise we are back to a situation where it is the loudest voice that is heard.

17
In and Out

Mila started with what Frank 'n' Stein said about Simmel's essay on 'the stranger' because she imagined that her own brief experience of assuming a false identity might make this an easy path into Simmel's theories. It turned out that the essay was not really about the experience of being a stranger but something unexpected: the way having a stranger around affected *other* people. If there was someone in a group who did not belong like the others, and might not stay for long, this affected the way the group functioned. For example, the members of the group could use strangers to bring them things that they could not provide for themselves. So strangers could be traders, for example. As the European Jews found, this was a role that those from outside could occupy when all the economic roles inside the group are taken.

Strangers were also useful because they could be objective. They were not insiders and could operate with a detachment that could be extremely useful. This might even give the stranger great power. Simmel talked about the:

> dominating positions of the person who is a stranger in the group; its most typical instance was the practice of those Italian cities to call their judges from the outside, because no native was free from entanglement in family and party interests.

It was uncanny: this was exactly what Mila and her friends had relied on Jasmine for. She was the one who they could always rely on to be honest – sometimes painfully honest – and scrupulously fair. They trusted her to be the objective one in disagreements or whenever they could not make up their minds about something. Up to now, it had never occurred to Mila that they might have given her this role because she was from another country, but she, and Tuni and Ana and Circe always thought of Jasmine as the neutral referee.

When Mila turned her attention back to Simmel, there were more surprises in store. He said the stranger's 'objectivity may also be defined as freedom.' The stranger could say what (s)he thought and had no stake in the status quo, no investment to protect. This meant that what strangers bring – like the outside agitators who so often are blamed for unrest – 'contains many dangerous possibilities.' Of course blaming strangers when things went wrong could be an excuse, a way of shifting the blame, but it would not work if people did not realise how dangerous the objective, uninvolved view can be.

Mila read on and found that, according to Simmel, we all have some things in common with the stranger, things we may have in common with many others, perhaps most of humankind, and this can tell us something profound about our relationships. What we think of any relationship is heavily influenced by the degree to which we see it as unique, or largely made up of things we have in common with lots of other people, including strangers of whom we know very little. Frank 'n' Stein seemed to like quoting Simmel.

> The stranger is close to us, insofar as we feel between him and ourselves common features of a national, social, occupational, or generally human, nature. He is far from us, insofar as these common features extend beyond him or us, and connect us only because they connect a great many people.

Simmel also said that some 'trace' of this kind of strangeness could be felt by people in intimate relationships, after they had got over the first flush of falling in love.

> In the stage of first passion, erotic relations strongly reject any thought of generalisation: the lovers think that there has never been a love like theirs; that nothing can be compared either to the person loved or to the feelings for that person. An estrangement – whether as cause or as consequence it is difficult to decide – usually comes at the moment when this feeling of uniqueness vanishes from the relationship. A certain scepticism in regard to its value, in itself and for them, attaches to the very thought that in their relation, after all, they carry out only a generally human destiny; that they experience an experience that has occurred a thousand times before; that, had they not accidentally met their particular partner, they would have found the same significance in another person.

Mila was irritated by this. She skipped a few pages of Frank 'n' Stein until she got to the discussion of his essay on fashion. She read this all at one go and it made her scream with laughter, because Simmel was obviously familiar with Tuni, their very own fashion queen. Soon Mila was chasing Tuni down the corridor trying to read quotes from Simmel's essay to her. Tuni locked herself in the bathroom to escape her, but Mila sat down on the floor outside and read to Tuni through the locked door while Tuni sang at the top of her voice in an attempt to drown Mila out.

'Where is that quote? It's just right, it's exactly like you, Tuni! Simmel says: "It is peculiarly characteristic of fashion that it renders possible a social obedience, which at the same time is a form of individual differentiation". Then she explained the quote while Tuni sang more loudly: 'He means that with fashion you can actually express your individuality *and* follow the crowd: it makes you feel both different *and* the same. The most fashionable people are able to carry this off with the most style, exaggerating the fashion of the moment just a tiny bit. They seem to be the most individual but are actually the most dominated by the fashion.'

Mila stood up to shout the next bit through the door at what she hoped was ear level. 'So, if you are leading fashion you are actually showing how dependent you are on the group, on the approval of the group. You are a sheep and it's the rest of us who are really individuals. That's what they mean by fashion VICTIMS!'

Ana came to tell her to keep the noise down. 'We're victims of your craziness. What do you think you are doing running up and down the corridor shouting bits of sociology at us, you mad woman?'

Well, thought Mila, that shows how much Ana has come out of her shell – she has become more self-confident and assertive in the last few weeks. She went back to her room and picked up her book again. Frank 'n' Stein said that, scattered through the odd collection of works Simmel had written, was a sort of theory. The first part of this theory seemed to rest on Simmel's conviction that everything that people did together, every human achievement, would sooner or later be turned against them.

Mila thought this meant that every creative impulse left us in the same position as the songwriter who came to hate the song that made her famous. As soon as she wrote the song, it became something outside her that other people could possess and it defined people's expectations from then on. The inevitable effect was that her opportunities for expression were constrained. When she stood up to sing, people wanted to hear that old song, the one they could sing along with. They didn't want to hear new songs, especially new songs which were in any way strange and different to the old ones.

Frank 'n' Stein said Simmel thought his theory applied to all forms of artistic self-expression and with other kinds of creativity, too. People would come up with religious belief because they were struck with wonder and awe and needed to assign meaning to the world. But then this became formal religion which severely limited, and even oppressed, individual creativity. If the theory could be applied to religion, it was even more relevant to bureaucracies and economic systems. People worked long and hard, and highly creatively, to make such systems but they turned into just that, objective *systems* that could stultify and oppress. They were always deadly to the individual's need to express themselves, to live out their uniqueness.

You could certainly see why Simmel had never got a proper job in a university, thought Mila. You would think he would also have kept away from the cities because it was there that he believed that people were least likely to connect with their creativity. Apparently, it was precisely *because* they had so much freedom and so much choice in the cities that people became dominated by objective culture and incapable of self-expression. Mila was not sure she completely understood the point about cities, and she wondered if Simmel was simply combining Weber's view of bureaucracy and Marx's view of the alienating nature of work under capitalism. Then she came to a discussion of Simmel's thesis in *The Philosophy of Money*, and she learned that it was probably reading Simmel that inspired Weber, rather than the other way round.

Simmel argued that money obliterated the differences between people that used to define traditional societies: not just differences that were ascribed by others – like being of low or noble birth – but also personal and subjective qualities of every kind. When you took money from people, or gave it to them, money made the exchange more impersonal: it might as well be anyone you were dealing with. Mila thought this was the same as the impersonality Simmel wrote about in relation to a trace of strangeness in our relationships – how, the more we thought of what people had in common with others, the less special and important our relationship with them seemed to be. As money became more important, that impersonality became characteristic of the sort of society we lived in: what other people might have thought of us (either because they paid attention to who our parents had been or because they made a judgement about our character) mattered less and less. Being of lowly birth no longer disqualified you from acquiring social esteem, as long as you had enough money. But then being thought a selfish or unscrupulous person was no longer a handicap either.

With money (and the complex division of labour that it made possible) we were more and more dependent on other people, but who those people were, what they were really like, mattered less and less. While money was changing the nature of our relationships with other people, it also intruded deeper and deeper into parts of our life which we were once sure had nothing to do with money. Even if we did not actually work out costs and benefits, money became an all-pervasive metaphor and we thought of all our dealings with other people as a kind of exchange. This fundamentally changed how we felt about others.

Mila thought that this bit had sounded like Durkheim as well as like Weber on rationalisation. Simmel said that irrationality gave way to reason because of the spread of money as the medium of exchange: it flattened cultural differences between people as everyone related between, as well as within, their societies in this impersonal way. Mila thought of how easy it was for people who had money to travel all over the world. Their little plastic cards had made people like her father at home everywhere, or perhaps they weren't really at home anywhere because money was the perfect medium for making connections between strangers – it was a very general kind of connection, something that most people would understand. You could see this linking up to Weber's idea of 'disenchantment'. There was no longer any possibility of being surprised or awed by another culture, by its irrationality and mystery and magic, because everyone had this one transparent and rational approach. In other words, thought Mila, money disenchants.

At this point Frank 'n' Stein mentioned 'globalisation' and the idea that societies in all corners of the world were becoming more and more similar. In Simmel's view, these supposed similarities between societies would refer to the impersonal stuff – the same snack bar on every corner, wearing the same fashions, the same silly songs in people's ears. These superficial things were pushing out opportunities people had for unique self-expression. This was, after all, where the real difference between cultures lay. When people thought of globalisation they usually thought of the new things that societies now had in common but they sometimes forgot about the things that were being lost. And, when people did say everything had become the same, maybe they did not realise that this was what money did. It made things impersonal and it levelled all the differences, which only occurred when people were motivated by other things like self-expression.

Mila thought she had finally understood the point about cities. In some parts of the world, when you got *outside* the cities, you could still find things that were surprising and strange. So, it was in the cities that everything was standardised first and that was because the cities were where objective culture, and particularly money, took hold first. And of course it was in the cities that people first started to assign power and position to others solely on the basis of money. Living in a society where money ruled, rather than religion or kinship, for example, also gave you a lot more freedom because money was neutral, did not make you submit to particular values, live your life in a set way, and so on. It was also in the cities that most people started to want more than their basic needs. This was also what Simmel meant by the cities offering freedom and choice.

It was a bit like what he had to say about fashion (the bit Mila had teased Tuni with). Intriguing possibilities were created when money became the universal, objective *standard of personal worth*, the yardstick against which everyone could measure themselves. You could buy things that showed other people how much money you had and this would allow you to manipulate how people reacted to you, and how they treated you. Mila thought this was like the way people usually thought of status competition and was surprised to learn it was not Weber who had come up with this but Simmel. Then it began to dawn on her that Simmel thought that, whatever the drawbacks, having money as a universal measure of worth was something we ought to celebrate.

Simmel thought money allowed us to see what the true value of things was. The price tag was determined by how much a thing was desired or, to put it in the language of the late twentieth century, by the choices consumers made. It was as if money was a fantastic invention for seeing in the dark, an infrared camera for disclosing the real value of one thing next to another. Of course, a necessary by-product of this invention was that the infrared camera became an object of our desires as well, in fact the most desired of all because it made everything else possible.

One of the most important possibilities for Simmel was that possessing money freed you from the group you were born into. In Weber's terms, Simmel was thinking of escaping from your status group and being able to buy your way into another one. Social conventions and rigid status boundaries could not survive this assault and no status group could keep out those who had money, no matter how its members railed against 'money made in trade' or, simply, 'new money'.

Simmel thought it was also marvellous how all the relations between people could be rationally regulated once you had money in charge. For example, if someone broke a contract by not supplying the worth of labour or goods that had been specified, then there would be compensation to pay, and it wasn't simply that relations were more rational. There were also more and more of them: money put us in touch with each other in a way we would not have dreamed was possible before, because it allowed us to buy and sell from each other. Think of how narrow and stultifying modern life would be without all those interpersonal relationships that money made possible, Simmel would say, and remember what we are buying and selling. We wander through this wonderland exercising personal choice, the ultimate freedom, in pursuit of the lovely things that mean so much to us.

Simmel thought that, because of the power of money, modern culture was full of possibilities which allowed us to design our own lives in ways that were never possible before. For instance, said Frank 'n' Stein, the mixing of cultures in globalisation produced new forms of culture. Mila thought that people like Tuni took most advantage of these possibilities, but wasn't it all a bit pointless? It was like colouring in a picture that had been mass produced. It was not really your ideas that you put into action, there was nothing really creative going on. Was this really going to make people feel that their lives meant something?

When you thought about it this way, Mila thought you could see Simmel was talking about the way money had taken over, or hollowed out, our innermost lives: our aspirations, expectations and fantasies. Simmel told us that money was the talisman of modern life with which the whole world and everything in it could be measured. There was nothing that could not be understood with money, or *tamed* with money, and nobody was above money. We had tamed the world and made it all sing to one tune, but we had torn away the foundations for human values in the process: what value had love and friendship if everyone had his or her price?

Frank 'n' Stein suggested that when people complained about materialism or hedonism this might be what they were trying to understand, but Simmel thought there was really a lot more to this than people abandoning themselves to their most basic desires, or maybe even their instincts. Simmel was working through the ideas of a philosopher, Schopenhauer, who believed that virtues like compassion were much more irrational than rational. It was reason that made us hungry for novelty and difference and we were permanently looking for the greener grass. Reason was responsible for materialism and hedonism: it was not that we were unhappy with what we had but, rather, we were always wanting more sensation and more excitement. This constant search for stimulation was what we had to do now we knew everything, and everyone, had their price.

Simmel thought there could be no freedom of choice without money but Mila wondered how those without it could be free to choose. She was becoming more and more convinced that money fundamentally changed how we felt about other people. She wondered whether this might, in some way, be related to the way people accepted inequality as an unfortunate effect of a rational system and could not be persuaded to do anything about it. In the world that Simmel described, people who were poor would be judged by their poverty: their lack of money would be a measure of their worth. You could then see very easily how people could come to believe that the poor deserved their fate in some way.

Perhaps the patterns that Simmel had found underlie all of the judgements people reached about inequality being unfortunate but inevitable? They simply accepted it as part of the same status quo that had us all wasting our time spending money in various silly ways in order to manipulate how others – who were just as much in thrall to the superficial world of money and what it could buy – thought of us. When you put it like this, you might conclude that failing to see that people could do something to put an end to inequality was no less deplorable than all the other effects of money on social relationships which Simmel had described.

Frank 'n' Stein explained that Simmel thought, on balance, it was all worth it, but his ideas were a warning that we were in danger of becoming simply the impressions we sought to give to others, with no core of things that we believed in. Wasn't this why we needed the money and the clothes and the rest of the things it could buy? Because we had lost all the things we used to believe in that made money unnecessary? Money gave us more freedom and less idea what to do with our time, other than go shopping. We could pay the prices, but we no longer had any values and so, even if we thought we could do something about inequality, did we really believe any longer that we *should* do it?

Mila wondered if that superficial connection we had with everyone because of money meant that there was so little shared between us and other people that we never really believed that they could be hurt like us. Was it any wonder that we forgot that the people who were poor deserved our compassion and, more to the point, should have their own dignity? We had completely lost the ability to empathise with those who were worse off than we were and the fact that money was our talisman had an awful lot to do with this.

Mila could now see that the economic system that legitimates inequality is our hopes and wishes and desires turned into objective culture which then seems to limit our options and frustrate our wishes. We set out to make people more prosperous and end poverty and want, but create a system which is unable to do this – just as Marx suggested – *and* which makes us wonder why we ever thought it could. Simmel showed that the culture that comes with the system smothers the hope we once shared that inequality could be reduced, and even eradicated.

This should have made Mila despair but it did not and what gave her hope was simply the existence of Simmel's theory. If the pre-eminence of money as a source of value was as assured as Simmel made out, it would have been impossible for him to come up with a theory to explain it. It would not have required explanation. It would have been so natural, so taken for granted, that no alternative could be imagined. But you had to imagine an alternative to understand what Simmel was saying. Simmel's alternative to money was a rigid, stultifying class system where personal freedom was impossible. For him, it was much better that we let the market decide what was valuable through the exercise of personal choice. But covetousness was surely not the only source of human values.

Mila thought you had to think of other sources of value, ideas like equality, to see what making money the measure of all things forced us to lose. That meant that despair was premature. Mila knew she was not alone in being able to think of other values, other ways of judging things, and she thought what was needed was not defeatism but a battle with those who could think of nothing else but money. She thought of this battle as an intellectual argument. Simmel, she hoped, had given her an insider's understanding of her opponent and, therefore, the opponent's weaknesses.

As far as she understood it, money was seductive for two reasons. First, it worked for lazy thinkers who did not want to waste time understanding, but were in a hurry to get on and act. Money made things simple for them because they needed only to understand one source of value. Is that good art? If you tell me how much it is worth, I can tell you how good it is. Is that person worth talking to? Again, how much is he worth? How should I spend my time today? Easy: how will you make most money? Second, money was the perfect solution for those who did not want to be told what they could not do: the ones who did not care for the rules and rigidities of conventional society, who would not be fenced in and would not be denied their right to choose.

So, money appealed to unreflective doers, rebels, people who did not care what others thought of them. Wouldn't they get caught out by their arrogance and lazy thinking? They would never imagine that anybody could have different values and sooner or later they would pay for this lack of imagination. And then it hit her: her father had paid for his lack of imagination. It was his inability to think there might be another way of seeing his actions, one more legitimate than his own, that had led him to deny any responsibility for his fraud. He simply could not imagine an alternative source of value than money and so was amazed and outraged when the mainstream judged him to be wrong. The flood of public judgement should have been a revelation but he saw it as an impertinent insult.

Mila did not yet know if this insight altered her relationship with her father but, before she thought about that, she had to follow her mind's workings through to the end. She could not stop now for fear of losing the elaborate architecture of ideas that she had built in her head. She needed to force her brain to a conclusion: what did all this mean for her understanding of sociology? Mila did not agree with Simmel's conclusions but she thought she had found the better theory she needed, the one that would not replace, but overtake, the other theories of Marx, Durkheim, and Weber.

She flicked through the pages she had just read, smiling to herself in the way she used to do as a child unwrapping a gift, then she noticed, among the pages she had skipped, a discussion of Simmel's observations on secrecy. This quotation caught her eye: 'Secrecy sets barriers between men, but at the same time offers the seductive temptation to break through the barriers by gossip or confession.' Mila started reading again.

***

The room in which Mila met her father was like one of the teaching rooms in the university. The lighting and furniture were the same but here two people sat on opposite sides of each of the tables. They had talked about Doni and her mother, and Mila had carefully avoided mentioning Lin. Now her father was asking Mila how she found living under an assumed identity at the university. She said simply, 'I've given up. They know who I am now.' Somehow, it did not surprise her that he seemed to be disappointed. While her mother had never offered an opinion, and had simply provided practical assistance, it was her father who had encouraged her to hide her identity. Indeed, it might even have been her father who planted the first seed of the idea in her mind.

Mila agreed with Simmel that, whatever the content of the secret, secrecy always had a mysterious attraction of its own. He said a secret is like a possession. If you have a secret you own something valuable and unique, something others can't even glimpse without your permission. This kind of possession might appeal to an acquisitive person. Maybe her father was not really like that, but he would appreciate, and expect her to appreciate, the other invaluable quality of secrecy that Simmel described. Whether you thought of secrets in terms of possessions or not, secrecy made you feel special and (here might be the strongest attraction for someone like her father) it gave you a feeling of being powerful.

Simmel said that sense of power was greatest when you made the choice to reveal the secret or keep it hidden. Knowing that you might reveal the secret at any moment allowed you to imagine how you might dispel illusions, spoil happiness, wreck lives – even if, as Simmel said, it was only your own life that you wrecked by revealing the secret. Mila thought that her father might not be able to understand how she had been able to relinquish such power.

Thinking of her own experience, Mila had no difficulty agreeing with Simmel that any secrecy was a way of disconnecting yourself, a trick to make you a kind of stranger among people who thought they knew you well. She now thought that this was also a way of making yourself feel important and mysterious. Mila was so glad she had not only given up her secret but avoided lingering over the telling of it.

Simmel said that the excitement of being found out was part of the thrill, and tension, and therefore attraction, of a secret but so was the inner temptation to give way and tell all. Mila had certainly felt this strongly at times when she was with her friends pretending to be someone else, but she had not felt that sense of power Simmel talked of when she had decided to tell. Of course Jasmine had swept her into it and given her no choice, but hadn't she just spat it out with a minimum of fuss when Jasmine led her into the kitchen? And hadn't she been tremendously relieved? But here was her father who was sorry she had done it – Mila thought she would try to explain to her father why she had been right to tell her friends who she really was.

'There were these women trying to connect with each other, making lifelong friendships and telling each other their deepest secrets, and I could tell them nothing. It made me really feel as if I was deceiving people, manipulating them. I felt much better after I'd told them, and I didn't have to wear those old glasses anymore.'

Mila's father smiled and told her how pretty she was without her glasses. It seemed to her that he could understand that vanity might be a good enough reason for giving up a secret but that the rest of her explanation had passed him by. This reminded Mila of all those times in the past when she had planned to tell her father something that was important to her and found the final experience disappointing and frustrating. It always seemed that what she wanted from him lay on the other side of an invisible line he would not allow her to cross. Now her father was telling her about one of his 'companions here' who: 'had over a thousand secrets, and each one of them was a work of art, literally. They let him keep up his art in here and so his room is like a ludicrously overstocked museum. There is hardly a place on the wall that is not covered by a painting – Modigliani, Chagall, that kind of thing. His name is Jean-Christophe, maybe you've heard of him? He was a famous art forger but it doesn't do him a lot of good in here. The idiot just can't stop painting.'

'Maybe he enjoys it; maybe it gives him a purpose. Does he paint anything of his own, anything that isn't a copy?'

'Oh, yes, very odd things. He gives them to the rest of us, for free. He even offered me one.'

'What's it like?'

Her father was surprised at the question. 'I didn't take him up on his offer – it was worthless.'

Mila was struck with the thought that this was an extreme example of Simmel's theory that creativity is stifled by the objective expression of art in artworks that are traded on the market. Of course, in this case the commercial value of the objects was a function of the success of the forger's deception, Mila thought, and now she was ready to ask the question she had come to ask. But she asked with less resolve than she could have relied on ten minutes ago. She had remembered the invisible lines and the way her father's expression would tell her when she was asking to be allowed to cross one. So she looked intently at him as she said: 'You had secrets too, didn't you, Daddy? Your Jean-Christophe is here because he deceived people. Did you deceive people?'

'You mean those people who lost money? I didn't rob them, you know. Nobody was making them give their money to us.'

'But you knew they didn't really understand and they trusted you to look after them.' But already her hopes of getting her father to talk to her in the way she had imagined were fading.

'I knew they didn't understand the world in the same way I do. That's why they paid me for my expertise. But you don't do these people favours by pretending the world is other than it is. They need to know how the world really works if they are going to survive, let alone prosper. Look how poor they are – it's because they don't know how to make money for themselves.'

'They are even poorer now.' But this was just one weak and pathetic line of the great speech she had intended to give. She had planned such a flight of righteous rhetoric to show him that his behaviour was morally wrong, that he would cast aside his defences. Then she would have taught him Simmel and he would have seen the error of his ways.

Her father's smile did not disguise his annoyance that the invisible line had been crossed. 'Look, I did them a favour – it was a lesson they needed to learn, otherwise they would always be poor. Maybe they haven't learned the lesson but it's not my fault. It's their own fault that they are poor. They simply don't realise how seriously you have to take the business of making money. I was teaching them to take it seriously.'

'Unless they become like you they will stay poor?' said Mila, almost hating herself. This was pandering to him, retreating to the respectful side of the line where her father's version of the world was left unquestioned.

'That's the way the world works, and it's cruel to pretend anything else.'

'Don't they deserve to be compensated for what happened to them?' Now her father was smiling at her naivety. 'Why do you want to compensate them? Because being poor is a problem?' Mila nodded. 'But why is it a problem? Because money matters, money matters above all. The poor are unable to live real lives, do what they want and have what they want, for one simple reason: they don't have enough money. Money is the only way to solve their problems, as you have just agreed.'

Though she knew it must be a trap, Mila repeated herself. 'So why can't they be compensated?'

'Where will you get the money to compensate them – the taxpayers perhaps, who have worked so hard for their own money? You want to steal from them but make it legal by getting the state to do it?' Mila was fumbling with her words but her father raised his hand to show her she must be quiet.

'I told you money is a serious business. It shows you what matters; it cuts through everything. Give them some money, you say, to make up for their losses. That's right, that's what money can do. It can make up for anything and everything. But it doesn't come out of thin air. That's why I was trying to *make* money for those poor people – to make everything possible for them – there is no other way to help them that doesn't involve stealing.'

Mila tried again but whatever effort she made to get him to empathise with the poor investors, her father simply repeated that money was the only reality. Mila began to believe that his certainty and scorn were so implacable she would have to back down completely, but she said: 'Your version of the truth's a bit convenient, isn't it? It's a reality that suits you and not them.'

'I can't help the way things are. Even if I wanted to change things, it would be impossible. I might have done well out of the system but it was open to anyone else to do the same.'

This might have been the point at which Mila accepted defeat. But there was something about her father's smugness that turned her frustration at being unable to say all that she had planned into anger. Her voice was barely under control. 'Can't the way that the system works be changed? The people who benefit from inequality seem to be very good at finding ways to change the rules whenever anybody shows signs of closing the gap. The new rules always justify their privileges just as well as the old ones. If the system can be changed to keep their excuses for inequality up to date, why can't we change it so that people can see other things matter than money?'

'I don't know what you're talking about.'

Perhaps his rudeness was meant to goad her into losing her temper, into bursting into tears. But Mila now had her voice under control. 'I know you don't, Daddy, but it looks to me as if everyone like you is so obsessed with a particular way of thinking, a way dominated by what they believe makes economic sense, that everything else, including human feelings, becomes of secondary importance. I don't think that it always has to be this way at all.'

***

As she took the elevator down to the entrance to the building, Mila was thinking her father was convinced he knew the world inside out, whereas he had only grasped one of its many threads. People could be tempted to see the world in quite narrow and impoverished ways. Even now, her father thought that financial success was the only judgement he needed to concern himself with. She did not excuse this, but at least now Mila could understand how money obscured his moral judgement.

Arun was waiting for her. He looked anxious. 'How did he take it?' Mila smiled, letting him know she was grateful for his concern. 'He was disappointed! That was a surprise but I guess it's not that hard to understand. He made those poor investors he robbed believe in a fiction with him as the hero who was going to give them a comfortable retirement. He must have liked the idea that I was living a fictional life too. Maybe, while I did it, he thought it meant I approved of his lying.'

Mila thought Arun still looked concerned and, as she turned to walk towards the entrance, he took her hand. 'While you were in there, one of their people came to tell me there are two photographers loitering by the entrance. Apparently they do that when they have had a tip-off about who might be visiting whom. Let's see if there's another way out.'

'No,' said Mila. 'I don't want to hide. But is that OK with you? You don't have to join in as well.'

'Yes, I do,' said Arun, and he squeezed her hand.

As they walked across the courtyard together towards the gatehouse, Mila spoke. 'Do you remember Charles Horton Cooley?'

'Yes, he was the guy who went on about how we only relate to each other in our minds.'

'Good, we will make a sociologist of you yet.'

'You want everyone to be a sociologist.'

'And so they should be. Anyway, Cooley said: "What, indeed, would society be, or what would any one of us be, if we associated only with corporeal persons and insisted that no one should enter our company who could not show his power to tip the scales and cast a shadow?"'

'You mean fictional characters can teach us something after all?'

'They can teach us anything, even sociology.'

Visit the companion website at **www.palgrave.com/companion/ Bancroft-And-Fevre-Dead-White-Men-2e/** to access additional learning resources, including seminar questions based on the chapter's coverage, a jargon buster that defines key terms used in the text and a timeline which provides an overview of the development of sociological thought.

● ● ● ● ●

1. As people become more the same the greater the need to state how different and unique each and everyone is becomes. Georg Simmel worried that differences in character are eroded by the impersonality of the monetary economy. He also saw the possibilities of modern society and a money economy which made a vast array of new relationships come into being, and that destroyed old hierarchies and bonds of class and place.

2. The danger was that there ended up being no core – individuals became a network of relationships based on rational, material value – and nothing more, at the end of the day. In that sense the more you seek to express your individual identity through the monetary economy, the more you are like everyone else doing the same thing.

3. Simmel thought that 'the stranger' was a special role, an outsider who can look objectively at a group, and whose ability to move across boundaries is both useful to society and the source of their strangeness.

4. The joy and the trouble of modern life is the same throughout. An economy can create great wealth and create great poverty at the same time. A culture can promote individuality and also have everyone conform in their insistence on being special. A state can allow its subjects' freedom and exercise power through the working of that freedom. Sociology allows us to understand these troubling contradictions.

1   In at the Deep End

Being a sociologist

Zygmunt Bauman and Tim May, *Thinking Sociologically*, 2nd edn. (Oxford: Blackwell, 2001)

Peter L. Berger, *Invitation to Sociology: A Humanistic Perspective* (Harmondsworth: Penguin, 1966)

M. de Certeau, *The Practice of Everyday Life* (Berkeley, CA: University of California Press, 2002)

Steve Matthewman, Catherine Lane West-Newman and Bruce Curtis, *Being Sociological*, 2nd edn. (Houndmills: Palgrave Macmillan, 2013)

C. Wright Mills, *The Sociological Imagination* (Oxford: Oxford University Press, 2000)

Why theory?

David Inglis with Christopher Thorpe, *An Invitation to Social Theory* (Cambridge: Polity, 2012)

Steven Miles, *Social Theory in the Real World* (London: Sage, 2001)

Chris Shilling and Philip A Mellor, *The Sociological Ambition: Elementary Forms of Social and Moral Life* (London: Sage, 2001)

Modernity

Bram Gieben and Stuart Hall, *Formations of Modernity* (Cambridge, UK: Polity Press, 1992)

To understand how the changes brought by modernity are experienced by people

Dean MacCannell, *The Tourist: A New Theory of The Leisure Class* (Berkeley, CA: University of California Press, 1999)

Daniel Miller (ed.), *Worlds Apart: Modernity through the Prism of the Local* (London: Routledge, 1995)

2   In the Café

Society and human behaviour

Émile Durkheim, *The Rules of Sociological Method*, 8th edn. (Glencoe, IL: Free Press, 1938)

Émile Durkheim, *The Elementary Forms of Religious Life* (Oxford: Oxford University Press, 2001)

Émile Durkheim, *Suicide: A Study in Sociology* (London: Routledge, 2002)

The idea of society in sociology

John Urry, *Sociology beyond Societies: Mobilities for the Twenty-First Century* (London: Routledge, 1999)

The division of labour

Émile Durkheim, *The Division of Labour in Society* (Glencoe, IL: Free Press, 1933)

Anomie in action

Robert E. Park, 'Human Migration and the Marginal Man', *American Journal of Sociology*, 33(6):881–93, May 1928

3   In the Picture

Emotions

Gillian Bendelow and Simon J. Williams (eds), *Emotions in Social Life: Critical Themes and Contemporary Issues* (London: Routledge, 1998)

Deborah Lupton, *The Emotional Self: A Sociocultural Exploration* (London: Sage, 1998)

Simon J. Williams, *Emotion and Social Theory: Corporeal Reflections on the (Ir)rational* (London: Sage, 2001)

Emotion and reason

Antonio Damasio, *Descartes' Error: Emotion, Reason and the Human Brain* (London: Vintage, 2006)

Freud and civilization

Sigmund Freud, *Civilization and Its Discontents* (London: Penguin, 2002)

Gender and emotion

Stephanie A. Shields, *Speaking from the Heart: Gender and the Social Meaning of Emotion* (Cambridge, UK: Cambridge University Press, 2002)

Emotional work

Arlie Russell Hochschild, *The Managed Heart: Commercialization of Human Feeling* (Berkeley, CA: University of California Press, 2003)

4   In our Genes?

Feminism

Jennifer Mather Saul, *Feminism: Issues and Arguments* (Oxford: Oxford University Press, 2003)

Black feminism

Patricia Hill Collins, *Black Feminist Thought: Knowledge, Consciousness and the Politics of Empowerment* (London: Routledge, 2008)

Performing gender

Judith Butler, *Gender Trouble: Feminism and the Subversion of Identity* (New York, NY: Routledge, 2006)

Gender order

Raewyn Connell, *Gender and Power: Society, the Person and Sexual Politics* (Cambridge, UK: Polity Press in association with Blackwell, 1987)

Relationships and equality

Lynn Jamieson, *Intimacy: Personal Relationships in Modern Societies* (Cambridge, UK: Polity Press, 1997)

5   In Cahoots

Signs

Charles S. Peirce, *Peirce on Signs: Writings on Semiotic* (Chapel Hill, NC: University of North Carolina Press, 1991)

Interaction

Charles Horton Cooley, *Human Nature and the Social Order*, Social Science Classics series (New Brunswick, NJ: Transaction Books, 1983)

Signs in the world

Roland Barthes, *Mythologies* (Paris: Éditions du Seuil, 1970)

6   In Doni's Club

Society in the mind

Herbert Blumer, *Symbolic Interactionism: Perspective and Method* (Englewood Cliffs, NJ: Prentice-Hall, 1969)

George Herbert Mead, *Mind, Self and Society: From the Standpoint of a Social Behaviorist*, Works of George Herbert Mead, vol. 1 (Chicago, IL: University of Chicago Press, 1934)

7   In the Night

Ethnomethodology

Aaron V. Cicourel, *Cognitive Sociology* (Harmondsworth: Penguin, 1973)

David Francis and Stephen Hester, *An Invitation to Ethnomethodology: Language, Society and Interaction* (London: Sage, 2004)

Harold Garfinkel, *Studies in Ethnomethodology* (Cambridge, UK: Polity Press, 1984)

Alfred Schutz, *The Structures of the Life-World* (London: Heinemann, 1974)

8   In the Morning

Erving Goffman, *Asylums: Essays on the Social Situation of Mental Patients and other Inmates* (Chicago, IL: University of Chicago Press, 1962)

Erving Goffman, *The Presentation of Self in Everyday Life* (Harmondsworth: Penguin, 1971)

Erving Goffman, *Stigma: Notes on the Management of Spoiled Identity* (London: Simon & Schuster, 1986)

Stigma at work

R. Parker and P. Aggleton, 'HIV and AIDS-related Stigma and Discrimination: A Conceptual Framework and Implications for Action', *Social Science and Medicine* 15:13–24, 2003

C. J. Pascoe, *Dude, You're a Fag* (Berkeley, CA: University of California Press, 2007)

9   In Control

Sex and the body

Michel Foucault, *The History of Sexuality* (London: Penguin, 1979)

Chris Shilling, *The Body and Social Theory* (London: Sage, 2003)

Bryan Turner, *The Body and Society: Explorations in Social Theory* (London: Sage, 2008)

Power on the inside

Michel Foucault, *Discipline and Punish: The Birth of the Prison* (Harmondsworth: Penguin, 1979)

Michel Foucault, *Madness and Civilization: A History of Insanity in the Age of Reason* (London: Routledge, 2001)

Michel Foucault, *The Birth of the Clinic: An Archaeology of Medical Perception* (London: Routledge, 2003)

Erving Goffman, *Asylums* (Chicago, IL: Aldine Publishing, 1961)

Sex and society

Jeffrey Weeks, *Sex, Politics and Society: The Regulation of Sexuality since 1800* (London: Longman, 1989)

Governing the self

Nikolas Rose, *Governing the Soul: The Shaping of the Private Self* (London: Free Association Books, 1999)

10 In Doubt

E. E. Evans-Pritchard, *Witchcraft, Oracles and Magic among the Azande* (Oxford: Oxford University Press, 1976)

Donald Mackenzie and Judy Wajcman (eds), *The Social Shaping of Technology* (Buckingham: Open University Press, 1999)

11 In Sickness and in Health

Deborah Lupton, *Medicine as Culture* (London: Sage, 2003)

Talcott Parsons, *The Social System* (London: Routledge, 1991)

Pills and identity

Nathan Greenslit, 'Depression and Consumption: Psychopharmaceuticals, Branding and New Identity Practices', *Culture, Medicine and Psychiatry* 29:477–501, 2006

12 In Two Acts

Habitus

Pierre Bourdieu, *Outline of a Theory of Practice* (Cambridge, UK: Cambridge University Press, 1977)

Pierre Bourdieu, *The Logic of Practice* (Cambridge, UK: Polity Press, 1990)

Pierre Bourdieu, *An Invitation to Reflexive Sociology* (Oxford: Polity Press, 1992)

Capital and status

Pierre Bourdieu, *Distinction: A Social Critique of the Judgement of Taste* (London: Routledge & Kegan Paul, 1984)

13 In essence

Gurminder K Bhambra, *Connected Sociologies (Theory for a Global Age)* (London: Bloomsbury Academic 2014)

14 In and Against

Karl Marx and Friedrich Engels, *The German Ideology* (New York, NY: Prometheus Books, 1988)

Karl Marx, *The Communist Manifesto*, ed. Friedrich Engels (Boston, MA: Bedford/ St. Martin's Press, 1999)

Class and self

Beverley Skeggs, *Class, Self, Culture* (London: Routledge, 2004)

15 In Between

Max Weber, *The Theory of Social and Economic Organization* (New York, NY: Free Press, [1947] 1964)

Max Weber, *From Max Weber: Essays in Sociology* (London: Routledge & Kegan Paul, 1970)

Max Weber, *The Protestant Ethic and the Spirit of Capitalism* (Harmondsworth, Penguin, [1902] 2002)

Status at work

Dale Southerton, 'Boundaries of "Us" and "Them": Class, Mobility and Identification in a New Town', *Sociology* 36(1):171–93, 2002

16 In Pieces

Feminist epistemology

Liz Stanley and Sue Wise, *Breaking Out: Feminist Consciousness and Feminist Research* (London: Routledge & Kegan Paul, 1983, 2nd edn, 1993)

17 In and Out

Georg Simmel, *The Philosophy of Money* (London: Routledge, [1900] 2004)

Georg Simmel, 'Fashion', *American Journal of Sociology* 62(6):541–58, [1904] 1957

Georg Simmel, 'The Sociology of Secrecy and Secret Societies' *American Journal of Sociology* 11(4):441–98, 1906

Georg Simmel, *The Stranger*, in Scott Appelrouth and Laura Desfor Edles, *Classical and Contemporary Sociological Theory: Text and Readings* (Thousand Oaks, CA: Pine Forge, [1908] 2008)

Georg Simmel, *Simmel on Culture: Selected Writings*, edited by David Frisby and Mike Featherstone, with an introduction by Mike Featherstone (London: Sage, 1997)

Examples

Stjepan Mestrovic, *Postemotional Society* (London: Sage, 1997)

Vivana Selizer, *Pricing the Priceless Child: The Changing Social Value of Children* (New York, NY: Basic Books, 1985)

Vivana Selizer, *The Social Meaning of Money* (New York, NY: Basic Books, 1994)

Here are references for the quotes Mila used:

p. 73   'If there is something in you ...', Charles Horton Cooley, 'Sociability and Personal Ideas', in *Human Nature and the Social Order* (New York, NY: Charles Scribner's Sons, 1922), p. 119

p. 76   'In order to have ...', ibid., p. 119; 'The imaginations which people have ...', ibid., p. 121

p. 84   'may do a miserable job in constructing his action ...', Herbert Blumer, *Symbolic Interactionism: Perspective and Method* (Berkeley, CA: University of California Press, 1986) p. 15

p. 109   '[w]hat is prison-like about prisons ...', Erving Goffman, *Asylums* (Chicago, IL: Aldine Publishing, 1961), p. 35); 'symbolic meaning of events in the inmate's immediate presence ...', ibid., p. 11

p. 123   'a state of conscious and permanent ...', Michel Foucault, *Discipline and Punish: The Birth of the Prison* (Harmondsworth: Penguin, 1979), p. 201

p. 147   'the valuation and its expression in recognition and status', Talcott Parsons (1947), 'Introduction', in Max Weber, *The Theory of Social and Economic Organization* (New York, NY: Free Press, [1947] 1964), p. 82

p. 158   'Objectively organised as strategies ...', Pierre Bourdieu, *Outline of a Theory of Practice* (Cambridge, UK: Cambridge University Press, 1977), p. 73

p. 159   'no innocent words', Pierre Bourdieu, *Language and Symbolic Power* (Cambridge, UK: Polity Press, 1991), p. 40

p. 161   'The ways of looking, sitting ...', ibid., p. 51

p. 185   '[t]he ideas of the ruling class ...', Karl Marx and Friedrich Engels, *The German Ideology* (New York, NY: International Publishers, [1845–1846] 1970), p. 64

p. 191   'rational ethic for the conduct of life', Max Weber, *The Protestant Ethic and the Spirit of Capitalism* (Harmondsworth, Penguin [1902] 2002), p. 366

p. 193   'an utterly clear conscience', ibid.

p. 219   'dominating positions of the person who is a stranger in the group', Georg Simmel, 'The Stranger', in Kurt Wolff (trans.), *The Sociology of Georg Simmel* (New York, NY: Free Press, 1950), p. 432

p. 220   '[o]bjectivity may also be ...', Georg Simmel, *The Stranger*, in Scott Appelrouth and Laura Desfor Edles *Classical and Contemporary Sociological Theory: Text and Readings* (Thousand Oaks, CA: Pine Forge, [1908] 2008), p. 260; 'The stranger is close to us ...', 'In the stage of first passion ...', ibid., p 261

p. 220   'It is peculiarly characteristic ...', Georg Simmel, 'Fashion' *International Quarterly*, 10(1), October 1904, reprinted in *American Journal of Sociology*, 62(6): 548–9, May 1957

p. 226   'Secrecy sets barriers between men ...', Georg Simmel, 'The Sociology of Secrecy and of Secret Societies', *American Journal of Sociology* 11(4):441–98, January 1906

p. 230   'What, indeed, would society ...', Charles Horton Cooley, 'Sociability and Personal Ideas', in *Human Nature and the Social Order* (New York, NY: Charles Scribner's Sons, 1922), p. 123